EMBRACING
ILLUSION

SUNY Series, Toward a Comparative Philosophy of Religions
Paul J. Griffiths and Laurie L. Patton, editors

EMBRACING ILLUSION

Truth and Fiction
in
The Dream of the Nine Clouds

Francisca Cho Bantly

State University of New York Press

Published by
State University of New York Press, Albany

Printed in the United States of America

For information, address State University of New York Press, State University Plaza, Albany, N.Y. 12246

Production by Marilyn P. Semerad
Marketing by Bernadette LaManna

Library of Congress Cataloging-in-Publication Data
Bantly, Francisca Cho, 1961–
    Embracing illusion : truth and fiction in The dream of the nine clouds / Francisca Cho Bantly.
        p.   cm. — (SUNY series, toward a comparative philosophy of religions)
    Includes bibliographical references and index.
    ISBN 0-7914-2969-5 (hardcover). — ISBN 0-7914-2970-9 (pbk.)
    1. Kim, Man-jung, 1637–1692. Kuunmong.   2. Buddhism in literature.   I. Title.   II. Series.
PL989.415.M3K8325   1996   96-3284
895.7'32—dc20   CIP
                          10 9 8 7 6 5 4 3 2 1

For my mentor and friend,
Frank E. Reynolds

Contents

Foreword
  Laurie L. Patton and Paul J. Griffiths ix

1. Illusion and Imagination 1

2. Narratives and the Autobiographical Process 35

3. The Symmetry of Illusion and Reality 69

4. A Metaphysics in Search of Expression 115

5. Philosophy in Narrative Action 151

6. Remythologizing the Comparative Enterprise 177

Notes 205

Selected Bibliography 239

Index 253

Foreword

The present volume, *Embracing Illusion: Truth and Fiction in "The Dream of the Nine Clouds,"* advances a significant agenda in the comparative philosophy of religions: the role of the constructive imagination in comparative textual study. Other articles and volumes in this series have begun the exploration[1], yet *Embracing Illusion* is the first full-scale exploration of the possibilities and limitations of the constructive imagination in the study of a single text—the *Dream of the Nine Clouds* of Kim Manjung, a seventeenth century official in the Chosŏn dynasty court of Korea.

Many of the authors contributing to the series have characterized the role of the constructive imagination in comparative work in terms of the "dialogical" metaphor. In "On the Origins of Philosophy of Religion," David Tracy examines the possibilities for re-reading, and thereby re-asking, the questions that inspired the traditional philosophy of religions of earlier centuries. In his treatment of David Hume, Tracy argues for the significance of Hume's choice of the rhetorical, dialogical form in his treatment of religion. As Tracy puts it, the dialogue form is "not an extended monologue nor a single argument but rather a sustained and implicitly comparativist conversation among genuine others"[2]. Such a dialogical form, then, allows for an expansion of the imagination and greater interpretive attention to the interest, dramatic setting, and passions of the characters. This expansion of the imagination is appropriate to the wider inquiry that must, in Hume's and Tracy's minds, constitute the study of religion.

Following Tracy's inaugural suggestion, the claim that our comparative imaginations must be dialogical in nature has been well explored (perhaps even over-explored) on a theoretical level—in this series and elsewhere. Yet such a claim has serious procedural implications for the present-day comparative philosophy of religions—implications that have only begun to be examined thoroughly in an actual study of a text. One of the most serious implications—and the one that the present volume takes up compellingly—is the real possibility that, in dialogue with the text of another culture, the scholar will not only talk to the text, but that the text will talk back to the scholar. To put it another way, if the scholar takes the categories of another culture seriously, those categories may not be polite. They may, in fact, rather rudely convince her of a new way of being philosophical—a way that pertains not only to the text itself, but to other texts, both in and outside of its particular genre. Put even more strongly, the categories of another's text may replace her own.

Francisca Cho Bantly's work shows the exciting possibilities of allowing a text to talk back, thereby taking to the farthest possible extent the use of the dialogical imagination in comparative work. She does this in three distinct ways. First, in showing the ways in which *The Dream of the Nine Clouds* has ontological force for its readers, she joins Martha Nussbaum and Michael Riffaterre[3], among others, in making a persuasive argument for narrative as a form of philosophy—only this time, from the perspective of the practice of an Asian tradition. While *The Dream of the Nine Clouds* does not offer the kind of verisimilitude that invites empathy and vicarious learning, it does provoke self-reflection on the question of certainty, thereby taking a place in the Taoist and Buddhist tradition of systematic speculation about the nature and utility of words.

Second (and relatedly), Bantly argues that *The Dream of the Nine Clouds* can teach us that fiction can be seen as a form of cultural "remythologization." In doing so she carries forward a specific speculation by Philip Quinn on the cultural dynamics of demythologization and remythologization. In his article in this series, "On Demythologizing Evil", Quinn wonders whether all cultures might evolve in the direction of demythologization, and if so, what might the dynamics of the evolution be.[4] Bantly's study of *The Dream of the Nine Clouds* provides the beginning of an answer. The answer involves the relationship between a culture's metaphysics and its metapractice. Ideally, a culture's metaphysics—the claims about what ultimately exists—and metapractice—claims about what ultimately works—should be in seamless harmony. Bantly argues that when there is a rupture between the metaphysical and metapractical aspects of culture, demythologization occurs.

In the specific case of China and Korea, Chan/Sŏn Buddhism charged that the practice of scholastic exegesis had become replete with wrong-headed claims about the ontological properties of language, and had thereby lost its credibility. Thus, the Chan critique of Buddhist practices was that they were out of alignment with their own metaphysical claims about the nature of illusion. Such a critique ultimately forced reconstruction on the metapractical level—a re-alignment of Buddhist metapractice with Buddhist metaphysics. This re-alignment can be characterized as a process of revalorization, or remythologization.

In the case of Korean Buddhism, Bantly argues, this revalorization included a turn to fiction. In that cultural context, fiction was a form of practice which, in its specific metaphysical awareness of the creativity of narrative (and perhaps of all illusion), could allow the revalorization of Buddhist philosophy as a whole. The move to fiction, then, was a conservative one in that it reinforced a perspective that pre-dated the practical innovation.

Bantly's suggestions about the Korean Buddhist process of demythologization and remythologization leads to her third, and even more daring, claim about the ways in which the text can talk back. Such a model has important implications for the present state of academic practices. The current malaise of the academy is that it lacks an ontology to justify its practices. If literature does represent a form of ontology, as *The Dream of the Nine Clouds* tells us, then it can also help us move out of the current demythologizing phase of comparative philosophy of religions. It can provide us a model for the constitutive and creative acts behind all understanding, including that of the academy.

With these three axes—the ontological power of fiction; the role of fiction as a remythologizing practice; and the relevance of fiction to the contemporary Westernized academy—Bantly has given us a compelling example of the way in which constructive imagination can be used in comparative work. Bantly's presentation of her conversation with the text, and its answers back to her, demonstrate that the imaginative redescription which is the stuff of the comparative endeavor is also the stuff of fiction. Even more importantly, it demonstrates that both can be powerful and persuasive agents of conceptual change.

While it is up to readers to decide what their rejoinders might be to *The Dream of the Nine Clouds*, for our part as editors, we find *Embracing Illusion* a welcome and refreshing voice in the scholarly conversation.

LAURIE L. PATTON
PAUL J. GRIFFITHS

Chapter 1

Illusion and Imagination

In Lee Yearley's side-by-side study of the philosophies of Mencius and Aquinas,[1] the author closes with a plea for the necessity of what he calls the "analogical imagination" in all comparative endeavors. He offers this formula as an antidote to the two extremisms of "univocal" and "equivocal" analyses, which form the outer limits of academic approaches to the study of other cultures. The first tendency affirms almost exclusively the similarities between cultures, whereas the latter emphasizes difference and uniqueness to the point of asserting the incommensurability of cultures. In Yearley's assessment, the very real differences between cultural orientations are what necessitates the scholar's use of his or her imagination in the construction of analogies. The emphasis here is on constructiveness, for "if we use the analogical imagination, the locus of comparison must exist in the scholar's mind and not in the objects studied."[2]

If comparisons are a product of our own imagination, this is not to say, as Yearley quickly notes, that this activity is not rule-governed nor subject to the criteria of proof and demonstration. But the observation that comparisons inhere in our own minds makes the salient point that the act of imaginatively juxtaposing diverse traditions is often a way of framing our own individual questions—ones that may never have occurred to the societies under examination. This raises more than the obvious point that, in Yearley's case, Mencius and Aquinas never met and therefore cannot be made to speak to Yearley's task of reconciling their conceptions of virtue. The more significant

1

implication is that the comparative enterprise is really a method for reconceptualizing the self—both individually and collectively defined. Yearley directly refers to this process in his assertion that, "Moreover, these inventions [comparisons] have the power to give a new form to our experiences. The imaginative redescription produced challenges our normal experience of the contemporary world in which we live and the often distant worlds we study."[3]

I choose to begin my own study of a seventeenth-century Korean novel with this short meditation on imagination because my enterprise is no different from the one Yearley describes. I too place my efforts under the rubric of the comparative philosophy of religions, with some notable variations. I will not compare the substantive thought of two discrete thinkers; instead I constitute the Western academic community (within which I operate) and its reigning conceptions of philosophical discourse as the context against which I offer the novel as a form of philosophy. The variation of my approach lies in the fact that I foreground my own questions to the point of placing my cultural milieu at one end of the comparative equation. This kind of comparison is perhaps more implicit than the kind Yearley engages in (others might prefer to call it an "encounter"), but its virtue is that it also highlights the extent to which imagination plays a role in the constitution of cultural knowledge.

The role of the imagination in my study is twofold, and thus supplies a double punch. In applying my own queries about the nature of philosophical discourse and the various forms it can take to the study of fiction, I make *The Dream of the Nine Clouds* answer questions it never explicitly encountered. Thus I supply an imagined arena in which the novel can talk back to our present time and space. To bend a premodern Korean work of literature to modern Western intellectual concerns, however, also forces me to use my imagination in the historical depiction of the novel's genesis. In other words, my questions heavily influence my interpretation of the society and religious history which made the writing of the novel possible.

Despite the fact of this influence, I will strive to demonstrate that my interpretation is justified rather than purely convenient. This will entail bringing to bear the insights of two well-established disciplines—Asian literary studies and the history of Buddhism in East Asia—on the present case. Although my engagement with these disciplines more often than not challenges some prevailing theories, my aim is to make my arguments satisfy the rules that govern scholarly debate within these fields. Finally, I will go beyond these disciplinary engagements to offer a more constructive thesis about the development of Buddhist philosophy in East Asia which is more properly in the realm of the philosophy of religions. This move will also entail an extensive discussion of what I feel is at stake in the constitution (or more properly, reconstitution) of this last discipline, particularly as it impinges on the existing field of the history of religions.

The Novel as Philosophy

Let us begin with a brief introduction of my main text and the major theses that will be argued in regard to it.

The Korean classic known variously as *The Cloud Dream of the Nine*, and *A Nine Cloud Dream*, is a translation of the Korean title *Kuunmong*, which I simply render as *The Dream of the Nine Clouds*,[4] or *KUM* for short. The novel was written by Kim Manjung (1637–92), a high official in the Chosŏn dynasty (1392–1910) court, and a member of the dominant political clan known as the "Westerners." Given this pedigree, Kim Manjung was, strictly speaking, a neo-Confucian. The dominance of neo-Confucian ideology in the political life of Chosŏn Korea was sufficient in and of itself to assure this sympathy. Kim's membership in the politically entrenched faction also gave him impetus to champion neo-Confucian orthodoxy in order to assure the survival of his clan's power. It is in this context that the unsubtle Buddhist vestments of *KUM* have proved a puzzle to many Korean interpreters.

The protagonist of the story is a Buddhist monk who lives on the sacred Lotus Peak of prehistorical China. The monk transmigrates in a frame tale into the mortal world of ninth-century China, where he experiences success in life and love and lives the idealized Confucian career, only to realize the brevity and emptiness of it all. He then wakes up back on Lotus Peak to realize that his life of glory had only been a dream, and spiritually awakens to the Buddhist equation of life with illusion.

If the philosophical thrust of the tale constituted a puzzle, and potential scandal, at the time of its creation, scholars of this century have chosen to explain it as an act of filial piety. Common scholarly lore has it that Kim Manjung wrote the novel to console his mother on the occasion of his political exile from the court. One can easily imagine as well Kim's own distress at the instability and frequent reversals of his political fortunes, and how this led to an observation of the vanity of life—particularly the life set on the Confucian model of government service. Daniel Bouchez's examination of Kim Manjung's surviving collection of private writings, known as the *Random Essays* (*Sŏp'o manp'il*), makes a convincing case for Kim's Buddhist sympathies.[5]

My interpretation of *KUM* builds on the assumption of Kim's underlying Buddhist sentiments but claims much more than the formulaic summary of the novel as the lesson that the glories and fortunes of life are nothing more than a spring dream. This may or may not adequately sketch Kim's sentiments as he composed the tale, but the text itself gives evidence of a larger historical process of development in the expression of Buddhist philosophy. The literary trope of "life as a dream" has a long history in East Asia which reached its fullest expression through the novel in the seventeenth and eighteenth centuries. Concomitant with this development is a maturation of Buddhist philosophical discourse which develops from and builds on prior intellectual practices. I refer mainly to early exegetical efforts on the part of East Asian Buddhists who attempted to digest Indian sūtras which were bewildering both in their array and style.[6] These efforts culminated in the scholastic tradition of Zhi Yi (538–597) and Fa Zang (643–712) who founded the Tiantai and Huayan schools, respectively, in China; and Ŭisang (625–702) who founded the Hwaŏm school in Korea (equivalent to the Chinese Huayan). I also refer to the early praxis-oriented efforts of Chan/Sŏn Buddhism which held to the futility of all speech and discourse in the realization of truth as dictated by the emptiness (*śūnyatā*) teaching of the Mādhyamika school.

To be sure, a mandatory task which lies before me is to articulate what constitutes criteria for being "philosophical"—a quality that I predicate of *KUM*. Indeed, my thesis about *KUM* is intended to probe some conventions regarding the nature of philosophy, both within the discipline of Western philosophy and within the history of Buddhism in China and Korea. To begin with the first, I have made no secret of the fact that the creation of my comparative study—as of all academic studies— has something at stake for the community that engages in such efforts. What is currently at stake in my enterprise is the recon- stitution of the comparative philosophy of religions through the attempt to discover different ways in which cultures constitute philosophical discourse. My assertion that fiction is a form of philosophizing offers just such an instance.

My use of the terms "philosophy" and "philosophical" en- compass a range of meanings which should be explicitly de- fined. In its most common meaning, philosophy can refer to a form of speculation that centers on ultimate concerns such as the nature and meaning of life as we know it. *KUM*'s lesson that life is nothing but a dream hence qualifies most generally as a philosophical statement. This usage is inexact, however, and insufficient for describing my thesis regarding *KUM*. Although a great part of my task involves demonstrating that the message of this novel derives from specific Buddhist metaphysical tradi- tions that speculate on the true nature of the world, my use of the term "philosophical" extends beyond references to world- views and also conveys something about how those worldviews are expressed.

This distinction is perhaps best expressed by the phrase "philosophical discourse." Most philosophical traditions evolve regularized and rule-governed forms of expression which are deemed normative. In the two communities that I am concerned with—the Western academic and Eastern Buddhist—systematic, exegetical, and textual expressions have been the norm. The term "discourse" can refer generally to a broad range of literary practices. I use the phrase "philosophical discourse," however, to mean those textual practices whose articulation of a worldview is compelling as much for the rigor and rhetorical prowess with which it is argued as for the argument itself. "Philosophy" as I most consistently use it refers not only to a view of reality; that is, metaphysical and particularly ontological speculation, but a system of articulation with internal criteria of satisfaction.

With this stipulative understanding of philosophy in mind, my goal of demonstrating that the novel *KUM* constitutes a form of philosophical discourse is faced with obvious challenges. Fiction, as generally understood within the two communities I am concerned with, does not fulfill the criteria of philosophical discourse. To be sure, fiction can concern itself with serious topics, even metaphysics to the degree that it explores questions of ultimate meaning and reality. But its *form* of expression—its discourse—follows a separate set of criteria and aims than that of philosophy. Admittedly, the aesthetic rigor of a novel can have an impact on the reader's metaphysical and moral perspectives, but this effect is distinguishable from the aim of philosophical discourse to make incontrovertible truth claims about reality. Inversely, given the temper of Kim Manjung's society—one which frowned upon fictive discourse as inferior and potentially decadent, the author's choice to philosophize through the vehicle of fiction is in need of some explanation.

My attempts to argue for the philosophical capacity of fictive narratives are immeasurably aided by similar thrusts within the current Western philosophical scene. The efforts of Martha Nussbaum in particular have clearly articulated just what is at stake in the act of reading fiction as philosophy.[7] Her suggestions are directly relevant to my reading of *KUM*. To begin, Nussbaum makes the readily observable point that the rich, engaging details of the novel, which are constitutive of its telling of specific and particular lives, reaches us far more intimately than the formal discourses of standard philosophy. This observation is much more profound than the obvious point that it is a lot more fun to read novels than abstract treatises. Our ability to be engaged by the novel is a direct reflection of the fact that narratives correspond most closely to the way we construct the meaning of our own lives. Philip Quinn, another philosopher who engages in the philosophical study of literature, makes the succinct observation that, "A life is a process with a narrative structure. The extent to which an ethical theory made in the image of the theories of science can generate a blueprint or model of life is problematic."[8]

The narrative structure of our lives suggests an evolutionary process within which our whole being is engaged. In defiance of rational models of knowledge, the truths conveyed by the novel affirm the necessity of going beyond pure reason and of engaging the emotions. In her own work, Nussbaum repeatedly invokes the "ancient quarrel between the philosophers and the poets" in Plato's *Republic* as an index to these two competing views of knowledge. In one aspect, the argument concerns the way knowledge is to be attained. Plato's ideal intellect aspires to the standpoint of the "real above" in which it is freed of physical appetites, emotions, and desires. Only the separated intellect is capable of attaining perspicacity, according to this view. On the other hand, the alternative that poetic engagement offers is an embodied form of knowledge that materializes in the particular *event*; a knowledge that only comes in the experience of living. Nussbaum relates this process to the knowledge of love:

> Here we would see the knowing of love, for example, as very different from a grasping of some independent fact about the world; as something that is in part constituted by the experience of responding to a loss with need and pain. Love is grasped *in* the experience of loving and suffering. That pain is not some separate thing that instrumentally gives us access to the love; it is constitutive of loving itself.[9]

These two models of knowledge—the one attained through separation from the world and its emotional entanglements, and

the other through embrace of the very same—present competing and fundamentally opposed epistemologies. The question
of how one obtains knowledge, furthermore, is tied to the basic
question of what counts as knowledge, which in turn implicates
a specific view of reality. The ideal of precision held out by
abstract, disembodied discourse assumes a world of certainty
that has been obscured by sloppy thinking. The world that is
revealed by poetry and narrative, however, rejects the ideal of
precision in favor of uncertainty. Thus the old quarrel between
the poets and philosophers was " . . . not just a quarrel about
ornamentation, but a quarrel about who we are and what we
aspire to become."[10]

What counts as knowledge in a world where by definition
certainty is not possible? To begin, this view of the world in and
of itself asserts something profound about ourselves—a profun-
dity which is revealed most virtuously by narratives. Nussbaum,
with her own poetic virtuosity, states:

> The novel's procedures do not bring everything about the
> soul into a perspicuous ordering; but this is part and parcel
> of its view that not everything about the human soul *is*
> perspicuous, that the deepest depths are dark and shifting
> and illusive. A form of representation that implied other-
> wise would be artificial and untruthful. Nor, in our own
> assessment or criticism of the view, should we claim to
> make everything perspicuous. If we did, we should be play-
> ing false the human mysteries to which it is our business to
> respond. The picture of the internal person cannot be para-
> phrased in the neutral language of the critic, dissected, ex-
> plained. It must be responded to in all of its painful violent
> mystery.[11]

My reading of the premodern Korean novel *KUM* may be
seen as a cross-cultural testing of Nussbaum's philosophical reading of literature. In the way of similarities, my reading of *KUM*
also emphasizes the necessary relationship between philosophical form and content. The reason why fictive narrative comprises the most judicious form of philosophizing has much to
do with what Buddhism has to say about the nature of reality.
Does this imply that even cross-culturally, to philosophize

through narrative entails a shared view of reality? My answer is most emphatically yes.

The Western philosophical desire for transcendence has often been expressed as an attempt to deny the very lives we live by insisting on our invulnerability to the usual hazards of being human. Much of this attempt to transcend our particularity as humans entails the desire to overcome our debilitating emotions in favor of a god-like self-sufficiency and completeness.[12] Buddhism is often and superficially characterized as just such a philosophy, wherein the emotions are rendered the primary human failing. The dominant Buddhist practice of meditation aims to overcome emotional attachments through mental discipline in order to create a completely autonomous being, untouched by the events of life. The repeated refrain from the *Mahāsatipatthānasutta*—a prominent meditation text from the Pāli canon—sums up the monastic ideal: "Independent he dwells, clinging to nothing in the world." This representation of the Buddhist spiritual path is in fact the view of the protagonist—the young novice monk—in *KUM*, which is ultimately surrendered after reflection upon his dream journey.

The legacy of Mahāyāna Buddhism, which is given voice in *KUM*, asserts the misguided nature of the human desire for transcendence. Straining against the monastic pursuit of disengagement, East Asian Buddhism has been particularly vocal in pointing out the metaphysical speciousness of distinctions between pure and impure, the worldly and the spiritual, and between illusion and reality. When the novice monk comes to full realization at the end of the novel, we are not told about the contents of his awakening—but we do not need to be, for the lesson is embodied in the contents of the novel itself. This lesson may be summarized as the novel's revocation of spiritual stasis; of the deluded view that one can achieve perfection or rest that is predicated on rejecting the world as we know it. The lesson entails, in fact, the revocation of spiritual certainty. The negation of certainty is one way of portraying a dominant strategy that has been used by Buddhists to convey the teaching of emptiness.

One must raise, however, an immediate concern regarding a significant difference between a reading of *KUM* and the reading of modern novels. As a premodern literary work, *KUM* does not exhibit the qualities of narrative that we have come to expect from novels. Some scholars have placed *KUM* within the classification of "romance," a genre prior to the development of the novel in the West.[13] Romances paint the world in an idealistic rather than realistic mode, where fantasy and improbable occurrences abound. Characters are cast in the image of universal types rather than as unique personalities; there is no character development nor psychological insights into the protagonist's conflicts or motivations. The immediate problem that is posed by the romantic qualities of *KUM* is obvious: Nussbaum and Quinn predicate the philosophical properties of the novel on those very qualities that distinguish it from the romance. In his reading of Shusaku Endo's *Silence*, for example, Quinn is able to overcome the cultural distance of this Japanese novel because of its narrative quality: " . . . by providing thick, rich and realistic descriptions of some of the possibilities for Christian life, they add to our resources for constructing in the imagination models of what it can be like to lead a Christian life."[14] On the contrary, a reading of *KUM* throws up the immediate barriers of embedded cultural archetypes rather than conveying our common humanity.

Much of these archetypes and cultural meanings can be explained. This is the function of some of the chapters to follow. The larger question raised, of course, is how one might proceed to define the narrative of *KUM* as philosophical. This task involves being more specific about how the metaphysical content of *KUM* is related to its narrative form. In fleshing out this answer, my primary strategy will be to sketch a structural rather than properly literary analysis of my text. Although the rhetorical and stylistic qualities of *KUM* will be referenced, I believe that these are insufficient for exposing the novel's self-reflexive, philosophical properties. It is the structural layout of *KUM*— particularly in its use of the frame tale—which, in relation to Buddhist views about the illusory nature of reality, makes the philosophical import of *KUM*'s narrative clear.

The interpretation of *KUM* to follow, then, begins with the concession that this particular novel lacks the rich, particularistic, and realistic details which invite empathy and vicarious learning. What is offered instead is a different strategy of reading which is no less self-implicating for the reader, and which provokes the same kind of self-reflection on the question of certainty. As I hope to demonstrate, the strategy that *KUM* utilizes stands within a long tradition of systematic speculation within the Taoist and Buddhist traditions about the nature and utility of words. Therefore, to appreciate fully the philosophical nature of *KUM* requires a consideration of the history of the religious use of literature in Buddhism. By placing *KUM* within this historical context, this study will hopefully add a cross-cultural perspective on current Western speculations on the philosophical significance of literature.

Interpreting the Asian Novel

The argument that *KUM* is capable of expressing philosophical concepts in a profound way must be grounded in a broader consideration of how East Asian narratives convey meaning. My discussion of *KUM* on this plane is greatly informed by the work of Chinese literary scholars. The applicability of this field of research to the Korean case needs little defense. Here I conform to Robert Buswell's observation in regard to East Asian Buddhism that an insistence on separating "Chinese," "Korean," and "Japanese" varieties inadequately represents the historical and intellectual contiguity of these Buddhist traditions, which warrants speaking of a pan-Asian religion. Buswell claims, " . . . in Buddhist studies we must look at Buddhism as the organic whole it has always been, rather than in the splendid isolation of our artificial academic categorizations."[15] In the case of literary traditions, Korea's conscious and eager imitation of Chinese forms, and the near exclusive use of classical Chinese as the language of the literati, makes Buswell's point even more apropos.

    KUM is perhaps Korea's best-known example of Chinese literature. Up until the middle of this century, however, Korean scholars have perpetuated the cherished belief that Kim Manjung composed *KUM* in Korean for the explicit purpose of demonstrating the literary merits of his native tongue. One need not doubt the existence of such sentiments on Kim's part; his other known work of fiction, *Sassi Namjŏnggi (NJG)*, or *The Southern Expedition of Madame Sa*, was composed in Korean and later translated into Chinese by his grandnephew Kim Ch'unt'aek (1670–1717).[16] Ironically, the Chinese translation of *NJG* aided the novel's survival through its mistaken attribution to Kim Ch'unt'aek, whereas nineteenth-century Korean translations of *KUM*, which ensured it a broad reading public, were essential to its eventual preservation as a Korean classic. The discovery of early Chinese-language manuscripts of *KUM*, in any case, has cleared up the debate concerning its original language of composition.[17] In addition, my analysis of the novel will stress its thematic unity with Chinese sources, both before and after its own composition.

The insights of modern Chinese literary studies have much to suggest for the interpretation of *KUM*. The views of Andrew Plaks, in particular, have informed much of my own work. Plaks' general theory of Chinese narrative, which contends that the patterns of Yin/Yang and Five Phases cycles comprise the most cogent "structure of intelligibility" within Chinese narrative,[18] offers much to be appreciated and also much that can be challenged.

I am indebted to Plaks for his persistent characterization of the Chinese universe of meaning, which is often sketched in opposition to the cosmological assumptions behind Western allegory.[19] Defining Western allegory most broadly as the dualism between surface meaning (of the text) and its more significant implied meaning (which is beyond the text), Plaks places Chinese cosmology in an anti-dualistic realm which does not distinguish between greater and lesser meanings, but rather constitutes meaning through the totality of the cosmos' constituent parts. The patterns of alternation and periodicity form the contours of these smaller cosmic events, whose meaning become intelligible only from the overarching, bird's-eye view. In his own words, "... the perception of intelligibility in this rather bewildering view of the phenomenal world comes in not at any given point in the system, but only in the *totality* of the system as a whole."[20]

A significant aspect of this system is its inclusive attitude towards oppositions. Given its emphasis on totality, rather than separation, all opposites are complementary possibilities, many of which (in accordance to the Yin/Yang system) exist in both temporal and spatial alternation. Plaks filters his interpretation of the dream theme, which dominates *KUM* and the Chinese novel *Dream of the Red Chamber*, through this perspective. The ambiguity between truth and illusion which is played out to maximum strength by the trope of the dream is resolved again by the larger perspective:

> That is, the spatial totality of the allegorical vision of the novel is of an order that includes both being and non-being within its scope, so that the apparent opposition of being and non-being emerges as an example of the sort of inter-penetration of reality and illusion for which the dream is the nearest analogue in human experience.[21]

Admittedly, there is nothing in this view that truth and illusion form complementary aspects of experience that contradicts the thesis of this study. The cosmological picture of co-dependent, holistic structures in fact conforms affably well with the Buddhist ontology of emptiness (*śūnyatā*), which is based on the broader doctrine of the co-dependent arising of all phenomena (*pratītya-samutpāda*). The Buddhist perspectives present in *KUM* agree with Plaks' version of the Chinese cosmos in seeing the causal linkage between all its constituent parts. Where my approach departs from Plaks', however, is on the question of the presence of religious meaning, particularly Buddhist, in East Asian fiction. Plaks' overriding emphasis on total *pattern* over and against discrete units of cosmic and literary meaning, reduces his structure of intelligibility to an aesthetic principle which does not allow for the integrity of religious/philosophical systems. He states,

. . . it may be said that the presence in Chinese narrative
of patterns of order and balance, reward and retribution,
the general conviction of an inherent moral order in the
workings of the universe, function more often as formal
aesthetic features than as thematic points of doctrine.[22]

In my view, the reduction of meaning to pattern regretta-
bly trivializes the impact of discursive thought on culture. Thus
although I have fully utilized Plaks' theory, with its focus on
patterns of alternation and periodicity, in interpreting the cosmology of the Chinese classic the Shijing (The Book of Poetry),[23]
I give fuller weight to the religious and ritual meaning of these
patterns.

In the investigation of fiction, which greatly antedates the
Shijing in historical time, the majority of literary studies ignore
the massive penetration and influence of Buddhist thought in
the intervening years. This disciplinary convention shows partial signs of wear in articles such as Anthony C. Yu's "The Quest
of Brother Amor: Buddhist Intimations in the Story of the
Stone."[24] Plaks, however, maintains the dominance of Yin/Yang
and Five Phases patterning in Chinese fiction, and to the extent
that philosophical thought is given any presence at all, the system
of choice is the syncretic musings of Ming neo-Confucianism.[25]

As an alternative view, I have already sought to demonstrate the coherence of Buddhist structures of meaning in the
Chinese novel. In a previous analysis of the sixteenth-century
novel Journey to the West, I have differed with Plaks' thesis
that the inclusive structure of Chinese meaning, wherein all opposites are united, disallows the notion of spiritual journey or
progress, which is considered more the province of dualistic
Western allegories.[26] If the subtleties of Buddhist soteriology
within the novel are allowed to speak, then the primacy of spiritual progress, which is allegorized in the tale of the five pil-
grims' journey to India in search of Buddhist scriptures, is plainly
heard without doing violence to Plaks' characterization of Chinese cosmology.

Needless to say, given my belief in the substantiveness of
religious meaning in certain works of Chinese fiction, my interpretation of the dream metaphor in KUM goes beyond Plaks'

strategy of using it to exemplify one sector of his cosmic design theory. This move is necessary also to go beyond the "life is but a dream" cliché I iterated earlier. To argue for the presence of religious meaning in *KUM* establishes a necessary prerequisite for proving the *capacity* of fiction to express philosophical ideas. Once such capacity is established, however, the burden of demonstration lies in the mating of *KUM* to a specific philosophical system which is able to bend narrative to the disclosure of its beliefs about reality. The specific system that *KUM* illuminates can perhaps be identified as the teaching of emptiness expressed in culturally seminal texts of the *Prajñāpāramitā* (*Perfection of Wisdom*) school, such as the *Heart* and *Diamond* sūtras. We will see later that the *Diamond Sūtra*, in particular, serves as *KUM*'s dominant historical and philosophical subtext.

An attempt to identify *KUM* with one particular school of East Asian Buddhist thought, however, is not necessarily the most illuminating approach to the novel and is hardly representative of Buddhist habits of the age. Similar to its counterpart in China, Chosŏn dynasty Buddhism subsisted in a neo-Confucian political environment which was overtly hostile to Buddhism. Suffering a dramatic decline in state support, Chosŏn Buddhism emulated the Chinese tack of propounding the unity of Buddhism with Confucianism and Taoism.[27] This syncretistic outlook is echoed in Kim Manjung's own thoughts, as revealed through his *Sŏp'o manp'il*. As a member of the neo-Confucian literati, however, Kim Manjung did not speak on behalf of the Buddhist community per se. Thus the extent to which Kim Manjung is representative of the Buddhist voice must be explicitly considered.

Interpreting the Buddhist Tradition

It is at this point that the discipline of Asian literary studies intersects with the field of Buddhist scholarship. We may further draw out the supposed antinomy between fiction and philosophy by attending to the realm of Buddhist studies in East Asia, particularly of the period in which *KUM* was composed. It is commonly proposed that East Asian Buddhism's

most philosophically creative efforts were the doctrinal synthe-
ses of the Tiantai and Huayan schools, which brought order out
of the chaos of competing Indian Buddhist traditions through
the principle of "dividing the teachings" (panjiao). The Chinese
scholastics' strategy for hierarchicalizing Buddhist doctrines into
greater and lesser revelations required them first to work out
their own philosophical and soteriological perspectives. The
dominant influence of such apocryphal texts as The Awakening
of Faith in this task demonstrates that Chinese and Korean exegetical efforts were not only creative and prolific, but pointed
and unified in their direction.[28] The ensuing development of
Chan/Sŏn Buddhism, although explicitly anti-textual in stance,
also produced a wealth of literature which was eventually proclaimed as canonical in status. The Platform Sūtra, attributed to
the sixth patriarch Hui Neng, is an example of Chan exegesis, as
are the poetic and homiletic devices known as gongans ("public
cases"). To be sure, the growth of Chan literature was eventually objected to as antithetical to the original spirit of Chan,
which proclaimed the ineffability of truth. The eventual overgrowth of commentarial and discursive Chan writings sometimes led to the reassertion of hostility towards philosophical
discourse and the emphasis on religious practice.

    Most studies of Korean Buddhism tend to focus on the pre-
Chosŏn context and on the Sŏn school. Institutional and ideological changes wrought by the founders of the Chosŏn dynasty
permanently altered the face of Buddhism from its prior forms,
ostensibly giving scholars much less to look at. The demotion of
Buddhism from official state religion to a practice banished to
the remote mountains had a discernible impact on its organization and visibility. Under the reign of Sejong (1418–1450), the
existing schools of Buddhism were stripped of their lineage
affiliations and reduced into two generic organizations—the
scholastic (kyo) and the meditative (sŏn). Court recognition of
even these remaining schools vacillated with the personal
policies of each monarch. The organization of Korean Buddhism
in this era is best described by abandoning attempts to identify
schools and doctrines and instead referring to an amalgamated

and syncretic tradition known generally as "mountain" Buddhism.[29]

My reading of *KUM* leads to suggestive reassessments of certain truisms within scholarly circles, particularly the wisdom that the cultural presence of Buddhism plummeted in stature and significance after the golden age of the Tang dynasty (618–907) in China, and the Silla (668–918) and Koryŏ (918–1392) dynasties in Korea. Stephen Teiser has already pointed out that this broadly accepted conclusion stems from a scholarly prejudice for institutional and doctrinal presence as evidence of cultural flourishing. He counters this habit in his own assessment of Buddhism in China by stating that " . . . the more pervasive influence of Buddhism on Chinese society is to be seen in domains that are not distinctively Buddhist."[30] I would elaborate on Teiser's point to argue that a penchant for limited forms of cultural discourse easily blinds the scholar to the dynamism of traditions; to the depth of variation and transformations that a system of thought can display over time. In the present case, the dispersion of Buddhist perspectives from historically and institutionally discrete settings into popular and even secular frameworks hardly diminishes their impact.

My point is not to challenge the assumption that classic exegetical traditions were a measure of the vitality of Buddhism in East Asia. Instead, I challenge the assumption that the parameters of Buddhist philosophical discourse were exhausted in the medieval period. This requires accepting the proposition that the practice of philosophy is influenced by history. From the sixth to tenth centuries, Chinese and Korean Buddhists rejected their prior attempts to emulate Indian scholasticism in favor of indigenous movements. The primary thrust of these efforts, which were guided by the *panjiao* system of doctrinal classification, was hermeneutical. The principle of "dividing the teachings" was a methodological tool for overcoming the challenge to understanding posed by the assertion that widely differing and opposing ideas were all part of one religious system.

The driving concerns of Buddhism in Kim Manjung's time differed significantly. The process of internal and doctrinal

systematization had already been completed, and subsequently
convulsed by the debate on the utility of language to convey
truth. Both of these phases of Buddhist history find voice in
KUM. The novel's primary impetus, however, stems not from
events internal to the Buddhist community, but from broader
intellectual currents. These currents have largely to do with the
interaction between Confucian and Buddhist philosophical
views—not in abstract textual discourse but in the minds of
men like Kim Manjung who utilized both traditions to shape
their own lives. In order to understand this phenomenon, we
must begin with a reconsideration of the viability of Buddhist
views in mid-Chosŏn Korea.

In Ming China, the cooptation of Buddhist views into neo-
Confucian discourse allowed for the expression of Buddhism in
controlled and altered forms. This compromised existence resulted in the near cessation of traditional scholastic Buddhist
tracts, which were normally tied to doctrinal lineage schools.
Scholars of Korea have tended to reach similar conclusions about
the fate of Buddhism in the Chosŏn dynasty:

> The fortunes of Buddhism had so dramatically changed that
> the religion had lost its ability to influence the nation socially
> or culturally, and had lost its ability to produce scholarly
> monks. These facts were the result of the various policies
> pursued by the Confucian monarchy over a century and a
> half. Buddhist Korea was a thing of the past.[31]

The formal if intermittent policy of state repression announced the depth of Buddhism's fall from favor as a protector
of the nation. More recent scrutinies of the transition between
the Koryŏ and Chosŏn dynasties, however, suggest that the supposed break between the two ruling houses has been somewhat
overstated. Recent studies suggest a continuity in the social and
political lineages that made up the courts of both dynasties.[32]
Consistent with this continuity, the official repression of Buddhism was often interrupted by the personal piety of Chosŏn
monarchs (King Sejo [1455–1468] and Queen Munjŏng [1545–
1567] being notable examples), which led to renewals in temple
building and the performance of Buddhist rituals.

To be sure, the loss of Buddhism's political status in the Chosŏn period should not be minimized. This dynasty was founded upon a self-conscious embrace of neo-Confucianism in its pursuit of social and political reform. This conversion entailed sharp but familiar criticisms of Buddhism on both institutional and doctrinal grounds.[33] The critical issue for this study, however, concerns the nature of Buddhism's altered form of existence itself. Within the monastic context, one can note the persistence of Sŏn Buddhism and the practice of scholastic study, which included the continued production of scholarly texts. *KUM*'s literary expression of Buddhist philosophy, on the other hand, is completely separate from traditional forms of Buddhist exegesis and represents a new mode of discourse altogether. An explanation of this new form of philosophical expression—which was produced separately and apart from the labors of professional monks—must be explicitly tied to an historical analysis of Kim Manjung's situation.

The Buddhism of Kim Manjung

The life of the neo-Confucian literati was paralleled by the supposedly non-intersecting lives of mountain-top Buddhists. It is not the case, however, that these separate callings were embraced by members of opposing social strata. The biographies of prominent Chosŏn dynasty monks reveal that they commonly came from aristocratic—or Yangban—backgrounds. In the process of attaining literacy, these Buddhist monks gained a proficiency in the Confucian classics, as well as engaging in the protracted study of Buddhist texts that was common to monastic training.[34] The ability to obtain an education was perhaps the most important factor in accessing both the Confucian and Buddhist worlds with some degree of skill. Hence, as the case of Kim Manjung himself demonstrates, it was also true that familiarity with Buddhist texts and ideas was well within the purview of Confucian scholar-bureaucrats.

Kim Manjung's collection of *Random Essays* (*Sŏp'o manp'il*) gives an account of his visits to Buddhist temples and conversations with monks. These visits took place during a period of political exile to Sŏnch'ŏn, near the Chinese border, from 1687 to 1688. These poetic reflections evince a philosophical interest in the Buddhist account of the nature and creation of the universe. The *Random Essays* are sprinkled with quotations from and references to Buddhist texts, such as the *Vimalakīrtinirdeśa Sūtra*, the *Lotus Sūtra*, and the *Platform Sūtra*. One reference to the *Śūrangama Sūtra* is contained in the line, "The mind is without emerging or entering. Thus the meaning of the *Śūrangama* is that the mind is not inside, nor is it outside."[35] The *Śūrangama Sūtra* is an apocryphal Chinese Buddhist text that was popular in Chan/Sŏn circles at the end of the seventh century. It is perhaps most known for expounding the theory of *tathāgatagarbha*, or the view that all sentient beings are fundamentally identical with the Buddha. In this particular passage, however, Kim Manjung's concern is with the Buddhist belief that all phenomenal experience is based on the mind. Kim Manjung's consideration of Buddhist theory here is passing and brief. It is not until the composition of *KUM*, with its frame tale of dream experience and reincarnation, that we get Kim's full elaboration of the view that all events are mental "travels," or realities constituted by the mind.[36] Kim's translation of Buddhist theory into narrative format is perhaps the most interesting aspect of his embrace of Buddhism.

The collected musings of the *Random Essays* is neither an exclusive nor systematic exegesis on Buddhist thought. In addition to religious reflections, there are essays whose contents are political and literary in nature. As for Kim Manjung's understanding of Buddhism, he generalizes it to the doctrine of emptiness, which he saw as the linchpin of the religion.[37] Many of the essays are devoted to defending Buddhism against the standard attacks of neo-Confucianism, particularly those that had been articulated by the philosopher Zhuxi (1130–1200). Kim demonstrates his capacity for critical thinking by exposing the inconsistencies, oversimplifications, and lack of philological rigor behind the Confucian attacks. In the course of this process, Kim displays a thorough knowledge of Buddhist, as well as Confu-

cian, textual and lineage histories. Echoing the syncretist sentiment of the age, Kim parallels the substantive concepts and
evolutions of the two traditions, but insists on the point that the
neo-Confucianism of the current age is derivative of Buddhist
thought.[38]

Kim's vision of Buddhism displays a unifying and totaliz-
ing perspective rather than the ability to finesse exegetical issues. Although this form of Buddhist erudition does not conform
with monastic standards, the author nevertheless demonstrates
sophistication in his ruminations. What is important to remem-
ber is that Kim's engagement with Buddhism was not a pursuit
of expertise, but rather a vital ingredient in a quest for an even
broader structure of knowledge. This structure cannot be demonstrated without taking into consideration the author's political and literary activities.

The title of *Random Essays* conveys the casual arrangement of this text, as well as its apparant lack of a unifying
thesis. Yu Pyŏnghwan suggests, however, a certain progression
of concerns which are replicated by the author's own life. Although the topics discussed in the essays are not offered according to any discernible scheme, Yu claims a logical flow from
political, to philosophical, and finally, to literary speculations.[39]
This progression of thought is mandated by Kim Manjung's
own life, which began with political ambitions (which led to
frustration and disgrace), then subsequently turned to theoretical reflections (as evidenced by *Sŏp'o manp'il*), which then culminated in literary creation (as evidenced by *KUM*). *Sŏp'o
manp'il*'s protracted consideration of Buddhism suggests "a long
evolution in Kim Manjung's thinking," confirming that its contents embody the author's response to the events of his life.[40]
The conversion of this response to the literature of *KUM* suggests that from the formless form of internal reflection arose the
drive to return to the ground through symbol. The range of Kim
Manjung's discourses perhaps demonstrates that theory often
requires enfleshment through narrative. In comparing the theory
and narrative of Kim Manjung, in any case, this study will suggest that whereas his essays were "in a rambling style, with a

quality of spontaneity, allusive in expression and at times enig-
matic,"[41] his narrative was far more systematic in form and hence
the better philosophy.

One can justifiably ask, however, what might have been
lost in the translation. Does not the literary expression of a theory
sacrifice certain standards of rigor in order to meet its own
internal, aesthetic demands? The end of chapter five will explicitly consider the question—through the evidence of *KUM*—of
whether or not religious and literary discourses are opposed.
Specifically, does the literary reading of the novel subvert the
Buddhist religious goal of detachment? The relationship between
Buddhism and literature partakes of the general complexity
Western theorists have encountered in attempts to delineate between religion and literature. Historical traditions around the
world have evinced the indivisibility of the two, in the sense
that all religious expression takes on literary formats and, inversely, much of the world's creative literary masterpieces have
taken on explicitly religious themes. It is still possible to point
to, however, a possible divergence between the religious and
poetic sentiments.

Hong Kisam's consideration of Buddhist literature in Korea,
for example, worries about simplistic tendencies to equate
Buddhist canon with Buddhist literature.[42] To collapse the two
together would be to confuse two different worldviews, Hong
contends. The poetic sentiment seeks integration of feeling and
images through inventiveness, whereas the religious sentiment
strives to transcend the individual and the subjective through
conviction. These divergent worldviews reiterate Martha
Nussbaum's depiction of the ancient quarrel between the poets
and the philosophers, respectively. But history demonstrates that
genres rarely remain pure. The vast majority of Korean scholarship on Buddhist literature has focused on one form of interaction: the Buddhist cooptation of literature in which the creative
arts were used to emotionally and aesthetically propagate Buddhism. Sŏn poetry is an example of this variety. But if Buddhists
are willing to utilize the seductiveness of art for the purposes of
religion, then it is only fair to speculate on the potential for

inversion—that the poetic means may consume the religious purpose to its own end. Hence, this version of Buddhist literature entails a precarious standoff between conflicting models of experience.

If one looks at the case of Korea, however, one detects an intimate tie between Buddhism and literature that is predicated on mutual dependence rather than hostile tolerance. Hong points out that Korean literary history is closely tied to Buddhism—an observation that Kim Manjung also made when he pointed out that Buddhist missionaries brought the Chinese writing system to Korea.[43] In a much later era, an important factor in the creation of the native *han'gŭl* script in the fifteenth century was King Sejo's desire to propagate Buddhism. The result was the publication of Buddhist sūtras and popular narratives in a written form that was accessible to those without the privilege of Chinese learning. These incidents suggest that the acceptance of Buddhism was fundamentally based on the creation of various literary media. The Korean literary tradition in turn not only owes a debt to Buddhism, but can even be said to be rooted in Buddhist *topoi*. Although the acquisition of Chinese characters entailed the study of Confucian texts and the emulation of Confucian-inspired historiographies, the realm of creative literature is seen by some scholars as a direct emanation from the Buddhist fold.[44]

This historical observation can be parlayed into a philosophical question: To what extent did the Buddhist worldview itself encourage the embrace and development of literary expression? Kim Manjung's own movement towards fictive narrative perhaps replicates a phylogenetic progression in the history of Buddhism and literature in Korea. That this culmination would occur at the hands of a Confucian official rather than a card-carrying Buddhist makes sense only in larger intellectual context. Given the ideological hegemony of neo-Confucianism within the Chosŏn state, it is perhaps no wonder that the primary scholarly output of Buddhist monks was an attempt to reconcile Buddhist theory and practice to Confucian principles. Armed with their Confucian educations, these monks were often concerned with justifying Buddhism within a broader

Confucian framework. The monk Hyujŏng (1520–1604)—perhaps the most famous of the Chosŏn dynasty—reiterated this era's version of political correctness when he proclaimed the unity of the three teachings: "Confucianists plant the root, Taoists grow the root, and Buddhists harvest the root."[45]

For Buddhists operating within an institutional context, the syncretic tack had obvious political expediency. Not all Buddhists (or at least individuals inclined to express Buddhist views), however, were constrained by considerations of institutional survival. For men like Kim Manjung who were readily ensconced in government careers, the impetus to embrace Buddhist attitudes was driven by different incentives, as well as a long tradition of using poetic literature as a form of political dissent. While professional Buddhists were largely invested in the project of reconciliation with the powerbrokers, many within this very same corps of privilege looked to Buddhism as a vehicle for another kind of agenda altogether. Despite the prevailing language of unity, the fault lines between Buddhism and Confucianism ran deep, and certain individuals found it useful to maintain and explore the bifurcation.

Upholding *KUM* as an example of Buddhist philosophical expression is predicated on the existence of a large, ongoing cultural conflict within which Buddhist views of life played a critical role. This role was created by a combination of neo-Confucianism's very dominance and its own limitations. The persistence of Buddhism in this context was based on its implicit criticism of Confucianism as a lived and experienced reality. These criticisms, as evidenced by their literary expression in *KUM*, were not driven by a single Buddhist sectarian perspective but by a much larger view—a view that challenged the perspectives and concerns of Confucianism from the moment Buddhism acquired a presence in East Asia.

At this basic level of conflict, *KUM*'s allegiance to the emptiness doctrine is not so much a reference to Buddhist scholasticism as it is an assertion of an anti-Confucian belief about the world. This belief is itself fundamentally pan-Buddhist in orientation:

The practice of wisdom . . . assumes a duality between the
surface and depth of all things. Objects are not what they
appear to be. Their true reality . . . is opposed to their appearance to common sense, and much strength of wisdom
is required to go beyond the deceptive appearance and to
penetrate to the reality [itself].[46]

KUM offers a literary incarnation of this basic Buddhist
belief about the world. I refer to this perspective as the Buddhist "ontology of illusion," an outlook which embraces a fundamental distrust of human perceptions of the world, as
suggested by *KUM*'s message that life is nothing but a dream—
not only because it is so brief, but because it is ultimately unreal.

The highest goals of both Buddhism and Confucianism may
be characterized generally as knowledge of the ultimate reality
of the world. The seemingly objective world we find ourselves
in, however, and the role that this world plays in the search for
true knowledge fundamentally differ in the two traditions.
Against the Buddhist concept of *samsāra*, which views surface
reality as something to overcome, Confucian optimism about
the perfectibility of society tended to assume that knowledge
was self-evident, provided that one knew where to look. Chartered by the philosopher Zhuxi's concept of "principle" (*li*),
Chosŏn state orthodoxy reinforced the Confucian premise that
moral principles operated within the world which could be discovered through self-effort. The assumed duality between the
surface and depth of the world in Buddhism, on the other hand,
requires one to pull away from the surface, questioning its reality, and to retreat to the cultivation of inner consciousness so
that this outer world may be ultimately transcended. To complicate matters, however, unlike Western dualism as Andrew
Plaks defines it, the Buddhist quest for transcendent knowledge
does not ultimately reject the ways of this world nor does it
seek a reality outside of it. This paradox forms a central ingredient in *KUM*'s own artistry.

The conflict between Buddhist and Confucian models of
reality rarely devolved into a simple matter of determining which
tradition was better or truer. The literatus of Kim Manjung's

day was an individual who lived in both worlds. The *panjiao* method within Buddhism demonstrated the principle of hierarchicalizing variant teachings in a way that allowed one to assert that each teaching was true in its respective domain. Similarly, the conflict between Buddhism and Confucianism that is expressed in *KUM* does not put them into head-to-head competition. The contention between these two worldviews consists in the attempt at cooptation rather than elimination. Which philosophy is capable of subsuming the other? While Buddhist exegetes were busy molding their tradition to a Confucian framework, *KUM* demonstrates the philosophical resourcefulness of Buddhism in integrating the Confucian life into its own structure of meaning. This mission was accomplished not by philosophy alone, but through its expression in narrative—that is, through the movement from theory to literature. Utilizing Buddhism's desire to go beyond surface reality, Kim Manjung deployed this impulse to do more than reject the surface by simply negating Confucianism. Instead, he used Buddhist-sanctioned fiction to arrive at a deeper understanding of that surface reality which was his life, which then led to a much needed reconciliation with it.

Interestingly enough, then, the strongest assertion of Buddhist orthodoxy in this era was not to be found in the traditional exegetical writings of late-Chosŏn Buddhist circles. For a personality such as Kim Manjung, in any case, the textual vehicle of career monks was not ideal for enabling him to speak convincingly yet securely from his position. Although the origins of the Buddhist ontology of illusion are best traced to Mādhyamika and Yogācārā texts, it is also possible to locate the theme of illusion in less scholarly and more literary manifestations. *KUM*'s embrace of the ontology of illusion in fact reactivated narrative traditions long-standing in Asia. These narratives are best described as tales whose truth or falsity is not so much the issue as the lesson that they are designed to convey. In this sense, it is quite possible to view Kim Manjung's own novel as simply a moralistic fable which stands within a long tradition of similar tales with similar messages. Take, for example, the Korean monk

Iryŏn's (1206–1289) record of the following legend in his *Samguk Yusa*.[47]

During the Silla period, a monk named Chosin is appointed caretaker of the manor of Hŭnggyosa temple in Kyŏngju. Chosin promptly falls in love with the magistrate's daughter who smiles upon him. She is, however, betrothed to be married to another man. On the wedding night, Chosin beseeches the Bodhisattva Guanyin in prayer in the Buddha Hall while racked by jealousy and grief. All of a sudden, the daughter appears to him in the temple, having forsaken her groom and they elope. Many years pass, and the couple are reduced to poverty so that they watch their own children fall dead. The wife turns to Chosin and states, "Coquettish smiles have vanished like the dew, and the pledge of our love has fled like the pussy-willows on the four winds. The passionate desires of our green youth have led only to this bottomless grief of the grey winter."[48] They agree to part in order to seek their own fortunes. At the height of Chosin's grief, he awakens to discover that it was all a dream.

The themes of the brevity of life, the parching of passionate desires, and the pedagogical function of the dream are given full representation in *KUM*. These elements serve as identifying markers of the narrative expression of the Buddhist ontology of illusion. As a substantive view of the world, an ontology is susceptible to both systematic and narrative modes of expression. My basic aim in the chapters to come will be to ultimately distinguish *KUM* from its earlier narrative cognates by demonstrating that this novel parlays its narrative discourse into an explicitly philosophical one. *KUM*'s transformation of narrative into philosophy forces our attention beyond the novel's beliefs about reality—its ontology—to its virtues as a mode of articulation.

Metaphysics and Metapractice

Given the contextual differences between Chosŏn dynasty Buddhism and its prior incarnations, a question arises as to whether or not each era of intellectual concerns can or should be measured by the same standards of discourse. A measure of sensitivity to the confluence of history and philosophical practices should confirm Araki Kengo's assertion about the late Ming: "But given the differences in the historical circumstances and the spiritual needs of the time, it is probably pointless to adjudge the Buddhist movements of this period as inferior to those in the Sui, T'ang, and Sung periods."[49]

To say that fictive discourse should not be held to the standards of exegetical discourse determines nothing about its philosophical capacity. The more important point is that philosophical discourse cannot be held to one stylistic standard. It is perhaps prudent at this point to be explicit about the criteria for philosophical discourse that I find *KUM* to satisfy. As stated previously, this set of criteria centers on the demand for integration between the form and content of discourse.

My emphasis will be on demonstrating that *KUM* is a superlative *form* of philosophical expression, rather than a vehicle for doctrinal innovation. Invoking Teiser's sentiments, I take issue with the criterion of innovation as the sole or even primary measure of philosophical creativity. I will give equal weight to the criterion of *expression*, or the ability of a system to integrate its philosophical ideas into a form of expression eminently suited to making those ideas manifest. By paying equal attention to the form as well as the content of a philosophical work, we will in fact be able to expand the concept of innovation so that it is applicable to *KUM*. This entails a further nuancing of my use of the term "philosophy."

My emphasis on forms of expression can be defined as a philosophical system's "metapractice." Metapractice refers to the methods of articulation, persuasion, and demonstration that are applied to promote a substantive worldview, defined most generally as metaphysics. To qualify as a metapractice, a method of articulation must exhibit a self-conscious logic and justification for its particular practices. As we will see in the case of *KUM*, its justifications for a narrative discourse arise from its own metaphysics; namely, its ontology of illusion.

The distinction between metaphysics and metapractice is necessary in order to specify my thesis regarding *KUM*. In my reading of the novel, an explicit literary question arises regarding how one is to discern meaning in art. Plaks' claims that " . . . such discussions have generally revolved around the question of whether meaning lies within the work of art itself—in the purely aesthetic experience of the artifact *in vacuo*—or in the manner in which the manipulation of form evokes some level of meaning not directly present."[50] My discussion of *KUM* casts a vote for the latter understanding. That is, the fullest appreciation of meaning in *KUM* necessitates looking beyond the text to its literary and philosophical context, which a reading of the narrative does not immediately reveal.

It is my intent to place *KUM* within a broader view of the evolution of Buddhist philosophical practices. This evolution must be highlighted by focusing on *KUM*'s narrative discourse as a metapractice rather than on its metaphysical views alone. Compared to the familiarity of *KUM*'s ontology of illusion, its narrative metapractice in the expression of this view of reality amounts to quite a philosophical innovation indeed. To recognize this innovation is to in turn affirm a particular definition of philosophy which pays equal attention to the form as well as content of its claims. To identify significant developments within this enlarged notion of philosophy also entails the broader forms of literary analysis I allude to above. The level of cultural perspective is key here, and amounts to a methodological organization which is determinative in my treatment of *KUM*.

The level of analysis I consider crucial to the following study is a plane of observable cultural phenomena that goes beyond the discrete historical consciousness of individual actors and institutions. Included in this is our author's individual consciousness and the account that it would give of itself and its motives as an historical agent. In other words, Kim Manjung never consciously set out to refashion the norms of Buddhist philosophical expression. He was not a Buddhist in any grounded institutional sense, and thus cannot be made to speak for mid-Chosŏn dynasty Buddhist orthodoxy. My claim that *KUM* represents an evolution in Buddhist discourse deliberately veers away from the standards imposed by institutional contexts. Instead, I counterpose a different set of criteria which is predicated on the formal definition of philosophy that I have proposed.

To make my thesis crystal clear, then, Kim Manjung's novel *Kuunmong* comprises Buddhist philosophical discourse because of the perfect symmetry that it attains between its metaphysics and its metapractice. This achievement satisfies my formal definition of philosophical discourse, but in the Buddhist context it offers a resolution to a particularly vexing paradox: Can one use words to express a wordless truth? The derivation and pervasiveness of this Buddhist dilemma will be explored in chapter four. The immediate point, however, is that the convergence of metaphysics and metapractice in *KUM* enables the resolution of a key Buddhist problem. It is on this basis that I claim that *KUM* is Buddhist. The qualifier "Buddhist" here is clearly philosophical rather than historical. Chosŏn scholastic and institutional Buddhism, in any case, has little bearing on the literary genius of *KUM*.

For the above reason, the assertions of this study are perhaps more properly in the discipline of philosophy rather than the history of religions. My interpretation of a late seventeenth-century work of narrative fiction makes claims for this entity that might prove puzzling in historical context—even to the author of the work. My intent is to explore the boundaries of Buddhist truth claims from *within* those claims. The benefits of doing so will hopefully go beyond formal definitions of philosophy to illuminating the Buddhist struggles with philosophical expression that I alluded to above. As my final chapter will show, this study of how Buddhist truth claims can be made is also an attempt to make Buddhist philosophy relevant to the discourse of the contemporary academy.

This should not be interpreted, however, as an abdication of all historical analysis. In order to make sense of how Kim Manjung almost unwittingly came to address a matter of immense Buddhist import requires exploring the context of his literary practices. This entails some understanding of the cultural use of narratives in Chosŏn Korea. Although Kim Manjung's literary practices have their social context, it is his philosophical understanding of the meaning of his activity that ultimately leads him to Buddhist ontology.

There is yet another front on which this study engages the question of historical analysis. To what extent is it necessary or even useful to define the Buddhist tradition in terms of its institutional boundaries? Understandably, historical studies tend to gravitate toward discrete entities that render themselves into manageable units of analysis. This is easier than dealing with the question of who or what is Buddhist from a larger cultural perspective. The question is particularly dicey when it comes to philosophical traditions, which were concerned with questions of legitimacy and lineage. Hence my efforts are perhaps an attempt to test the limits of Stephen Teiser's assertion that the most pervasive Buddhist influences can be seen in domains that are not "distinctively Buddhist." Can we say this of philosophical discourse as well?

In the field of recent Buddhist studies, the anthropologist Stanley Tambiah has most consistently and virtuously portrayed the Buddhist tradition in a holistic manner. His field work on modern Thai Buddhism has straddled the numerous bifurcations within scholarship that have threatened the organic totality of this historical tradition. The most relevant polarity that Tambiah has battled is the division between the philosophical abstractions of canonical and elite traditions and the mythical and popular practices of folk traditions. The division has been and still is mirrored in the organization of Buddhist studies, which is arranged into the dualisms of anthropology and Buddhology, and the studies of text and context.[51]

This division of labor can be blithely applied to *KUM* as well. Given the dubious status of fiction in Kim Manjung's own day, it would be easy to toss this novel into the ring of popular amusement cloaked in facile and empty Buddhist garb. Tambiah's point, however, that a religion's high literary tradition is varied, cumulative, and changing, and that popular religion in turn incorporates much of the orthodox literary tradition is particularly apropos.[52] Tambiah argues for this balanced perspective by asserting the historical connection between the past and present of a religious tradition. Tambiah describes this connection through the terms "continuities" and "transformations." He states, "By continuities I mean the *persistence* of certain structures or customs from the past into the present; and by transformations I mean *systematic changes* in forms over time, . . ."[53] In my own use of the categories of metaphysics and metapractice, the former will be used to demonstrate the continuity of *KUM* with prior Buddhist philosophical discourse, and the latter will be used to demonstrate the transformation the novel effects within the same realm, which ultimately forces a reevaluation of the criteria of what constitutes a philosophical text.

To look for the persistences and systematic changes in a tradition over time in the way Tambiah espouses assumes a view of history as integrated and meaningful. Inasmuch as a continuum of social phenomenon exists, its very recognition by the scholar amounts to a commitment to the belief that herein lies the most significant and interesting information. Therefore, against Thomas Carlyle's notion that all history is the history of great men (and women, presumably),[54] I do not elect to offer *KUM* as a work of singular merit. On the contrary, I will demonstrate its lodgment in a continuum of literary and philosophical development. Even in my portrayal of the author, Kim Manjung, I will show how his biography is more typological than unique. The manner in which he chose to reveal his personal self, as evidenced by his literary works, employs some common *topoi* of Asian literature. Thus the writing of literature for Kim formed a double loop which served as a vehicle not only for self-expression, but for a culturally patterned self-conception as well.

This strategy of interpretation is not to deny the distinctive literary merits of *KUM*. My aim is to place *KUM* within a developmental path of philosophical practice. This development, to reiterate a point made above, is located on a level of significance that transcends the individual. But to claim that the author and work in question are instantiations of points of historical development is not to belittle them. I will hopefully demonstrate that far from being a minor pitstop, the novelistic form which *KUM* represents can be considered an historical culmination.

Before attending to the nature of *KUM*'s philosophical practice, we must first explore its literary qualities. In order to substantiate my argument that narrative can be constituted as an explicitly philosophical metapractice, one must explore Kim Manjung's awareness of narrative's capacities. The following chapter will primarily be devoted to Kim Manjung's use and practice of writing fiction. This investigation entails examining the attitude of the author's own society towards the writing and consumption of various literary genres, and some recent scholarly theories regarding the particular significance of the rise of fiction in China as a distinct literary mode.

This kind of historical inquiry is a prerequisite for understanding how the merging of narrative and philosophy was made possible in this particular place and time. The substance of my argument will be that Kim Manjung's practice of fiction demonstrates the fact that narratives have the power to model real lives, conforming to Philip Quinn's observation that "A life is a process with a narrative structure."[55] I will refer to this power as narrative's ontological capacity. This capacity refers to more than the ability of narratives to ponder the meaning of our lives. Here one must distinguish two senses of the term "ontology." I have thus far referred to *KUM*'s ontological capacity in terms of its specific outlook on the world, an outlook that I have identified as the ontology of illusion. In the following chapter, I will develop a much more substantive notion of narrative's ontological capacity by showing that Kim Manjung uses narratives not only to express a view of reality but actually to create that reality. The use of narratives to create reality suggests a greater and more active notion of ontology which will be critical in pushing *KUM* beyond the boundaries of metaphysical expression to the realm of metapractice. The third chapter will be devoted in large part to exploring *KUM*'s metaphysical heritage, but it will also demonstrate the novel's awareness of its own ontological powers. With these preliminary yet critical investigations in hand, the subsequent two chapters will focus on *KUM*'s internal philosophical mechanics.

Chapter 2

Narratives and the Autobiographical Process

Public versus Private Selves

The attempt to define and trace the emergence of the Korean classic novel (*kososŏl*) is no less problematic than in the Chinese case. Standard anthologies of Korean fiction will point to Kim Sisŭp (1435–1493) and his collection of tales known as *Kŭmo Sinhwa* (*New Stories from Golden Turtle Mountain*) as heralding the emergence of the Korean novel.[1] These stories, of which only five survive, are clearly modeled on the Chinese *chuanqi* ("transmitting the strange") tales and fall distinctly short of the full-length novel. The most likely explanation for the attention given to *Kŭmo Sinhwa* in the study of Korean fiction is that its stories are set in Korea. The Chinese provenance of many of the literary narratives known to Koreans explains why *Kŭmo Sinhwa* represented a departure. Story collecting had been in vogue since the mid-Koryŏ dynasty, inspired by the translations of Chinese *chuanqi* and Song and Yuan dynasty narratives. These tales naturally featured China as their setting. The *Kŭmo Sinhwa* offered, then, a Korean internalization of the *chuanqi* genre and the incorporation of indigenous sources and contexts.

The first full-length narrative produced in Korea came a full century later with Hŏ Kyun's (1569–1618) *Hong Kiltong* (*The Life of Hong Kiltong*). This work too is based on a Chinese model—the *Shuihuzhuan*'s (*Water Margin*) tale of banditry—

but its setting and the social issues that it examines are clearly Korean. Although Korean literary scholars uniformly recognize *Hong Kiltong* as representative of Korean fiction, at least one amongst them, W. E. Skillend, has disputed the authorship of Hŏ Kyun and the dating of the novel, calling it a "patently late nineteenth century work."[2] Skillend asserts that the production of Korean novels did not occur until the nineteenth and twentieth centuries, with the sole exception of the works of Kim Manjung in the late seventeenth century. Calling Kim Manjung an "oasis in a vast desert," Skillend claims that there is no knowledge of any Korean prose author before him and no prose for at least one hundred years after him.

The difficulty in talking about the Korean novel results in large part from its indebtedness to the Chinese tradition. Kim Manjung's own fiction writing was influenced by Chinese classics such as *Xiyouji* (*Journey to the West*) and *Sanguozhi Yanyi* (*Romance of the Three Kingdoms*). For this reason, it is a rather forced enterprise to speak of his fiction as a part of some specifically Korean narrative tradition. This is not to suggest, however, a dearth of literary activity inspired by and reflective of the native Korean scene. Two popular modes of fiction, for example, were historical novels depicting the Japanese and Manchu invasions of the sixteenth and seventeenth centuries, and palace memoirs written by court women. Although these works might be identified as Korean fictive traditions, the authors were largely anonymous and the manuscripts existed only in private collections. As Skillend points out, there is very little evidence that these works circulated in printed form before the late nineteenth century. Hence the question arises as to whether or not one can speak of a Korean novelistic tradition before this period.

Certainly in the case of Kim Manjung, his literary efforts had little to do with participation in a tradition that was propelled by a wide reading public or intertextual development. Although *Kuunmong* is now revered as a Korean classic, this designation and broad public consumption did not occur until, again, the nineteenth century. Thus perhaps the more important question to ask about novels in pre-nineteenth-century Chosŏn Korea is their significance relative to the small numbers of literati who produced them. Peter Lee points to a process of social awakening touched off by the Japanese and Manchu invasions, during which the king and court proved their ineffectiveness. Lee suggests an ensuing rise of class consciousness on the part of the politically dispossessed which led to a new literary movement that allowed for "spontaneous expressions."[3] If Kim Manjung and Hŏ Kyun are to be taken as representatives of this trend, however, one is necessarily tempered from overstating the case for class stratification. Both were denizens of the literati rank, although both had clear reasons for political dissatisfaction. It is perhaps the voices of discontent from *within* the privileged and literate ranks that are most clearly heard in their prose.

The association between the novel and political dissension is undoubtedly the reason why the same literati class, this time speaking in the voice of neo-Confucian orthodoxy, uniformly condemned the novel as specious history and a corruption of traditional morals—particularly in the realms of male-female relations and social hierarchy. The conflicting standing of the novel—its immense popularity and its morally suspect nature— is the very characteristic that enabled its authors to speak with a new voice.[4] This was in great part enabled by the use of the vernacular tongue, defined in the Korean case by the native Korean language (as opposed to classical Chinese) and the native *han'gŭl* script. More importantly, however, as a form of expression simultaneously embraced and feared, the novel provided an arena in which individuals could explore some marginal options for identity in the name of idle amusement. The novel offered the shelter of play, but unleashed the power of self-renewal. To fully appreciate the nature of this renewal, one must turn to a consideration of the philosophical significance of fiction.

Although *Kuunmong* was written in Korea by a Korean, its broader narrative meaning cannot be illuminated without recourse to a study of Chinese fiction. Given that my central intent is to establish the presence of philosophical meaning and practice in *KUM*, it is particularly important to have some sense of what significance current scholars attach to the rise of fiction in China. In exploring this literature, I will hone in on a general theory of fiction—particularized to sinological traditions—that explores the *philosophical* significance of narratives. More specifically, I will focus on what I refer to as the ontological capacity of narrative—a capacity utilized by Kim Manjung to imagine the meaning of his own life.

To consider narratives from this perspective makes a considerable contribution to the question of how fiction conveys meaning, or, more generally, to the consideration of meaning in art. As we will see, Kim Manjung's narrative practices suggest a view of reality and art that is chartered by specific metaphysical perspectives. These perspectives ultimately lead the philosophical reader of *KUM* to question the metaphysical status of fiction itself. By first making explicit the possible relationship between narrative and certain philosophical functions, we will then be able to see how these themes are specifically encoded within *KUM*.

Most meditations on Chinese narrative begin by situating fiction opposite the culturally dominant genre of history, and then attempt to determine when fiction diverged from the latter as a self-conscious form. Although the full-blown novel did not appear in written form until the Ming dynasty with such classics as the *Xiyouji, Shuihuzhuan,* and *Jinpingmei,* the roots of the novel have been traced back to Song and even Tang popular narratives. Many would push back the origins of fiction even further to the *zhiguai* ("describing anomalies") tales of the Six Dynasties (220–581) which, while proposing to be accounts of true events, nevertheless diverge from "properly" historical matters. There are those, too, who point out the fictive creativity of monumental histories, such as Sima Qian's (146–86 B.C.E.) *Shiji* (*Records of the Historian*), which is evident in spite of early China's high degree of historiographical sophistication.

Corresponding with the problem of dating fiction in China, the more interesting question concerns the broader meaning or impetus behind the rise of fiction. Uchida Michio, for example, assumes that the chief criterion for fiction is a self-conscious authorial intent to create a realm of imaginative discourse liberated from a slavishness to "facts." Building on this, he claims that fiction was initiated with the Tang *chuanqi* ("transmitting the strange") tale, and emphatically not with the *zhiguai*, because the former is an intentional literary creation while the latter still claims for itself the rubric of history.[5] The important point here is Uchida's definition of fiction, which hints at a cultural liberation of the imagination from the droll, pragmatic demands of didactic history. The result is a widening of possibilities for both the form and function of literary narratives.

Others have made the same kind of observation, but have focused on different eras and literary bodies. Kenneth DeWoskin, for example, agrees with the spirit of Uchida's definition of fiction, but emphatically disagrees with his conclusions about the *zhiguai*. DeWoskin notes that the Six Dynasties, which spawned the rise of the *zhiguai*, was a period which witnessed

> ... the first widespread acceptance of writing as a private act, writing as literature, writing as an art. Energy once expended in justifying writing, usually in terms of its public good, was invested in efforts to understand its special workings and its unique aesthetics, and to explore its potential for personal expression and edification.[6]

Opinions may differ as to when exactly the liberation of literature from constraining pedagogical ends can be fully documented, but I choose to focus more narrowly on the *fact* of this process itself. In this vein, Victor Mair offers perhaps the most provocative thesis about the rise of fiction in China. He asserts that the development of fiction, both in the sense of a favorable view of the "created" and hence the open, willful use of the creative imagination, did not attain fruition until after the influx of Indian Buddhist literary themes and, much more importantly, the justifying ontology of Indian thought which proclaimed that all the world is illusion/creation (*māyā*).[7] This justifying ontology was arguably a necessary ingredient for countering the native preference for history and its supposed concern with true events. In the Chinese mind, real events demonstrated eternal principles. To fabricate events would necessarily distort ethical truths and the laws of human relations. The semantic meaning

of *xiaoshuo* ("novel") as "small talk," or "minor discourse" conveys a long-standing suspicion that fictive narratives create
worlds which, in departing from historical truth, distort reality.[8]
Given this context, the Buddhist view of reality posed a challenge to both the form and content of truth discourse.

Mair's thesis is an argument that I will make consistent use
of throughout this study. An important aspect of this discussion
is the tyranny of history, which must be grappled with in any
account of the rise of fiction. The early dominance of history, or
shi, as a literary and political genre gave it a cultural weight
that threatened to relegate all other literary modes into an or-
bital path around it. Non-historical narratives were recognized
and sanctioned by the extent to which they related, conflated,
and extended themselves to and from orthodox historiographical functions. In this broad division of literary genres, fiction—
to the extent that it departs from history—is perhaps more
properly styled *wen* (belles-lettres).[9]

Others, however, have questioned the benefits of polariz-
ing Chinese narratives along the "truth-illusion" axis, as represented by history and fiction. Rather than insisting on these two
opposing categories as true genres, Andrew Plaks suggests that
they represent a division of labor in which a question of content
rather than form comes into play:

> That is, for want of a differential truth-function or sharply
> contrasted narrative form, the major observable difference
> that conspicuously separates the two branches of Chinese
> narrative is the simple fact that historiography (and histori-
> cal fiction) deals primarily with affairs of state and *public
> life*—military, political, diplomatic, court-related—while fic-
> tion takes up the slack to cover the more individualized
> and intimate details of the *private lives* of figures of vary-
> ing roles or status.[10]

The impetus for positing a weak "differential truth-function" in Chinese literature is aided not only by the observation
that histories contain fictive narratives, but that inversely, fiction often "continued to prefer the garb of history, even if only
imaginary history."[11] This observation accurately describes the

Ming novels *Shuihuzhuan* and *Jinpingmei,* as well as the Tang *chuanqi* tales, which are often supplemented with the author's assurances that the disclosed events were personally related to him by the tale's main character, or through a reliable source.[12] From a critical perspective (both East and West), Anthony C. Yu has questioned the inherent viability of the truth differential, stating, "Once the historian's craft is conceded to be constitutive of its object both formally . . . and ontologically . . . , it will not be long before one reaches the conclusion that the process of reading history is similar to that of reading fiction."[13]

This suggestive development in the analysis of fiction and history holds out a productive option in the interpretation of *KUM.* Although the truth-illusion differential is an ontologically constituted theme within the novel itself and a mainstay of my discussions to come, the polarity of public and private expressions as offered by Plaks creates a framework for depicting the fluid boundaries between *KUM* and its author, Kim Manjung. Since an historically and dialectically situated interpretation of *KUM* is just as critical to my project as an internal criticism, such a framework is indispensable.

My strategy revolves around depicting the relationship between the novel and its author, not only from the perspective of how the work flows from the author's biography, but the manner in which the work constitutes his biography within a larger, more public context. I therefore believe that *KUM,* while obviously not an autobiography in the sense that the author either directly or allegorically offers a self-accounting, nevertheless performs an autobiographical function. What comprises such a function does not ensue from the outpouring of personal views as much as it derives from the use of public symbols and images in the construction of that personal self. In *KUM,* the most dominant public symbol that Kim Manjung, or Sŏp'o,[14] chose to utilize was that of the dream. His use of this theme is hardly idiosyncratic or notably original. In fact, it is rather conventional. The greater significance of his use, however, inheres in the manipulation of literary themes and forms in order to give vent to a personal expression on the meaning of his own existence—an expression that was necessarily veiled in presentation.

I will begin, then, by training our sights on the private and public selves of Sŏp'o as created and constituted by his fiction. This route begins with a consideration of some dominant aspects of Sŏp'o's life and leads to an investigation of how this life came to hold meaningful form through the use of literary motifs. The latter process imbues narrative with an ontological significance in the strong sense of ontology that I defined at the end of the last chapter. As Mair points out, the rise of fiction signals the liberation of the creative imagination—to imagine the world, life, and even the self—which is underscored by the implicit understanding that beyond the imagination, nothing else may exist. Thus narratives create and conjure the world in a sense that surpasses the symbolic. It is, for all intents and purposes, ontologically creative.

The manner in which Sŏp'o's own life exemplifies this kind of literary magic is also historically constituted. Korea inherited China's literary traditions along with its writing system, both of which gave voice to the smaller nation's own historical consciousness. Thus as in China, the literary representation of the self—genres that we would today label as biography and autobiography—was formally assigned to the realm of historical writing. In Western understanding, autobiography is preoccupied with a meditation on one's private life, and is expected to disclose what a public persona will not admit. In sinological traditions, biography/autobiography falls into the realm of purely historical and therefore didactic discourse, rendered not as a private disclosure, but as a model exemplar of predesignated categories: the morally irreproachable statesman, eminent monk, virtuous woman, filial son. These exemplars are delivered not as individuals but as recognizable and socially sanctioned types. They strive not for a private divulgence, but to fulfill a mandatory public paradigm.

The contrast in modern Western and classical Chinese notions of selfhood offers a polarity that is historically comprised. The individuality of the self which mandates that each person fulfills a unique and internally justified potential is an attitude that scholars of autobiography agree in calling "modern" (since the close of the eighteenth century). It is intimately tied to a peculiar experience of history. In particular, the modern Western experience of diversity has been critical for overcoming fixed standards of being human. The concept of individuality reflects a culture that ventures to explore alternative visions of the self and that accepts heterogeneity as a positive value.[15] In contrast, traditional societies both East and West display a tendency to look to static models of self. These are worlds that stress living up to preordained ideals: "They offer man a script for his life, and only in the unprescribed interstitial spaces is there room for idiosyncrasy."[16]

On the Chinese and Korean scenes, this strategy of self-representation was reinforced by the general Confucian emphasis on community and the demand that each individual fulfill his or her designated function within it.[17] This accounts for why the depiction of individuals most often became the task of the historian. According to Robert Hegel:

> Histories were intended as manuals of precedents for Confucian administrators; this explains the tendency to group subjects in terms of their moral function in a particular social role, both roles and functions described in terms congruent with Confucian conceptions of social order intended to facilitate governing.[18]

Sŏp'o's standing in his own world—a status conscious world populated by patrilineal descent lines and pedigreed by records of government service—virtually assured his future within the elite pathway of education, examinations, and political appointment. Sŏp'o occupied a social position, in other words, that was considered foundational to the moral order of his day—that of the scholar-offical. Sŏp'o also lived in an era, however, in which sociopolitical contradictions and uncertainties gave the men of his class much reason for discontent. The resolutely public and rule-governed nature of their existence assured that any desire for private expression was steered towards the *wen* side of the literary spectrum.

Long before Sŏp'o's birth in seventeenth-century Korea, the association of fiction with the private domain was exemplified by the rise of popular narratives and drama during China's Song dynasty (960–1279). Given the limited focus of histories, the private life was an experience that laid outside the purview of the classical Chinese language. Popular narratives, on the other hand, readily embraced the vernacular tongues and increased the vocabulary for expressing one's inner life. Recent studies of Song drama suggest the ontologically creative nature of these narratives. In noting that theater is particularly oriented to the task of self-presentation, Pei-yi Wu states:

> The dramatist's art is predicated on the articulate and energetic egocentrism of the characters in his plays. They must project themselves on stage: they begin with a self-introduction to the audience and in their own voices unveil their inner feelings and narrate events not convenient to enact. . . . Thus a performer on the stage is the very opposite of a writing historian: the performer is nothing if he fails to project himself through his words while the latter has to operate under the convention of the selfless compiler, mute and invisible.[19]

Although the self-projection of the actor on the stage may be understood as the creation of a false and momentary persona, the greater effect perhaps lies in the integrity and reality of the life that he portrays. In this sense, the ready compatibility between creative fiction and the task of representing coherent, meaningful identities should be apparent. Similarly, the modern study of autobiography has noted the easy convergence between memory and imagination in the creation of life stories. Memory is committed to its own creativity the moment it orders its disparate glimpses into a linear narrative. Add to this the fact that fictional characters can have greater consistency than people or selves in real life, and the affinity between fiction and autobiography surfaces. In the explanation of one observor of the genre, "Autobiography as much as novels depend on narration, provide explanations, and insist on the comprehensibility of life."[20]

Sŏp'o's practice of fiction writing, then, must be seen as a convergence of two critical factors—the philosophical and the historical. The philosophical is comprised of the apprehension that narratives have the power to create lives by structuring them into meaningful patterns and progressions. The need to invent one's life has always existed, perhaps, in the "interstitial spaces" of even those classical societies where relatively static concepts of self prevailed. Thus in Korea, poetic and literary practices often gave voice to alternative visions of self.[21] In time, these alternatives themselves became a part of the cultural canon. Historically speaking, however, Sŏp'o emerged at a time when the pursuit of self took on a heightened urgency, thus compelling him to plumb fully the decentered zones of the canon. The end result is not the embrace of true innovation—of individuality and autobiography in our current usage. Instead, some familiar motifs of rebellion are recycled with a new and heightened consciousness of the *process* of such self-representation; in fact, in *KUM* this process is itself the philosophical message.

Sŏp'o supposedly produced many works of fiction but only two survive. Presently, I will focus on how Sŏp'o chose to represent himself through his other surviving novel, entitled *Sassi Namjŏnggi*, or *The Southern Expedition of Madame Sa* (*NJG*).[22] The French scholar Daniel Bouchez has conducted excellent studies of this novel, and I owe much of the following analysis to him. *NJG* is worth our attention because its autobiographical sensibility is much more obvious than in the religion- and fantasy-encrusted narrative of *KUM*. By first rehearsing the dynamics of public and private selves as they get composed in the fiction of *NJG*, we will facilitate our perception of a much more private self in *KUM*, which in its use of Buddhist religious themes, also implicates a broader historical development in the evolution of Buddhist discourse.

The Internal Theodicy of NJG

It is difficult to understand the autobiographical sense of *NJG* without first digesting the highly politicized life of its author. Sŏp'o was born in the first half of the seventeenth century, just a few years before the fall of the Ming dynasty in China and the official establishment of Manchu rule. Korea's recognition of the new regime was grudgingly given only after it itself suffered two direct assaults—the first in 1627, and the second in 1636. By the time the Manchus founded themselves as the Qing dynasty in 1644, Korea's submission was an established political fact but a source of lasting consternation.

Korea had existed in a tributary relationship with Ming China since the founding of the Chosŏn dynasty in 1392. The policy of *sadae*, or "serving the great," articulated Chosŏn Korea's ritual capitulation to the Chinese court as the supreme power. The emperor resided only in China; the Chosŏn monarch styled himself merely as a king. The Korean court had been deliberately put under the Ming umbrella by Yi Sŏnggye, the founder of the Chosŏn dynasty and a military leader seeking legitimation for his rule. The prestige of investiture by the Chinese emperor came at a nominal price. The Chinese court by and large stayed out of the internal affairs of its satellite nation and was content to receive its thrice-yearly tributary missions, frequently augmented by additional envoys on special ritual occasions.

For the Korean side, regular trips to the Chinese capital provided welcome opportunities for economic and intellectual exchange. The Chosŏn court's ardent interest in neo-Confucianism received regular infusions from contact with the mainland. Indeed, the scrutiny and interest aroused by all intellectual currents emanating from China assured that even heterodox ideas—such as Catholicism—eventually found their way into Korean territory. Korea's overriding ideological embrace, however, was of neo-Confucianism—initially articulated by the founders of the Chosŏn dynasty as a desire to replicate Chinese institutions on Korean soil.[23] This commitment to neo-Confucianism would become a major vehicle by which internal factional politics were played out within the Yangban aristocracy.

Sŏp'o's career as a public official and a member of the literati class is just one story that stems from this larger political and ideological framework. Sŏp'o was born of the Kim clan of Kwangsan, one of the pillars of the so-called "Western faction" which held continuous title (with the exception of periodic interruptions) as the most powerful bureaucratic party in the royal court. The intrigues of the Chosŏn court, like most of Korean politics, was something in the nature of a family affair. The acquisition and preservation of power was not solely predicated on clan status, however; it also cloaked itself in neo-Confucian philosophical rhetoric. Hence the designation of "Westerner" (Sŏin) and "Easterner" (Tongin) not only indicated one's clan affiliation, but the school of neo-Confucianism with which one was aligned.

The primacy of neo-Confucianism in Chosŏn Korea was supposedly an expression of reform based on Chinese institutions, and also supposedly signaled the demise of the kind of Buddhist influence that characterized the Koryŏ dynasty. Although neo-Confucian discourse supplied the Chosŏn with its ideological clothing, the actual institutional structures of the state revealed long-standing indigenous struggles—particularly the balance of power between the king and court bureaucrats, and the struggles amongst the bureaucrats themselves to gain the upper hand as members of the king's inner circle. The scholar-official's advantage, however—both against the king and against other scholar-officials—was most often embodied in claims of superior Confucian learning, earned through the state examination system that entitled them to office. The establishment of three censorate bodies allowed these scholar-officials not only to play watchdog to the king's ministers, but to admonish the monarch himself.[24] Confucian learnedness therefore became a powerful political instrument in the preservation of self-interest.

The scholar-officials, nevertheless, was a body divided against itself. As a social class, it comprised the Yangban aristocracy, whose wealth was based on the land granted to it as payment for office. Yangban status was strictly hereditary and a prerequisite to holding office. Chosŏn society's status consciousness manifested itself through the Yangban ranking system, which divided the Yangban into nine classes and strictly determined the level of office one was entitled to hold. Implicit in this system already was a stratification process that inevitably set its members off against each other.

The most immediate fracture within the Yangban class was drawn between the so-called meritorious elite, who formed the closest circle around the king, and the broad literati, many of whom formed their power bases in the provinces. The meritorious elite was initially comprised of subjects whose support had proven critical to Yi Sŏnggye's dynastic enterprise and who subsequently vaulted to power in the new political order. These newcomers rivaled the long-established clan powers, who now found themselves in competition for their prior privileges.[25] Those lucky enough to find themselves within the faction, however, were not guaranteed security. From time to time the king would find it necessary to break the power of the inner court by recalling the countryside literati (*sarim*). King Sŏngjong appointed many of these *sarim* during his reign (1469-1494), thereby bringing into his fold many scholar-officials whose ancestors had initially refused to serve the Chosŏn out of loyalty to the Koryŏ. The introduction of this faction touched off a series of intense struggles between the meritorious elite and the *sarim* which carried over into the middle of the sixteenth century.[26]

The names of those who rose and fell with the political winds changed with the years but the class of the politically frustrated was a continuous and growing entity. The *sarim* of the provinces were comprised not only of those initially displaced by the Chosŏn dynasty, but those who lost succeeding court battles, or those who for one reason or another did not succeed in gaining office. One significant example of the latter were the sons of concubines or secondary wives, who as a group were categorically denied the privilege of political service.[27] In addition, the increased ranks of the literati, with no attendant increase in the number of government positions, ensured a growing class of failed examination candidates. Most of these ostracized or would-be officials found it to their advantage to remove themselves to their ancestral provinces, where they could take up positions as local elites and assume responsibility for the community's moral and political leadership.[28]

One outgrowth of such local gentry activity was the establishment of private Confucian academies (*sŏwŏns*). These acad-

emies functioned as the center of Confucian rites and education—a prerogative that was monopolized by the localized literati. Serving as both spiritual and educational institutions, the
sŏwŏns acted as a holding ground for clan factions who were
biding their time. The practice of recognizing worthy sages of
the past as emblems of the schools lent them an aura of moral
authority which was instrumental in eventual bids for political
ascendancy. The practice also rendered the *sŏwŏns* into lineage
shrines, ensuring the perpetuation of factional disputation
through the imparting of clan loyalty from master to disciple.

What is perhaps the most interesting about the *sŏwŏns* is
what they illustrate about the Yangban strategy of political rebellion. Those dispossessed of power and position had sufficient reason—and means—to test the winds of change; to use
their own power base in the countryside to assert opposing
ideologies in an attempt to restructure society. Indeed, increasingly throughout the seventeenth and eighteenth centuries, a
body of scholarship known as *Sirhak* ("practical learning") voiced
censure of the status quo in favor of a new order based on
commerce and industry, and a social structure that recognized
individuals on the basis of merit alone. Those who articulated
this school of thought came in large part from those factions
excluded from political participation. The burgeoning of *sŏwŏns*
in the sixteenth and seventeenth centuries, however, reveal a
much more conservative response to political displacement.
While the literati of the provinces overtly took the stance of
rejecting the corrupt machinations of the court—of deliberately
opting out of an unworthy reign—they actively groomed themselves for an opportunity to assert themselves back into the
political center. The success of this bid could be predicated on a
showing of Confucian purity—a purity proven by one's prior
disdain of government service in the pursuit of classical learning and moral impeccability. The laments of these self-styled
"hidden sages" were frequently voiced in poetry and song and
provide a pertinent context for Sŏp'o's own literary efforts.

In turning to Kim Manjung the scholar-official, Sŏp'o
boasted one of the most privileged of lineages. His great-

grandfather, Kim Changsaeng (1548–1631) was a leading disciple of Yulgok (1536–1584), the prominent neo-Confucian philosopher who served as the authority for the Westerner faction. Kim Changsaeng's own commentaries on the official texts of family rites and mourning services were recognized as authoritative by the court. Sŏp'o was born shortly after the death of his father, a junior official who committed suicide after the Manchu invasion of Korea in 1637. He was raised by his mother, a woman who exercised profound influence over her son and his education. She was a Yun of the Haep'yŏng clan, reputed for its adherence to Confucian principles, and a great-granddaughter of King Sŏnjo (1567–1608).

Sŏp'o's own career reads like a catalogue of model accomplishments. He placed at the top of the government service examinations in 1665 at the age of twenty-eight. He served at high level positions, beginning as a provincial inspector, and moved on to posts in the Ministry of Rites, Public Works, and Justice. He was also appointed director of the prestigious Office of Special Counselors in 1685. This censorate body was scholarly in orientation, maintaining a library, drafting documents, and advising the king on the Confucian classics and other literary matters.

For all of his success, Sŏp'o's political life also reflects the ups and downs of his faction, the Westerners. The underside of this existence is documented by the political disfavor Sŏp'o suffered, all in the form of exile, in 1674, 1683, 1687, and 1689. The last exile, which came after a close brush with execution, was the worst—banishment to a remote island. It is here that Sŏp'o perished in 1692 at the age of fifty-five, much saddened by the news of his mother's death just three years before, and weakened by illness. The last years of Sŏp'o's political life, including the final exile, seem to have been the period in which both KUM and NJG were written.[29] In 1698, when the Westerners had regained power, Sŏp'o was posthumously reinstated and honored with titles for his filial piety and literary skills.

NJG has been known mostly in its Chinese version, but in fact was composed in Korean. Sŏp'o's grandnephew, Kim Ch'unt'aek (1670–1717), who made the translation while himself in exile on the island of Cheju between 1706 and 1710, gave the following reason for doing so:

> Sǒp'o composed a rather large number of novels in the vulgar language. Amongst them, the one entitled *Namjǒnggi* offers comparisons which are far from trivial. That is why I have undertaken to translate it into literary characters (Chinese).[30]

Most Korean interpreters of this novel, as Bouchez notes, have taken Kim Ch'unt'aek to mean that *NJG* is an allegorical novel based on the political events which sent Sǒp'o to his exile in 1687 and 1689. Furthermore, it has been assumed that the allegory was designed to affirm Confucian principles and instruct its readers, particularly the king at the center of the affair. The author's grandnephew undertook the Chinese translation of the novel, it is reasoned, so that it would be preserved and read by those most suited to benefit from its instructions. This didactic interpretation of *NJG* is not unwarranted given the established tradition—beginning in China and emulated by Korean literati—of justifying the writing of fiction on the premise that, like history, fictive narratives can morally edify. Here we have evidence indeed of the weakness of the differential truth-function in the Chinese/Korean view of these two literary genres. What separates them is not that one form of narrative is true while the other is false. Rather, it is that the first educates while the latter can potentially corrupt. The writing of history is a rule-governed affair where norms of identity and behavior are clearly predetermined. The writing of fiction, on the other hand, gives license to the imagination and can unleash the depiction of deviant models. If one can demonstrate the didactic properties of fiction, however, the objection is overcome and the distinction between history and fiction is erased.[31] Sǒp'o's own evaluation of the Chinese classical novel *Romance of the Three Kingdoms*, to be examined later, offers evidence that he was familiar with, and himself perpetuated, the didactic use of fiction.

The political affair to which *NJG* directly points is King Sukchong's (1674–1720) attempt to crown his concubine (Lady Chang) queen in 1689 after she bore him a son, thus effectively

deposing the reigning Queen Min. The queen had been unsuc-
cessful in bearing children, and Lady Chang had for some time
found favor in the king's eye. The Westerner's family ties to the
queen led to their vehement opposition to the plan, for which
many suffered disfavor and even death. The eventual discovery
of Lady Chang's association with court intrigues led to a charge
of sorcery and the reinstatement of Queen Min in 1694, along
with the revival of the powers of the Western faction.

In the tale of *NJG*, which is set in China, the scholar Liu
Yanshou and his wife, Lady Xie, are troubled by the latter's
inability to produce a son. The lady persuades her husband to
have a child by a concubine named Lady Qiao. After the deed is
done, Lady Qiao slanders Lady Xie in a bid to replace her altogether. Lady Qiao succeeds, and Lady Xie is forced to leave her
home and travel in the southern province of China. In the meantime, Lady Qiao and her lover, a man named Dongqing, politically frame the scholar Liu so that he is sent into exile. He stages
a comeback, however, and Lady Qiao is eventually executed
and his legitimate wife, Lady Xie, is restored to her happy home.

The parallelism of fictive and historical events seems to be
made more cogent by the fact of Sŏp'o's personal participation
and sufferings in the affair of Queen Min's deposition. It is
credible to conclude that *NJG* was written to give vent to the
author's more than dispassionate views of the incident, and to
confer moral triumph on his political clique nearly a decade
before its historical actualization. It is interesting to note that
later literary history would also vindicate Queen Min, and her
associated Western clan, through another novel—the historical
fiction known as *The True History of Queen Inhyŏn*.[32] The author of this work is unknown, and the work itself appears to
have been derived from previous texts composed within a century after the relevant historical events. The folkloristic version
of the political affair offered by this novel depicts in typical
fashion the Confucian constancy and irreproachability of the
queen, who represents the model virtuous woman. The degree
to which Queen Min is allowed to play this role, however, also
betrays the absoluteness of the Westerner's ensuing dominance.

Indeed, the faction which the concubine Chang Huibin represented—the "Southerners," which was a subfaction of the Easterners—never managed to stage a comeback after this defeat.

NJG's reference to political events, and its function as political vindication, has appeared to be palpable to most Korean interpreters. Here is an instance in which the autobiography of the author and his literary creation mesh seamlessly. The author clearly strives for some resolution of the events that landed him in the desolate setting of Namhae, an island off the southern coast of the Korean peninsula. The question that remains, however, is whether or not this reading does full justice to the metaphorical finesse with which Sŏp'o set about his literary task. To be sure, even the most ardent and progressive defenders of fiction in Ming China highlighted its educative capacity rather than its literary merits. One modern observer notes that "didacticism seemed to have provided men of letters with a convenient justification for any writing that deviated from what was deemed orthodox literature."[33] This defensiveness perhaps limited the extent to which fiction could be truly appreciated. One must keep in mind, however, the limited degree to which such appreciation could be explicitly articulated. In the case of Sŏp'o and NJG, one may argue that the political allegory on the affair of Queen Min was a concession to public discourse. If one looks more deeply, however, one can detect another level of allegory which eschews the didactic for a much more personalized concern with self-presentation.

Daniel Bouchez is less partial to the overtly politicized reading of NJG. The context in which his doubts are posed points to the interesting puzzle of the title. If the events depicted in NJG are mainly concerned with King Sukchong's troubles with women, Bouchez asks, then why does the title, The Southern Expedition, refer exclusively to the second half of the novel, which has little to do with the relevant events and which has always been ignored in the traditional interpretations?[34] The second half of NJG recounts Lady Xie's journey to the south, where she travels to the city of Changsha in the province of Hunan. There, on the banks of the River Xiang, Lady Xie contemplates suicide, until Heaven intervenes and puts her under the care of the Immortal of the South Sea. There she bides her time until events vindicate her purity and restore her back to her household.

A detail of significance concerns the identity of this Immortal of the South Sea. The unusual designation represents none other than the Bodhisattva Guanyin, and it is this Buddhist deity to whom Heaven entrusts the virtuous wife. This devotional touch, notes Bouchez, is surprising in a Confucian Yangban.[35] If nothing in Sŏp'o's own background suggests the sincerity of this detail, geographical associations are perhaps more helpful. Lady Xie's travel to the south renders Sŏp'o's invocation of the Bodhisattva Guanyin a plausible move given the *Avataṃsaka Sūtra*'s statement that this particular deity resides in the South Sea. The proof of East Asia's awareness of this geographical designation is offered in the frequent citings and/or establishments of the so-called island of Potalaka in the southern waters off of China, Korea, and Japan.

The addition of this religious and folkloristic detail is even more suggestive if one cares to notice that it refers back to the author's own location on the island of Namhae (itself meaning "South Sea"), which had long been identified as the Korean Potalaka. Geographical sources document that a hermitage of Guanyin existed on the island. Legend also recounts that it was built by the preeminent Korean monk Wŏnhyo (617–686). The suggestion of homology between the author and his heroine Lady Xie is deepened by the fact that they are both in exile, unjustly accused—so the suggestion goes—and made to suffer for their virtues. This analogy has the unexpected result of profoundly personalizing the novel's level of allegory. Lady Xie does not represent Queen Min, who in turn symbolizes a political group that Sŏp'o wishes to champion. Instead, as Bouchez convincingly argues, Lady Xie stands in for Sŏp'o himself.

In the Confucian penchant for homologizing, the honest minister who is unappreciated, mistreated, and rejected by his sovereign is likened to the virtuous woman who is cast out by her husband. The earliest literary instance of this association is offered by the poet Qu Yuan who lived in the southern state of

Chu in the third century B.C.E. Qu Yuan represents perhaps one of the earliest historical figures cast in the mold of the honest counselor who speaks his mind and is then banished from court for his efforts. He offers his own analogy of the situation in his famous poem *Lisao,* "Encountering Sorrow," where he compares himself to a wife unjustly forsaken by one to whom she remains true.[36] Lines 33 to 48 of the poem state:

> 'The fools enjoy their careless pleasure,
> But their way is dark and leads to danger.
> I have no fear for the peril of my own person,
> But only lest the chariot of my lord should be dashed.
> I hurried about your chariot in attendance,
> Leading you in the tracks of the kings of old.'
> But the Fragrant One refused to examine my true feelings:
> He lent ear instead to slander, and raged against me.
>
> How well I know that loyalty brings disaster;
> Yet I will endure: I cannot give up.
> I called on the ninefold heaven to be my witness,
> And all for the sake of the Fair One, and no other.
> There once was a time when he spoke with me in frankness;
> But then he repented and was of another mind.
> I do not care, on my own account, about this divorcement,
> But it grieves me to find the Fair One so inconstant.[37]

Bouchez states of this poem:

> The two figures, the banished minister and the outcast woman, are mixed together in a deliberate ambiguity. Sima Qian praises the poet for composing a work which is at the same time a love poem and a political poem, avoiding the defects of each of the two genres. The allegory of the forsaken woman has been often revived in China after Qu Yuan by poets unhappy in public affairs.[38]

Sŏp'o's consciousness of this tradition is spoken for in *NJG*, again through geographical association. Lady Xie's journey to the south allows the heroine to enter the historical domain of the ancient kingdom of Chu, where Qu Yuan served as minister to King Huai (r. 328–299 B.C.E.). Lady Xie's attempt to throw herself into the River Xiang also points to a paradigm: Qu Yuan supposedly drowned himself in the Miluo (a tributary of the Xiang) after completing the *Lisao*. Following the account in the *History of the Former Han Dynasty* (*Hou Han Shu*), the narrative in *NJG* recounts, "Qu Yuan, the virtuous minister of Chu, served King Huai with complete loyalty but was slandered by a minor official. He composed the *Lisao*, then he threw himself into the river and was drowned." (楚之賢臣屈原， 事懷王盡忠，爲小人所讒，著離騷經投水而死)[39]

When Madame Xie decides to attempt suicide in the river, the apparitions of E Huang and Nu Ying, the two wives of the legendary Emperor Shun, appear to her and state, "You wish to follow in the footsteps of Qu Yuan, but that is not the will of Heaven." (欲追屈原之蹤甚非天意)[40] The direct invocation of Qu Yuan in this particular instance does not represent a culmination; the references to this archetypal figure reverberate throughout the novel. The incorporation of the two wives of Shun as agents of Heaven who counsel Lady Xie against taking her own life offers a subtler manner of literary and historical association. Emperor Shun supposedly died on campaign in the south and was followed there by his grieving wives. They drowned themselves at the mouth of the Xiang River and were transformed into river goddesses. They became objects of a major local cult and Shun himself, buried on Doubting Mountain (Jiuyishan), was greatly venerated by the Chu people. Sŏp'o's allusion to this history is actually a redoubling of Qu Yuan's poetic action. In lines 143 and 144 of the *Lisao*, Qu Yuan states,

> And crossing the Yuan and Xiang, I journeyed southwards
> Till I came to where Chong Hua was and made my plaint to him.[41]

Chong Hua is another name for Emperor Shun. Qu Yuan's move to seek him out makes implicit reference to the cult of Emperor Shun. It is the associated cult of the river goddesses E Huang and Nu Ying that is invoked by Sŏp'o in order to save Madame Xie. Bouchez draws attention to these poetic lines of Qu Yuan in a different but complementary way: It is the account about crossing the Yuan and Xiang and *journeying south-*

ward, he claims, that served as Sŏp'o's inspiration in titling his own novel.[42]

The double homology of the *NJG*—Sŏp'o as Lady Xie, Lady Xie as Qu Yuan—justifies the view that Sŏp'o's ultimate aim was to cast himself as a latter-day embodiment of Qu Yuan. The *NJG*, which refracts this process of self-conceptualization through the figure of the virtuous but estranged wife, makes use of what is by now a prevailing cultural trope and replicates Qu Yuan's own act of self-conception. According to this model, Sŏp'o is a loyal minister unjustly banished, and he comforts himself by writing *NJG*, just as Qu Yuan wrote *Lisao*.

Sŏp'o undoubtedly conceived this strategy through the example of those before him. The habit of invoking Qu Yuan in exile poems experienced one culmination in the Korean poet Chŏng Ch'ŏl (1536-1593), who is credited with the perfection of the Korean lyrical poem known as the *kasa*. Chŏng Ch'ŏl, whom Sŏp'o recognized as the only reputable poet of Korea, was also a Westerner who ran afoul of favor during the succession debate in the reign of King Sŏnjo (1567–1608). His two poems, *Sa miin kok* ("Mindful of My Seemly Lord"), and *Sok miin kok* ("Again Mindful of My Seemly Lord") evoke the *Lisao* in fusing the love and political plaints of his address. The first poem, which Peter Lee translates as "Hymn of Constancy," begins with these lines:

> I was born to serve you
> By happy affinity, Heaven's wish.
> My youth was spent for you; you loved
> me alone. What can match
> this undivided mind, this rare love?
> I wanted to spend my whole life with you.
> Why do we live apart in our later age?
> Once I repaired with you to the Moon Palace;
> but then I was left here below. Three years now
> since my hair has become disheveled, unkempt.
> For whom should I dress?
> My mind, tied in knots of anxiety,
> and grief, piled fold upon fold,
> only produces sighs, tears.
> Life has an end; only sorrow is endless.[43]

Chŏng Ch'ŏl's poem gives ample evidence of the cultural embeddedness of Qu Yuan as an archetypal figure, as well as the strategy of evoking him through the literary mode.

A close examination of Sŏp'o's *NJG*, then, reveals a deeper and subtler allegorical stratagem than traditional interpretations have allowed for. Bouchez argues that Kim Ch'unt'aek was aware of Sŏp'o's intended allegory between himself and Lady Xie. In a study of Kim's preface to his Chinese translation of *NJG*,[44] Bouchez contends that Kim's statement that *NJG* "offers comparisons which are far from trivial" in fact referred to Sŏp'o's double homologizing process. Bouchez notes, however, that the corruption of Kim Ch'unt'aek's translation, which was frequently copied back into Korean, led to misinterpretations of the novel, as well as misconstruals of the significance that Kim attached to it.[45]

To be sure, the process of frequent recopying assured the novel's literary presence in Korean culture. It first circulated amongst the ladies of the royal court, then branched outward as a popular novel amongst the literati. Through these variant texts, *NJG* was consumed within all literate circles. "Such success," Bouchez avers, "contrasts with the lesser estimation with which it is held today by critics, particularly compared to that which is accorded to *Dream of the Nine Clouds*."[46] The work of the copyists, on the other hand, subverted Sŏp'o's original intentions. The novel "lost its finesse and brilliance [and] its literary allusions disappeared."[47] What is most interesting about the course that this process took is that the popular readings of Sŏp'o's novel moved away from his autobiographical purpose and approached much more closely the function of histories. In other words, *NJG* was foisted with a didactic message and categorized as a moralistic novel. The most common rendition of this assumption was the view that Sŏp'o wrote *NJG* to admonish King Sukchong and "enlighten his heart and mind." The contents of the lessons that Sŏp'o supposedly wished to teach are classically Confucian in concern: how to run one's household, which is akin to running a state; how to choose a concubine, which is also akin to choosing a counselor; and the ideals of conjugal harmony and feminine chastity.[48] Bouchez notes that these values are evocative of the *Great Learning* (*Da Xue*), a classic Confucian text which imposes "the necessity of putting one's own house in order before governing the state," and also the "well known parallel between the fidelity of a wife and the loyalty of a grand officer."[49] Given this homology, it is understandable that *NJG* was also read as a biography of an exemplary Confucian woman.

The simultaneous enactment of political and personal allegories in *NJG* invites another consideration of Andrew Plaks' assertion that the polarity between history and fiction draws a division of labor between public and private expressions. If we wish to preserve this schema, then we must be profoundly grateful to Daniel Bouchez's research, which rescues *NJG* from reduction into history—with its didactic and political intentions. What the case of *NJG* demonstrates, however, is that Plaks' distinction between the formation of public and private selves is perhaps too neatly drawn. For the autobiographical conception that Sŏp'o perpetuates in his fiction is very much modeled on public Confucian ideal types—the virtuous wife and loyal minister. This underscores the fact that narrative genres have fluid boundaries. We have already determined that fiction can be put to political purpose as readily as history. We may further conclude that the public selves of history can also be privately consumed in the act of self-conceptualization. Like history and fiction, public and private selves appear to have similarly ambiguous boundaries.

Sŏp'o's choice to follow in the footsteps of Chŏng Ch'ŏl (and many others) instantiated an archetypical form of self-conception. Sŏp'o's decision to view himself through culture-governed patterns was an act that went beyond the use of literary themes. By employing the metaphor of the virtuous wife, Sŏp'o incarnated a cultural paradigm that allowed him to take on a distinct and condonable historical identity. This identity in turn allowed him to effect an internal theodicy, a way of imagining himself to himself that would overcome and create meaning out of his political sufferings. The most interesting aspect of Sŏp'o's use of narrative, then, is that it is distinguishable neither along the truth-differential nor the public-private axis. Instead, Sŏp'o's deployment of narrative is single-mindedly focused on the autobiographical process. Although this study concurs with Pei-yi Wu's thesis that fictive narratives were better suited for self-expression, the more general point here is that all narratives have this capacity.[50] Here the distinction between history and fiction manifests the least possible significance. It is replaced by a cultural process in which history and fiction often share the same *topoi* to create both public and private selves that at times converge.

The prototype of the banished minister, especially as homologized to the virtuous wife, has traversed the gulf between the public and the private from the earliest stages of Chinese and Korean discourse. This figure is not a simple model of political success, but one who has a complaint to vent. The political purpose is accomplished by privatizing the plaint. By likening the disgruntled officer to a loyal and wronged lover, the suggestion of political sedition is mitigated. The historian Sima Qian praised Qu Yuan's deftness in spanning the realms of public and private identities: "The Songs of the States are sensual without being licentious; the Lesser Ya poems are plaintive without being seditious. *Lisao* may be said to combine both virtues."[51] Understandably, it is when the public and private selves are so thoroughly combined that the distinction between history and fiction is at its most fickle. In the case of Sŏp'o, fiction is used to reactualize history within his own situation in order to conceive himself. But this "history" is itself a literary creation.

The case of Sima Qian, who wrote a biography of Qu Yuan, offers another way of imagining the fusion of public and private lives. In the telling of Qu Yuan's public tale, Sima Qian acknowledges the life of a personal hero and analogizes it to his own private sufferings. As David Hawkes explains:

> Ssu-ma Chien was obsessed by the belief that all great literature is the product of great suffering. The reason for this

is easy enough to discover. He had himself suffered the horrible and humiliating punishment of castration for having dared to speak up on behalf of a victim of the Emperor Wu's wrath. After undergoing mutilation, he felt that he ought to have committed suicide, and explained to his friends that he had not done so because he wanted to finish his great History. It is not surprising, therefore, that he should have found both a defence and a consolation in the reflection that all his literary heroes had been men who, like him, had known suffering and humiliation.[52]

Here the figure of the banished minister is further fleshed out as the prerequisite for literary genius—a progression which is present in Sŏp'o's own self-consciousness and made evident by his decision to enact his life through the composition of *NJG*. Sŏp'o's participation in this cultural habit resonates with long-standing patterns but also suggests a certain turning point in the practice. Scholars of seventeenth-century China have called attention to the frequency and deliberateness with which angry would-be statesmen with a strong sense of their own abilities and literary talents took up their literary brushes.[53] The political conditions of Chosŏn Korea during this era provided equal incentive for expressing grievances. The development of the full-length narrative offered unprecedented avenues for the subtlety and artfulness with which one's unhappiness could be voiced. In *NJG* we have an example of how the novel is capable of combining the rather divergent tasks of addressing contemporary political problems and probing the meaning of one's individual existence. One may choose to see the former, more public task as an imposed constraint which was necessary to simultaneously enable and veil the expression of the latter, more private exploration. In my estimation, however, the significance of the novel as a literary format is not limited to its ability to navigate conflicting cultural demands. In its use of the full range of cultural symbols—both orthodox and heterodox—in the exploration of identity, the novel demands awareness of the malleability of self and the processes which go into its composition.

Convergence of Narrative and Philosophy

The abundant cultural and historical references in Sŏp'o's novel give evidence of a persistent dynamic in the sinological tradition in which the production of literary works are preceded by certain forms of self-conception. Life takes on preconceived modes and follows archetypes which are both created and perpetuated by literary formats. Chinese history is full of statesmen who turned to versification, and later, prose, to tender their personal feelings. Their actions soon generated public prototypes of selves. The example of statesman and poet Bo Zhuyi (772–846) provides a succinct and versified sample of some choices for self-conceptualization. In the last lines of one poem, a comparison is made between a common cultural polarity, the Confucian official and the Taoist hermit:

> Yesterday his counsel was sought by the Throne;
> To-day he is banished to the country of Yai-chou.
> So always, the Counsellors of Kings;
> Favor and ruin changed between dawn and dusk!
>
> Green, green—the grass of the Eastern Suburb;
> And amid the grass, a road that leads to the hills.
> Resting in peace among the white clouds,
> Can the hermit doubt that he chose the better part?[54]

The frequent actualization by historical men of culturally patterned self-conceptions suggests the pertinence of Victor Mair's ontological theory of fiction. The rich subtlety of Mair's thesis suggests not only the creative process in which literature conceives of lives, but also a philosophical awareness of this process on the part of those who implement it.

This awareness is of critical importance for the analysis of *KUM* to come. One might pose this factor as a question: To what extent does the ontological process of fiction itself become an object of consciousness? I have interpreted Sŏp'o's use of narrative along the lines of Mair's ontological theory of fiction—that narratives in fact bring the self into being. This assertion may be summarized as the formula that illusion creates reality.

This analysis, however, is an inverse telling of the Buddhist ontology of illusion, which offers the wisdom that reality is illusion. Hence if narratives are capable of defining the contours of one's existence, one must also entertain the proposition that that existence is quixotic and pliable, with its range of options limited only by the range of narratives that cultures choose to apply to it. The ontological theory of fiction and the ontology of illusion, in other words, form a mutual equation. Although each part is capable of being understood and appreciated on its own, the particular philosophical virtue of *KUM* is that the two are made to converge.

I describe this convergence in terms of the harmony of *KUM*'s metaphysics and metapractice. The ontology of illusion, as a view of reality, formulates the novel's metaphysics. To express this metaphysics, Sŏp'o' utilizes fictive narrative, which in his hands, demonstrates an understanding of the ontological theory of fiction. Hence, Sŏp'o's use of narrative to espouse the ontology of illusion creates a seamlessness between the author's view of reality and his articulation of it. This articulation is his metapractice, or his ability to make his mode of expression conform to what is expressed.

To qualify it fully as a metapractice, however, one must demonstrate the self-consciousness, rather than fortuitousness, of *KUM*'s unity of metaphysics and mode of discourse. Sŏp'o's narrative practice in *NJG* argues for his awareness of the ontological capacity of fiction. To further this argument, one might end with one known instance in which Sŏp'o explicitly expressed his opinion about the function of fiction. Daniel Bouchez reports that in Sŏp'o's collected writings (*Sŏp'o manp'il*), the author makes a comparison between the Chinese Ming novel, *Romance of the Three Kingdoms,* and its official historical account, the *Sanguozhi.* Sŏp'o concludes that the novel is superior to the history for the purpose of instructing the young and the common people.[55] Bouchez notes that this is an opinion that is rather original for the era. What Bouchez alludes to is Chosŏn Korea's neo-Confucian temper, which disapproved of the creative imagination and its potential for engendering and glorifying social deviance. Assurances regarding fiction's didactic powers might have proven expedient, but Victor Mair, as we have seen, argues on the contrary that the real reason for the ascendancy of fiction in East Asia was based on the influence of Buddhist ontological views. Nevertheless, Sŏp'o's reading of the *Three Kingdoms* demonstrates that the didactic and metaphysical considerations need not conflict. Let us briefly consider Sŏp'o's treatment of this work.

The *Three Kingdoms* is a military epic based on third- and fourth-century historical records of the fall of the Han dynasty in 220 C.E. and the subsequent rise of the kingdoms of Wei, Wu, and Shu. The fiction centers around the heroic efforts of Liu Bei to restore the Han dynasty to its former glory and dynastic position. When Luo Guanzhong wrote his novel during the reign of the first Ming emperor, he culminated a popular tradition begun during the Southern Song in which Liu Bei, the would-be dynastic restorer, came to symbolize resistance to foreign invasion. Luo Guanzhong's own era—the early years of the Ming— represented the successful overthrow of the Mongol Yuan dynasty and the restoration of legitimate Chinese rule. The romanticized sentiment surrounding Liu Bei and the Han becomes more cogent in light of these events and the Chinese habit of using past events to allegorize and comment upon the present. Zhu Yuanzhang, the founding emperor of the Ming, is but one example of a stateman who used such allegories to full personal advantage: He identified himself with the first Han emperor, paralleling the Ming with the Han, and thereby suggesting the legitimate and "indigenous" nature of his own reign.

It is no wonder that Sŏp'o, as a Korean, took the *Three Kingdoms* and its approbation of resisting foreign rule to heart. Less than a century before, his country had suffered the devastating Japanese invasions of 1592 and 1597 led by Toyotomi Hideyoshi. The incursions produced one of Korea's own larger-than-life heroes, the naval commander Yi Sunsin whose famed turtle boats succeeded in turning the tide of the war. More recently and more significantly, the Manchu invasion of China had encroached upon Korea's own borders and ultimately undermined Korea's loyalty to Ming China. The Western faction had staunchly counseled a pro-Ming, anti-Manchu policy, but this was vetoed and they were overrun by those who urged submission in order to spare the country from further invasion. A month before his birth, Sŏp'o's father, a member of the royal court, had killed himself in the wake of the 1636 invasion in order to protest his country's submission. The events that deprived Sŏp'o of his father succumbed to an era of festering hatred for the Qing court. In Korea, the succeeding reign of King Hyojong (1649–1659), himself a Manchu hostage for eight years, harbored designs to launch a revenge attack on the north and raged with debate concerning Korean foreign policy. Bouchez points out that these issues "marked the infancy and youth of Kim Manjung and were ones to which he could not remain indifferent."[56]

In favoring the fictionalized account of the *Three Kingdoms* to its historical documents, Sŏp'o recognizes the primacy of the popular symbolic associations evoked by Liu Bei and the Han. Through this recognition, Sŏp'o focuses on the cultural mechanisms by which meaning is conveyed. In other words, Sŏp'o is fully aware of, and furthermore sanctions, the use of fiction to provide moral commentary upon contemporary events. Bouchez demonstrates how Sŏp'o's preoccupation with the *Three Kingdoms* centered around a literary character—the Taoist-inspired figure of Zhugeliang. This character served as Liu Bei's adviser and as a paradigm of the true Confucian. Zhugeliang is a figure characterized more through fiction than fact, but it is he who represents, in Sŏp'o's mind, the man of action to which all Confucians should aspire. Ignoring standard Confucian assessments of Zhugeliang's capacities, Sŏp'o notes the persistence with which the counselor carried out the restoration enterprise long after the death of Liu Bei himself. He also surmises that had this minister been in charge of Korea during the Manchu aggression, the course of passive submission would never have been countenanced.[57]

The use of fiction—particularly fictionalized history—in order to reflect upon the meaning of the present is an activity that

inevitably presents itself as didactic. The search for an illuminating perspective upon current political events naturally sends
one in search of parallels from the past. With the presence of the
formidable Chinese historiographical tradition, moreover, looking to the past immediately implies the digestion of previously
articulated lessons on the meaning of human affairs. The present
can be clarified only by the extent to which it is made to
reinstantiate past events which are, ostensibly, perspicuous and
absolute in their significance.

So too, in the realm of personal identity, the past offers
definitive models of being:

> Whenever he is in doubt, a Chinese is bound to look to the
> ancients for moral support or spiritual illumination. Indeed,
> it can be said categorically that so long as one is mindful of
> the teachings in any of the Three Schools, be it Confucian-
> ism, Taoism, or Buddhism, no Chinese should feel at a loss
> in any given situation as to what to do with one's life.[58]

The weight of the past, to be sure, imposes a burden with
its tenacious ability to assert itself into fresh situations. The visions of self that are created even in the novels of Korea and
China tend on the whole to be continuous with prior types. It
would be erroneous, however, to confuse this perpetuation with
a mindless conservatism that prefers mere repetition over cultural innovation. The criterion of innovation need not demand
complete rejection of one's cultural legacy. My consideration of
Sŏp'o's novel, *The Southern Expedition*, suggests a narrative
creation that is aware of the peculiar quality of literary allegories. It suggests that the use of fiction to invent one's life is the
creation of allegory at its most dependently symbolic level. This
is so because the contours of that life are almost solely predicated on the allegory. The use of narrative to signify one's life
suggests an entity which does not exist beyond that act of imagination. The deployment of narrative within this framework of
understanding suggests innovation in a different vein—an innovation that does not inhere in the revolutionary nature of the
self that is imagined, but rather in the awareness and articulation of this process of imagination.

This innovation perhaps amounts to no more than Paul Ricoeur's observation that "there is no human experience that is not already mediated by symbolic systems and, among them, by narratives."[59] Sŏp'o's appropriation of narrative, in particular, underscores and magnifies this cultural truth in that he re-animates ready-made symbols as a form of autobiography. The modeling of the self to the virtuous wife in *NJG*, and from that back to the ancient poet Qu Yuan who originally made the homology, ripples backwards in an endless chain of self-imaginings passed on through countless generations of disillusioned statesmen. The historical veracity of Qu Yuan as the archetypal wronged minister—that is, the facticity of the original created self, is of little or no importance in comparison to the act of creation. The need to imagine the meaning of one's life through recognizable formats derives from what Ricoeur calls the "prenarrative quality of experience," which underdetermines our lives and which therefore yearns for concrete expression:

> . . . a life story proceeds from untold and repressed stories in the direction of actual stories the subject can take up and hold as constitutive of his personal identity. It is the quest for this personal identity that assures the continuity between the potential or inchoate story and the actual story we assume responsibility for.[60]

Composing *The Southern Expedition* was clearly an instantiation of this cultural process. To speculate on how *The Dream of the Nine Clouds* participates in this process is more involved and more interesting. There is, to be sure, a distinct flavor of rebellion against the Confucian model of self in Sŏp'o's embrace of Buddhist sentiments in *KUM*. We must be careful not to read a simple assertion of religious or political choice into the situation: that is, the rejection of Confucianism in favor of Buddhism. Sŏp'o's use of narrative is the same in both novels despite their uses of opposing ideological symbols. In my reading, the opposing symbols do not signify the author's divided loyalties as much as each novel's differing philosophical prowess—that is, the extent to which the author's narrative practice is internally recognized and ontologically accounted for.

The virtuous wife/banished minister theme of *NJG* lacks the metaphysical relevance that makes the question of self-consciousness possible. This is not an inherent failing of the image, but rather a reflection of the limited concerns of the Confucian tradition within which the image subsists. Thus it is incapable of allowing the author to incorporate a consciousness of itself and the role it plays in framing a life. For this, Sŏp'o was forced to turn to a different figurative image altogether— the metaphor of life as a dream.

The self-consciousness that I desire to attribute to *KUM* arises from a common cultural fund, and is not a product of Sŏp'o's singular creation. This time, however, the substance of the metaphor in use is specifically philosophical. To narrow it even further, it is ontological in its insistence that life, meta-physically examined, amounts to nothing more than a passing illusion, a dream. In the following chapter, I will attempt to match the narrative elements of *KUM* with the Buddhist onto-logical views. The attempt will be to discern how the structure of the novel provides a translation of the Buddhist view of life. By creating this match, it will become clear how *KUM* conjures a self-conscious discourse, which, in its self-reflexivity, comprises a sophisticated form of philosophical practice.

Chapter 3

The Symmetry of Illusion and Reality

The Dream of the Nine Clouds opens with a panoramic inventory of the five sacred mountains of China, and then immediately focuses on the southernmost range known as Hengshan. It is stated that Lotus Peak, which is located on Hengshan, not only is home to Lady Wei, who became a Taoist adept in the time of the Jin, but to an old Buddhist monk from India who arrived during the time of the Tang and established a monastery for his six hundred disciples. This old monk is known as the Great Master Liuguan and he expounds the *Diamond Sūtra*, one of the seminal texts of the *Perfection of Wisdom* (*Prajñāpāramitā*) tradition of Mahāyāna Buddhism.

Amongst Liuguan's coterie of some thirty advanced disciples, the youngest is known as Xingzhen—the fairest and most accomplished of all, and whom Liuguan intends to appoint as his successor. One day Xingzhen is sent on a mission of thanks to the Dragon King of Dongting Lake, who frequently transformed himself into a white-robed scholar in order to come to the monastery and listen to the Master's sermons. Xingzhen is greeted with great festivity by the Dragon King and cajoled into drinking three cups of wine, despite the Buddhist injunction against drink and Xingzhen's own great reluctance. Feeling flushed and fearing discovery by his Master, the adept decides to rest by a stream on his return journey, where a delicious fragrance leads him to the enchanting sight of the eight fairy

69

girls of Lady Wei. They too are returning from a courtesy call, their's to Xingzhen's own Master Liuguan, and are lingering on the way home to enjoy the scenery of the peak.

Xingzhen and the fairy ladies engage in a spirited and flirtatious dialogue, and afterwards each party makes its way home. That evening, the adept is spiritually and mentally disturbed by the memories of this encounter. He reflects on the difficult and lonely life of the monk and thinks longingly of the pleasures and rewards of those who pursue the Confucian path of fortune and renown. Quite suddenly, he is summoned by his angry Master, who rebukes him for his sin of drink and idle thoughts, and turning a deaf ear to all of the young novice's pleading, condemns him to hell and the judgment of King Yama.

In the underworld, Xingzhen again encounters the eight fairies, who too have been condemned by Liuguan. King Yama, reluctant to judge all these accomplished adepts too harshly, commands that they be returned to the land of the living. Xingzhen is sent to be reborn as a child to the hermit Yang and his fifty-year old wife in the province of Huainan. Xingzhen is named Shaoyou, or "brief sojourner" (小遊) by the hermit, who proclaims, "This child is a heavenly being come to live among men." (此兒必天人摘降也)[1] When the child is still in early youth, Hermit Yang, who is somewhat of an immortal being himself, states that his term of karma which bound him to the world of dust is up and he departs with fellow immortals to Penglai, where all immortals dwell.

What follows from this point in the tale is an account of Shaoyou's adult life, in which his karmic affinity with the eight fairies (contracted in his previous life) is brought to fruition in courtship and marriage. At the age of fifteen, Shaoyou decides to embark upon the capital city in order to try his hand at the imperial examinations. On his way, he stops to rest in a thicket of willow trees, which he finds so poetically inspiring that he sings several spontaneously composed verses. His clear voice is carried to the upper window of a nearby house—the abode of Government Commissioner Qin—where the commissioner's daughter Caifeng (Phoenix) had been napping. Phoenix is enchanted by the song, and upon peering out the window, the two destined lovers' eyes meet in silence until she withdraws.

Through the medium of Phoenix's nurse, more verses and a vow of marriage are exchanged, and although highly contrary to the modesty expected of ladies of proper upbringing, Phoenix agrees to a love meeting for the very next day. Unfortunately, Shaoyou's eager anticipation is frustrated by the outbreak of political rebellion in the capital, which forces him to flee to the mountains. Here he meets a Taoist immortal who is personally acquainted with his father, the former Hermit Yang. Shaoyou stays for the day and the Taoist teaches him a few immortal tunes on the lute. The next day, unable to locate Phoenix, and hearing that her father had been implicated in the rebellion and executed, Shaoyou returns home. The fulfillment of their fate together will not take place until much later in Shaoyou's career, when he has achieved renown and the position of royal son-in-law. (Shaoyou will learn then that Phoenix is present in the palace, having been carried off as a maid after the execution of her father. At that point, she will be appointed as one of his concubines.)

The following spring, Shaoyou sets off once more for the imperial examinations. Taking a different route from the previous year, he passes through Loyang where he happens upon a drinking party of young literati engaging in a poetry contest. Amongst the dancing girls, the fairest of all—Gui Chanyue (Moonlight)—is renowned for her skills in verse and is the apparent prize for the most talented composer of the evening. Moonlight picks out Shaoyou's verse as the best and follows with a pledge to bind herself to him after he has established the position and rank that she knows is his due. Shaoyou continues his journey the next day.

When Shaoyou reaches Changan, he discovers that there is plenty of time before the examinations to carry through his mother's wishes of finding a proper wife. Through a relative—a Taoist priestess—he hears of Qiongbei, the daughter of the high ranking Minister Zheng. Determined to have a look at her for himself, Shaoyou disguises himself as a young Taoist priestess and manages an invitation into the Zheng home to play the lute. At the meeting, Qiongbei's knowledge of music is equal to Shaoyou's skill in playing. A suggestive song, however, leads her to see through Shaoyou's disguise, and she flees in mortification.[2]

At the examinations, Shaoyou places on top and his name is immediately heralded throughout the capital. Shaoyou submits a marriage proposal to the Zheng household which, despite Qiongbei's lingering anger, is accepted by her parents. Much to Shaoyou's delight, Qiongbei's maid Chunyun (Cloudlet) is thrown into the bargain as a secondary wife, as the two women had sworn sisterhood and vowed never to be apart from each other.

As Shaoyou makes preparations to bring his mother to the capital for the wedding, an uprising of governors in league with the Tibetans in Hobei forces a hiatus in plans. Shaoyou is given the rank of general and commissioned by the Emperor to make a diplomatic trip. He is successful in bringing the parties to submission and on his return route, he passes through Loyang where he is reunited with Moonlight. The general is given another opportunity at double-dipping when Moonlight makes a secret substitution of beautiful Jinghong (Wildgoose) for herself one night. Wildgoose is another famed dancer with whom Moonlight had made a pact: if one of them were to find a worthy man, she would immediately share him with the other. Satisfied with this arrangement, Shaoyou continues on to the capital.

Shaoyou's success in Hobei brings upon him a heap of honors and dignities, including a royal marriage proposal from the emperor on behalf of his sister, the Princess Orchid. Because of his previous contract with the Zheng family, he attempts to refuse. Before matters can be resolved, Shaoyou is once more pressed into military service by an uprising by the Tibetans. The campaign that he leads gives him occasion for two more love adventures. While planning strategy in his military tent, a would-be assassin appears to him in the person of a lovely swordswoman. When the general displays fearlessness, Niauyan (Swallow) throws down her weapon to the proclamation that he is her destined lover, foretold by her sword instructor. After sporting together a good many days (during which Shaoyou all but forgets his military goals), Swallow departs, promising to follow him eventually to the capital.

In the meantime, the campaign advances. Arriving at Taishan, the soldiers discover that the lake water is brackish and causes them all to be ill. Pondering what to do, Shaoyou falls asleep. In a dream, two girls come to him to tell him that the daughter of the Dragon King requests his presence at the Water Palace. There the daughter informs him of how a fortuneteller had foretold their union. All is not well, however, for the Prince of the Southern Sea had pressed his suit, and upon her refusal, had threatened to wage war. The princess had fled and her cries to Heaven moved it to make the lake waters so forbidding that the prince's army did not dare enter it. Acting upon her pleas for protection, Shaoyou fights a battle with the watery army and emerges in victory. After an immense victory celebration at which the Dragon King is present, the king and the general approach a mountain where they stumble upon a Buddhist temple. The chief priest who greets them informs Shaoyou, "the day of your final coming has not yet arrived," and tripping, Shaoyou awakens from his dream.

The situation for Shaoyou's army has changed: it is discovered that the water of the lake has turned sweet and the soldiers are able to drink of it. Afterwards, they wage a successful campaign. While Shaoyou is in service, Princess Orchid decides to resolve her marriage impasse by having Qiongbei adopted as her sister so that both can be married to the unsurpassed hero as equal royal wives. The princess disguises herself as a commoner in order to befriend the minister's daughter. Upon swearing sisterhood, the princess reveals her identity and spirits Qiongbei off to the palace, where the old empress-dowager adopts the latter as her own daughter.

It is decided to accomplish this double-marriage through a trick on Shaoyou. He is told upon his return that Qiongbei has died of grief, so that there is no need to refuse the Princess Orchid as his bride any longer. He is offered both Princess Orchid and her "sister," Princess Blossom, along with Phoenix, now a palace maid with whom he is happily reunited. With Shaoyou believing that Qiongbei is really dead, the women continue their merry deception of the imperial son-in-law until they are accidentally discovered.

The rest of the tale is occupied with an idyllic life of dancing, poetry, and archery contests. Moonlight and Wildgoose permanently join Shaoyou when he returns to Changan with his mother, and Swallow and Whitecap (the Dragon King's daughter in the dream) also appear shortly thereafter. More honors and titles are heaped upon the son-in-law, and he becomes a cherished minister of the state. His two wives and six concubines bear a horde of children, all of whom attain high government rank or get married off to royalty.

One day when Shaoyou and his wives are admiring the view from the high tower of Green Mountain Castle, Shaoyou draws forth his jade flute and plays a tune so plaintive it draws tears from the women. Asked the reason for his sadness, Shaoyou proclaims the brevity of life and vows to seek the way beyond life and death. He declares that this is his last evening with them before he goes off to seek the Merciful Bodhisattva of the Southern Seas and Mañjuśrī of Wu Taishan. As they raise glasses to toast farewell, the sound of a staff is heard on the stone pavement and an old man with long white eyebrows appears. The monk Liuguan reminds Shaoyou of his former existence, and then disappears into a mist. When it clears, Shaoyou discovers himself in a little prayer cell with a freshly shaven head, kneeling on the floor. He is Xingzhen once more, and his life as Shaoyou had all been a dream.

With clear memories of his dream, Xingzhen attributes it to the wisdom of his Master. When the novice thanks Liuguan, however, the Master bedevils the disciple's sense of reality by questioning which of his identities is real—Shaoyou or Xingzhen? When pressed for an answer, Liuguan merely preaches from the *Diamond Sūtra*, for which the eight Taoist fairies are also present. Xingzhen achieves supreme enlightenment. Liuguan turns over his rosary, rice bowl, water bottle, staff, and the volume of the *Diamond Sūtra* to Xingzhen and returns to the West.

Reality and Realism in KUM

This summary sketch of *KUM*, for all its brevity, raises certain points for consideration. The first is that given our modern views of love and ready disquisitions on human psychology, the tale of one man's evenly harmonious love affairs with eight women understandably raises doubts about the novel's sense of realism. To be sure, moderns are quite aware of the historical veracity of concubinage in East Asia. What gives cause for doubt, however, is the apparent cheerfulness of it all. Not only do all the wives of Shaoyou get along, they positively aid and abet his amours. In his first meeting with Moonlight, the dancer recommends Minister Zheng's daughter Qiongbei and the famed dancer Wildgoose to him for their virtue and beauty. Moonlight later puts her words into action when she allows Wildgoose to stand in for herself in Shaoyou's bed. Qiongbei is in turn willing to offer her maid Cloudlet to her husband-to-be because of the closeness between the two women. Finally, Princess Orchid is willing to raise a commoner to the status of her older sister just so she can share a man between them.

At times one can detect a degree of rationalization for such actions. Moonlight proclaims to Shaoyou, "You will become either a minister of state or a general, and all the pretty women of China will run after you. I cannot expect to be the only one who loves you." (丞相印綬，大蔣節鉞，非久當歸於郎君手中，天下美女，孰不願從於郎君乎).[3] This seeming admission of feudalistic reality is echoed by Qiongbei when she proposes giving Cloudlet to Shaoyou as a concubine. She queries her parents, "Do you think a man of that sort is going to be satisfied with only one wife? Once he gets a high post with a fat salary, how many Chunyuns (Cloudlets) do you think he will provide himself with?" (其氣象豈獨守一女子，而終老乎？ 他日據丞 之府，享萬鐘之祿，則堂中將有幾春雲乎?)[4] The theme of female harmony also functions to illustrate the unequalled virtue of these women. When Princess Orchid insists that Qiongbei must be adopted by her mother, the Empress reflects, "The natural thing is for women to be jealous of one another's cleverness and beauty, but my daughter loves another girl's intelligence as much as her own and honors her virtues as though she were thirsting for water." (妬才忌色，女子常情， 吾女兒愛人之才，若己之有，敬人之德，如渴求飲.)[5]

However much these utterances may reflect the family system of the author's society and the qualities it sought to ingrain into its women, it is difficult to ignore the overwhelmingly idealistic depictions of this novel. Some scholars have been led to brand *KUM*, in fact, as an "idealistic novel" (*isang sosŏl*) which seeks to justify the "one master, many wives" model of monarchical feudalism. According to Wei Xusheng's introduction in the Mainland Chinese edition of *KUM*, this idealistic portrayal betrays not only Kim Manjung's background as a feudal literatus, but politically approves of his social system through the tacit demonstration of how benign feudalistic rule can be.[6] It is also worth noting that the perfect harmony that reigns between these eight idealized women suggests a homology for the relations that ought to govern ministers of the court—a setting which as Sŏp'o well knew was rife with jealousies and personal contention. Wei further argues that although the main character is made to mouth the superiority of Buddhism over Confucianism and Taoism, the great bulk of the novel paints a picture of the ideal Confucian way of life.

Political considerations aside, the literary recommendations of the idealistic novel, if one chooses to characterize *KUM* with this rubric, seem less than given. In one assessment, Kim Kidong asserts that the idealistic orientation of *KUM* "leads to the overusage of romanticism and reliance on fortuitous chance, causing the novel's events to unfold in an unrealistic manner."[7] This judgment appears to place *KUM* outside the fold of those qualities of the novel that make its case as philosophy. According to Martha Nussbaum, philosophy should create a link between historical particularity and our common, universal humanity. Novels do this well:

> . . . by enlisting the reader as a concerned participant in the adventures of the characters, novels take our common humanity for their theme, implying that what is at issue is not merely some idiosyncratic event that actually happened, but a possibility or possibilities for human life.[8]

One can perhaps contend that *KUM,* too, paints a possibility for human life, albeit in an overly idealized manner. The personal biography of Sŏp'o should account for why this author chose to maximize in fiction the life he never got the chance to live out. Or one can perhaps look to Korea's social and political history in order to explain why its classical fiction hangs so much upon visions of a perfect world. Chung Chong-wha, for example, considers the thesis that given the legacy of political turmoil caused by foreign invasions and internal corruption, the difficulties of life resulted in "people longing for an ideal world beyond and also seeking consolation in the dream world offered in the classical fictions."[9]

As another case in point, Chung points to the novel *Hong Kiltong,* which he attributes to Hŏ Kyun. This tale of banditry tells the story of an able son of a concubine who is led to rebellion because his lower birth denies him the social rewards that his talents demand. He eventually establishes a utopian society on a remote island where there is no blood lineage discrimination. This new society does not look much different from the Confucian milieu of the author (himself a third and dispossessed son of the minister Hŏ Yŏp), but it is a place where the hero can flourish within the given structure.[10] *Hong Kiltong* instantiates the East Asian practice of using the literary to voice social and political criticism. In seventeenth- and eighteenth-century Korea, fictive and poetic narratives were frequently utilized to express the social discontent of both the Yangban and lower social classes.[11]

One must ask, however, whether or not this use of literature as political commentary suffices as philosophy. The answer hangs not so much upon what themes are proper to explore in fictive literature as on the salutary effects of reading. Sŏp'o and Hŏ Kyun may have derived some satisfaction in venting their utopian visions against their personal experience of Chosŏn dynasty Korea, but do they engage us as "concerned participants," or offer up to us an actual "possibility for human life"? To be sure, cultural differences must be negotiated. Premodern Korea confronts us with a glut of historical specificities that must be considered. Nevertheless, such barriers should not pose an insurmountable divide—in fact, if the novel succeeds in doing its job, the historical particularities should only reinforce the lesson of our common humanity. The novel should hone our imagination and empathy so that we see the generality of the characters' dilemmas, and so that they become our own.

The primary obstruction that *KUM* erects—which keeps us from achieving this desired empathy and universality—seems to inhere in its literary quality rather than its cross-cultural distance. Chung Chong-wha categorizes *KUM*—and Korean classical fiction generally—as a romance rather than a novel, deriving both these terms from the Western theory which traces the evolution of narrative from epics, to the romance, to the novel proper. This continuous literary development suggests a movement from the elevated realms of mythic gods to ordinary people. The successive phases of epic, romance, and novel increasingly train narratives on people and situations with which we ourselves can immediately identify. Along with this augmented interest in the common, close-to-the-ground experience, there is a greater degree of specificity and realism in the way that characters and situations are portrayed. The modern novel displays the greatest degree of depth in this regard by plunging into the world of the human psyche, no longer content with surface descriptions of daily life.

The romance, in this scheme of things, falls in the middle of the spectrum defined by the epic and the novel. Flourishing mostly in the Medieval and Renaissance periods, the romance traces a simplistically linear tale of the adventures of a larger-than-life hero. Events move along with little attention paid to the nature of causality or the development of character. In merging Korean classical fiction with this phase of Western narrative, Chung points to an archetypal pattern in the Korean variety:

> The protagonist is usually the son of an aristocratic family, extremely handsome, clever in his study, good at poetry, loyal to his parents and the king, righteous in his social and political outlook, courageous and victorious in war. He marries a virtuous and most beautiful girl, and he is

extremely happy. But his idyllic life is interrupted by an evil opponent. The cliche pattern follows, moving towards the obvious happy ending, with the defeat of the villain (often by the means of supernatural phenomena and miraculous chances) and the hero's ascendency in the social hierarchy. He and his family become happy forever after.[12]

The inner tale of *KUM*—the one which narrates the life of Yang Shaoyou—falls all too easily into this generic pattern. The story of a most exceptional hero and his mating with eight beauties recalls the "talented scholar–beautiful maiden" (*caizi-jiaren*) tales, which go back to the *chuanqi* genre of popular narratives from Tang China.[13] Although some scholars trace the beginnings of the Chinese fictional impulse to this tradition, the *chuanqi* nevertheless constitutes its own genre of narrative which continued after the rise of the classical Chinese novel.[14] Its distinctiveness is indicated by its genre designation—"transmitting the marvelous," or "transmitting the strange" which deliberately eschewed verisimilitude in favor of the fantastic (although it initially and ironically claimed historical veracity).

Chuanqi tales are commonly populated by fox-fairies, spirits, and ghosts; they entail dream journeys to the underworld and visits to the Dragon King in his underwater palace. The romantic tales of love and adventure between the scholar and beauty exhibit repetitive conventions such as the exchange of poems, ghost wives and lovers, and didactic commentary at the end of the tale. Most of these formulas are utilized in *KUM*. The Korean novel's apparant continuity with the *chuanqi* is reinforced by Chung Chong-wha's claim that the beginnings of Korean classical fiction can be traced to Kim Sisŭp's *Kŭmo Sinhwa*, which dates two hundred years before Sŏp'o's novel and which comfortably fits into the *chuanqi* genre.[15]

KUM's embrace of elements of the *chuanqi* narrative suggests surface similarities between the Korean novel and the Western romance in that both fail to sustain an abiding and convincing sense of the real. Although speculations on what distinguishes the novel from other narratives have considered a variety of options, one consensus has centered on the requirement that

novels must sustain credibility in its portrayal of motivations
and personalities. The expectation of "realism" is present in both
Western and Chinese contexts.[16] Thus the perfect comparative
foil to *KUM* is perhaps Cao Xueqin's *Dream of the Red Chamber*, another novel in the dream tradition but easily the culmination of Chinese classical fiction, recognized as so in large part
because of its painstaking detail and vivid portrayal of aristocratic life in late imperial China.

The criterion of "realism," however, can prove to be rather
fickle upon closer examination. In eighteenth- and nineteenth-
century Western spheres, the standard of fictive realism was
readily fulfilled by certain conventions relating to subject matter (the lives of common people, the details of daily life) and
narrative style (historically specific descriptions, logical temporal progression, consistent narrative perspective). As Andrew
Plaks points out, however, twentieth-century developments in
the novel have defied these conventions of realism. Perhaps as a
direct result of the literary pursuit of the depths of individual
consciousness, aesthetic innovations such as impressionism and
surrealism have given artists license to explore and ultimately
confront reigning assumptions about the nature of the real.[17] To
judge Sŏp'o's work against the obsolete Western sense of realism is then peculiar indeed, and also points to the dubiousness
of aligning Korean classical fiction with one isolated phase in
the continuum of Western literary history.[18]

The deliberate explorations and distortions of the notion of
"realism" that have been expressed in twentieth-century philosophical and aesthetic circles seem to complicate the term and
vitiate its usefulness as a literary criterion. If we observe the
evolution of "realism" in Western novelistic portrayals, however, one may posit a certain constancy—not in the way that
realism has been defined, but in the persistent exploration of
the nature of reality itself. Plaks' attempt to give some universal
definition to the novel as a unique literary form points to this
overriding concern. In doing so, he liberates the comparative
study of the Chinese and Western novel from the impasse of
divergent structural and literary histories and locates their com-

monality in their respective intellectual orientation. Plaks theo-
rizes that the rise of the novel in both East and West coincided
with an elevation in critical consciousness which forced intellec-
tuals to examine some problematic aspects of human existence.[19]
Much of this consists of a reexamination of standard conceptions of reality. At particular issue in the creation of fiction is
the author's ironic awareness of his own role, of his own subjectivity, in his mimetic representation of reality.

As early as the Tang dynasty, the composition of fictional
biographies raised to self-consciousness "the problems and dilemmas of the historical representation of human beings."[20] Meditation on the nature of representation cannot help but critique
superficial models of realism. In Confucian historical narratives,
an aesthetic of realism dominated which disallowed for ambiguity; which insisted that life has transparent principles that are
simultaneously objective and normative.[21] In contrast, the Buddhist mandate to pull back from surface reality—to explore its
nature and ask what, if anything, lies beyond it—would seem to
be inherent to the process of writing fiction. Hence we might
effect a reconciliation between the literary qualities of *KUM* and
the more facile demands of realism. Although the narrative texture of *KUM* does little to foster a sense of verisimilitude, it is
maximally engaged in a consideration of the nature of reality.

The impetus for this query undoubtedly originated in political discontent—as so much of fiction during this era in both
China and Korea had. The specificity of the historical conditions
that gave rise to the discontent, however, is transcended by
what the novel explores. As Robert Hegel states, " . . . the novelists of the seventeenth century ultimately reveal their own minds
through serious discussion of the human problems nearest their
own experience."[22] In exploring the life that might have been,
Sŏp'o pursues the larger question of how lives are constructed.
As I attempted to show in the last chapter, this quest is framed
by Sŏp'o's implicit awareness of the ontological capacity of fiction. Sŏp'o demonstrates this self-consciousness much more forth-
rightly in *KUM* than in *The Southern Expedition*. This
self-consciousness cannot be adequately revealed, however,

through immersion in the surface narrative or through a search for literary texture and depth. Instead, we must be guided by the peculiarities of Asian classical fiction and its own literary mode. Here again, Plaks' observation of the Chinese scene is invaluable:

> ... in the history of the Chinese novel, one observes an increasing self-consciousness in the use of various storyteller's devices (e.g., chapter titles, post-chapter summations and forecasts, narrator's intrusions, etc.) which superficially refer to the contingencies of circumstances involved in a given plot, but actually indicate precisely those points at which the author calls attention to his own problematic role in the imposition of a credible structure on the flux of human events.[23]

The use of literary devices serves as an index to the author's rising awareness of the intersection between his narrative practice and ontological imposition. The use of conventional rhetorical devices become an exploration of how culturally designated patterns form instruments for the presentation of truth. This assumption is key in my interpretation of *KUM*, and also determines my interpretive approach. The storyteller's devices that Plaks makes reference to are rather common, as are the ones that Sŏp'o employs. Their banality makes them easy to overlook, but my assumption will be that Sŏp'o's self-conscious use renders them into vehicles of explicit meaning. In the remainder of this chapter, I will look at two devices that Sŏp'o employs: the literary device of karma and its integration into the structure of the dream tale.

Kim Kidong's criticism of *KUM* that was previously cited—with its reference to "reliance on fortuitous chance"—undoubtedly has in mind the frequent use of karma as an explanation for Shaoyou's encounters with his numerous lovers. The ready use of this device is signaled whenever the narrative turns to talk of the destiny, or affinity, of two lovers. The term *yuan*, which is used in every such narrative instance, denotes not only the general meaning of karmic destiny, but the specific love destiny of two people to meet and wed. As Shaoyou explains to his own wives in reflecting upon his life with them, "If it were not for the unresolved karma of a previous life, we surely would not have come to this. Male and female meet through the agency of karma, and when it is spent we return—this is the constant way of heaven." (非前生未了之緣，必不及於是也，男女以緣而會，緣盡而歸，乃天理之常也.)[24]

The narrative often states that during the youth of Shaoyou's various lovers, it was foretold that the mistress would encounter the young, amorous hero under certain circumstances so that she may recognize him and then, devote herself to him. The case of Princess Orchid's predestined affinity with Shaoyou is particularly poetic in design: In her youth, it is discovered that only she can play upon the unearthly jade flute which was presented to the palace as tribute from the West. When she played, the cranes would flock to dance. Thus it was determined that the male who displayed a similar ability would be her destined mate. When Shaoyou plays upon his jade flute (his gift from the Taoist immortal) during a stay at the palace, the cranes are also observed to gather and dance, thus revealing the two characters' affinity.

In my view, the karmic mechanism offers the most plausible, and most internally consistent, explanation for the maximal success that our fair hero experiences in love. It is important to look at both the structural and religious meaning that the agency of karma conveys. To begin with the structural meaning, karma offers a binding mechanism between the inner tale, in which karmic destiny is played out, and the outer frame, in which karma is first contracted (the meeting of the novice with the eight fairies on the bridge and the emotions that are engendered by it). The thread of karma produces a literary coherence in the frame tale. The dream sequence follows directly from the prologue as a result of karmic necessity, and the denouement (Xingzhen's final enlightenment) is made to hinge on the lessons learned as a result of having dreamed the dream.

The tightly woven tripartite structure of *KUM* in turn foregrounds the process of religious awakening by novelistically paralleling the religious journey that is more abstractly

understood in Mahāyāna Buddhist philosophy. The Buddhist
novice of the tale—Xingzhen—is incarnated as "before" and "after" identities whose spiritual transformation comes about only
as a result of his sojourn in the world of dust. If the novice who
originally dwelt on Lotus Peak represents a pure self untainted
by knowledge of the world, it is only through the forging process of worldly experience that he is completely healed and
made immune to the specter of temptation. The journey, then,
has a point from both a structural and religious perspective.
The successive incarnations of our male hero simulaneously unfold and circle back on themselves in mutual dependence. For
this reason, Hwang P'aegang has called the structure of the
novel "systematic."[25]

Through its systematic quality, *KUM* gives form to Buddhist doctrinal views of the ultimate contiguity of spiritual and
mundane realms. Here one witnesses the concretization of Buddhist attempts to come to terms with, indeed, positively to sanc-
tify, the ordinary world as part of the process of spiritual
transformation. The novelistic expression of a religious teaching
that was normally declared in abstract terms is an historical
development in the practice of philosophy. If this philosophy is
to be properly represented, one must first understand the point
of view—the notion of reality—that is struggling to emerge,
and the manner in which the literary traits of the novel serve as
its vehicle.

With this consideration in mind, the second point to be
made about *KUM* is that the dream motif is the novel's most
prominent symbol of the Buddhist ontology of "emptiness"
(*śūnyatā*). I make this assertion over and against modern scholarly tendencies toward diluting the presence of Buddhist meaning in Asian fiction. In his study of the *Dream of the Red
Chamber*, Andrew Plaks generalizes the significance of the dream
as a literary trope for the interpenetration of illusion and reality,
which is only one of all balances of opposites in the Chinese
allegorical universe.[26] In Plaks' reading, the dream is an experi-
ential analogue of this cosmic reality, rather than an index to
the specific Buddhist teaching of emptiness. To argue for a direct

correlation between the Buddhist teaching and the meaning of the dream requires an examination of the philosophical concepts of the doctrine of *śūnyatā*, as well as of the dream itself. The philosophical investigation will be deferred to the next chapter. The following discussion will attempt to sort through some of the dominant dream motifs of Asian literature and to identify which strands appear in *KUM*.

The Dream Adventure Tale

Any attempt to distill the definitive meaning that a culture gives to dreams is likely to oversimplify. Although dreaming (like love and death) is a cultural constant not only experienced but also reflected upon by societies, the interpretations themselves are rarely univocal. Michel Strickmann points out that in China, the dream has as many meanings as there are interpreters, although the interpreters are finite in number and usually representative of a social function.[27] The ancient tradition of "professional" dream literature can serve as a catalogue of these professional occupations. There are dream manuals that were used by specialists in dream interpretation, as well as medical literature that used dreams as a diagnostic tool for pinpointing both physical and mental ailments. Taoist literature also documents the belief that dreams constitute visions or visitations from spirits, and Buddhist tales attest to a widespread use of dreams as a means of prognostication.[28]

The notion of the dream as an instrument of communication from ghosts and dead ancestors, or as a divine disclosure which predicts events, is commonly encountered in fiction, where it becomes embedded as an integral portion of the narrative structure. Dell Hales points out that the short story, drama, and novel in China owe much to dreams, which perform a range of simple to complex literary functions.[29] In Korea, from ancient times dreams were also believed to be messages sent by spirits, or the experiences of the soul when separated from the body. These views of the dream—which were commonly imbued with the same meaning and significance as phenomenal, waking reality—are reflected in Korean narratives from the fable to the novel. Most generally, two kinds of dreams are featured—the birth dream and the prognostication dream.[30] The birth dream is used as a device to announce the auspicious birth of the main character. In the dream, typical objects such as stars, dragons, or flowers enter into the chest or mouth of the mother, signifying the mystical conception of the main character. Cross-culturally, we can immediately recognize this brand of dream in the story of the conception of the Buddha: Mahāmāyā dreams that a white elephant enters her right side; the king calls upon prognostics to interpret the dream, whereupon they tell her that she is with child who is destined to be either a universal monarch or the Buddha.

The birth dream is contiguous with prognostication dreams generally, which are broadly used to predict the future fortunes of the protagonist—usually a character who is currently mired in the worst of circumstances. Such a dream sequence is embedded within one of the best-known and beloved of Korean stories, the *Tale of Ch'unhyang*, which originated sometime in the eighteenth century with the oral narrative performances known as *pansori*. The tale concerns the beautiful daughter of a *kisaeng* (akin to the Japanese geisha), who remains faithful to her departed husband despite the lecherous overtures of the new governor. Severely tortured and imprisoned, Chunhyang dreams a dream in which her make-up mirror is cracked; cherry blossom falls outside her window; and a corn-dolly is suspended on her threshold. Fearing that they are portents of death, she calls upon a blind male shaman to interpret the symbols in her dream. He informs her that they in fact predict that she will be reunited with her husband and form a happy home.

Although the dream is a common motif in Korean literature, it is possible to classify subgenres of relatively discrete dream tales. The birth dream and prognostication dream tales exhibit the widely held belief that dreams encode numinous messages or even directives from forces beyond. The reflection of this belief in dream tales can be seen across Asian cultures, and forms a tradition that is too broad to be of particular relevance in the study of *KUM*. A more specific variation of the dream tale in Korea is two distinct brands of the dream travel narrative.[31] The first, often designated in its title as a "dream travel record" (*mong yurok*), is a variety of the *chuanqi* tale. Little relationship is established between "reality" and the events of the dream, and there is no serious reflection on the meaning of the strange events of the dream. The second, which is designated more vaguely as a "dream tale" (*mong charyu*), is more common and can be identified by the karmic tie that is established between the dream and waking worlds, and the intense speculations on nothingness that are provoked upon waking from the dream.

This second body of stories might be designated the dream adventure tale, and can be assigned a uniform Buddhist-Taoist origin. Rather than communicating the intentions of spirits, the dream here becomes a device through which the author conveys a moral about the nature of life. Most typically, this moral is the pseudo-philosophical observation that life is illusory like a dream. Employing the reality-dream-reality structure, the dream adventure tale typically begins with the protagonist who is engaged in some kind of struggle or pursuit. He enters a dream in which he attains his every desire, but after awakening he realizes the acute nothingness of the dream, which is also no different from his real life.

KUM stands within a long tradition of dream tales in Asia which can be categorized together on the basis of structural similarities. David R. Knechtges has written an article in which he claims that the "dream adventure" tale can be found worldwide, in European and Islamic/Arabic sources as well as Chinese. Knechtges posits three determining features of this kind of tale: (1) A "vision of grandeur" in which the dreaming hero achieves great success in attaining his goals; (2) a temporal illusion of time in which the dream seems to occupy a long period (in most instances, a whole lifetime) but, it is discovered upon awakening, has occurred in a very brief time; (3) and a time measuring device to show just how brief the dream actually was—the dream occurs, for example, in the span of time required to cook a meal, wash hands, or saddle a horse.[32]

Technically, *KUM* lacks the third element, but I believe Knechtges casts his markers too restrictively. This leads him not even to consider the vast tradition of Indian dream tales, which form an important body of evidence for my own arguments. I am reluctant to offer an alternative definition in view of the fluidity of all cultural artifacts, but as a working definition I simply posit the dream adventure tale as a frame narrative in which the dream functions as a didactic tool to awaken the hero to the illusory nature of life. The story of Chosin from the *Samguk Yusa* that I recounted in the first chapter offers Korea's earliest example of the dream adventure tale. The presence of this tale genre in Korea, however, traces itself back to Chinese influence.

One of the earliest Chinese examples of the dream adventure tale is found in the *Soushenji* ("Record of Spirits"), a Six Dynasties narrative written by Gan Bao. Within it, the tale entitled, "The Pillow of Jiaohu" (which can also be found in *Taiping Guangji*) tells a story set in Jiaohu Temple, which houses a jade pillow with a small crack. One day the merchant Yang Lin arrives at the temple to offer prayers. Guessing that Lin is seeking a wife, the temple priest leads Lin to the pillow and causes him to enter it through the crack. Once inside, Lin discovers a street lined with magnificent buildings, one of which belongs to the high minister Zhao. Lin marries Zhao's daughter and fathers six children, all of whom grow up to hold important government posts. Passing many years without any thought of returning to the outside world, Lin suddenly awakens as if from a dream and finds himself still standing beside the pillow, much to his lasting grief.

The simple plot of this tale became elaborated upon in Zhen Jiji's Tang tale called, "The World Inside a Pillow" (*Zhenzhongji*). In it, a Taoist priest named Lu Weng stops at an inn where he meets a young man named Lu. Lu complains of his failures in life, whereupon the Taoist lends him a pillow to sleep on just as the innkeeper is putting on some millet to cook. Lu dreams that he marries into the rich and powerful Cui family, passes the examinations, and is appointed to high posts. He is sent to fight the Tibetans, which he does successfully. The jealousy of fellow officials, however, brings him demotions, imprisonment, and exile, all of which he survives and overcomes to be finally enfeoffed as a duke. He fathers five sons, all of whom achieve great success. Lu attempts to retire, but his petition is refused; he finally falls sick and dies. Lu awakens with a start at the inn to discover it had all been a dream. He then thanks the Taoist, saying, "Of the ways of favor and disgrace, the vagaries of distress and prosperity, the patterns of accomplishment and failure, the emotions of life and death, I have thoroughly been made aware. In this way, sir, you have checked my desires."[33]

Elements that appear in *KUM* are quite recognizable in this tale. Not only is the basic structural and didactic thrust of *Zhenzhongji* the same, but details such as the campaign against the Tibetans and the denied petition for retirement are also identical. Although it is impossible to prove Sŏp'o's specific familiarity with this tale, its probability can be safely argued for given the broad circulation of Tang tales in Korea.[34] *Zhenzhongji* was itself the basis of one of the best-known stories composed in Tang China, Li Gongzuo's "The Magistrate of the Southern Branch" (*Nanke Taishouzhuan*, which can be found in *Taiping Guangji*). Here a jaded soldier of fortune named Chun Yufen is given to a life of drink, and one day he falls asleep in a stupor while his drinking buddies wash their feet and tend their horses. He dreams that he enters an ant kingdom located in an acacia tree. He marries the king's daughter, attains high position, and has children. His good fortunes are reversed, however, when he is defeated in battle, and his wife dies. The king decides to send him away (over twenty years have passed), and Chun awakens to find that his friends are still washing their feet.[35]

The cultural pervasiveness of the dream adventure tale, particularly as embodied in this narrative thread beginning with the pillow stories, is evinced in its further elaboration by the famous Ming playwright Tang Xianzu (1550–1616), who is known best for his work *The Peony Pavilion* (*Mudanting*). Some

of Tang's last plays were based on "The Magistrate of the Southern Branch" and "The World Inside a Pillow," entitled, respectively, *Nankeji* ("The Tale of the Southern Branch"), and
Handanji ("The Tale of Handan").

In the currently known corpus of Chinese tales, there is
one more story which fits under the rubric of the dream adventure, Ren Fan's "The Cherry Maid" (*Yingtao Qingyi*, in *Taiping
Guangji*), which was composed in the Tang as well.[36] Here yet
another scholar named Lu who is unhappy with his career comes
upon a Buddhist monastery, where he falls asleep during the
course of a sūtra chant. He dreams of meeting a girl carrying a
basket of cherries, who turns out to be from the eminent Cui
clan. She leads him to her mistress, and Lu marries the woman's
niece. He passes the examinations, becomes powerful, and has
many children. After thirty years, Lu returns to the monastery
where he had met the cherry maid to listen to the priest, when
he suddenly awakes to find that the chanting has just finished.
Realizing what has happened, Lu resolves to abandon the world.

The most consistent binding element of these dream adventure tales is the didactic perspective on the illusoriness of
life as learned through the dream. At its most diffuse level of
meaning, the dream is an automatic cultural reflex which signifies a general observation about the vanity of life. Such an observation transcends the parameters of discrete religious
traditions and functions as common cultural property. This generic function is visible in one tale of Lu Dongbin, the most
popular of the coterie of Eight Taoist Immortals whose tale tradition began at the end of the Tang dynasty. The emphasis in
this story is not so much the character's Taoist affiliation, but
rather the mechanism of the dream which causes him to turn
away from the path of high officialdom to religious practice.
The story states that Lu Dongbin:

> ... had a deep interest in the ways of the wise men and of
> the immortals. Whenever he could, he would study the an-
> cient writings and meditate on his life and its purpose. But
> official duties left him little time for such reflections and he
> was still too dazzled by the hoped-for glories of power to

seriously contemplate giving everything up and becoming a hermit.[37]

In the space of time that it takes to heat a bottle of wine, Lu Dongbin dreams that he achieves powers that cause governments to quake, but he is eventually undone by the jealousy of fellow officials. He is sent into exile and his whole family is exterminated. Awakening in shock, he realizes that the path of power is empty and embarks upon his study of the immortal way.

In another narrative example of the dream adventure, the author demonstrates how it can be given a lucid Buddhist coloring. *The Tower of Myriad Mirrors* is an English rendition of the Chinese work simply entitled *Xiyoubu*, or *Supplement to the Journey to the West*.[38] It was written by Dong Yue (1620–1686), a contemporary of Sŏp'o. Dong Yue took it upon himself to expand the original Ming classic *Journey to the West* by inserting a dream episode centering around the story's most popular character, Sun Wukong, or Monkey. To be inserted between chapters sixty-one and sixty-two of the original novel, *The Tower of Myriad Mirrors* is the tale of Monkey's dream adventures which are cast as a series of surrealistic events in the aforementioned tower. The author's intention, as plainly indicated in his own preface, is to shift the original novel's focus on Monkey's physical powers to his mental journey in the quest for Buddhist enlightenment. Through this strategy, Dong Yue fully plumbs the Buddhist metaphor which likens the untamed and unenlightened mind to the restless monkey that leaps among the limbs of a tree.

Dong Yue's use of the dream to illustrate the Mind-Monkey's journey perhaps offers one more instance of the dream being used as "a foil dramatizing the ephemeral quality of human life."[39] The Buddhist intentions of Dong Yue, who was reportedly a Chan master, are in fact quite explicit. When Monkey is roused from his dream, an elder identified only as Master of the Void plays on the pun of Monkey's name by crying out, "Is Wu-k'ung (Aware-of-Vacuity) no longer aware of vacuity? Is Wu-huan (Aware-of-Illusion) no longer aware of illusion?"[40] The

Master of the Void reveals that the Tower of Myriad Mirrors was a creation of the Qing Fish Monster, a name that is homophonous with the *qing* meaning "desire." Dong Yue explains this device according to the Buddhist dictum that desire is the root of delusion:

> To become enlightened and open to the Great Way, one must first empty and destroy the roots of desire. To empty and destroy the roots of desire one must first go inside desire. After going inside desire and seeing the emptiness of the root of the world's desire, one can then go outside of desire and realize the reality of the root of the Way. *The Tower of Myriad Mirrors* deals with the Demon of Desire, and the Demon of Desire is the Ch'ing (Qing) Fish Spirit.[41]

Dong Yue's fortuitous decision to record the intentions of his novel offers historical evidence of the praxeological connection between the dream device and Buddhist instruction. The author's conscientiousness about employing the dream extends to carefully including the time measuring device in order to demonstrate the brevity of the dream—when Monkey awakes "he saw that the sun above the peony tree had not moved."[42] The significance of Dong Yue's novel is not only that it maintains the traditional elements of the dream device. The discontinuities of reality, and the distortions and discrepancies that Monkey experiences in his dream, create a narrative which explores in unprecedented detail the actual nature of dreaming. Unlike previous dream tales which unfold in straight linear progression, *The Tower* presents a narrative that replicates the incoherence of dream experiences.[43]

Dong Yue's sophisticated depiction of dreaming offers further elaboration of the Buddhist message that all perceptions are distortions of the mind. In presenting this message through a deliberate manipulation of his narrative, the author conveys his awareness of the possibilities of his art. For the dream, of course, can easily be homologized to the novel itself—both Dong Yue's and Sŏp'o's. The latitude of the dream trope, which can be reinvented as fiction, suggests that in the Buddhist calculation, narratives can be plied to the service of religious lessons.

The Tower of Myriad Mirrors underscores both the theme and utility of the dream by multiplying its appearance. In chapter thirteen, Monkey sits and watches play performances, amongst which *The Tale of the Southern Branch* is included. At the end of the dramatic performances (which are all about dreams), a performer recites, "A Taoist who wished to save the ignorant fully explained men's desires and the ways of the world. Keep this in your hearts when you wake from your dreams, you people of the world."[44]

The comparative length and sophistication of seventeenth-century narratives such as Dong Yue's *Xiyoubu* and Kim Manjung's *Kuunmong* raises questions about their inclusion into the dream adventure genre. Their complexity relative to the shorter tales allows them to be appreciated on other grounds. Korean literary scholars are in fact apt to classify *KUM* as either an "idealistic novel" (*isang sosŏl*), or "family novel" (*kajŏng sosŏl*), grouping it with the plethora of dream novels that came after it such as Nam Yŏngno's (1810–1858) *Ongnumong* (*Dream of the Jade Chamber*). I agree with Pak Sŏng'ŭi's position, however, that *KUM* cannot be classified with these later dream novels. *Ongnumong* borrows heavily from *KUM*, but it incorporates many other elements from Chinese novels and imparts the feeling of summarizing all reigning literary conventions.[45] KUM, on the other hand, exhibits its own departures from the dream adventure tale but nevertheless can be seen as a culmination of the genre. It combines traditional elements of the dream tale with the biographical details of the military romance, resulting in a much more sophisticated hybrid which Sŏl Sŏnggyŏng calls the "Sŏn (meditation) dream tale" (*sŏnmong sosŏl*).[46] The complexity of this narrative structure hinges on the deliberateness with which the dream adventure is produced *within* the novel. The tale of Shaoyou, which follows the conventions of the military hero novel, is an empty creation of mind, or meditation, that was deliberately provoked by the master Liuguan. In juxtaposing the military and dream travel traditions, Sŏp'o creates a narrative whose elements are syncretic but whose effect is philosophically far more profound. As Sŏp'o's literary inspiration, Sŏl points to the *Journey to the West*, the *Zhuangzi* and *Liezi*'s tales of illusion (to be elaborated upon shortly), and the emptiness philosophy of the *Diamond Sūtra*. The presence of the *Diamond Sūtra* in *KUM* will be focused upon in chapter five.

To be sure, the evidence of Chinese and Korean literature confronts us with how often and how readily authors took up the dream device. Situating *KUM* within the broader spectrum of East Asian dream tales is useful but it will not explain the significance of Sŏp'o's own manipulation of this common motif. In ascertaining the philosophical import of *KUM*, however, a consideration of the literary origins of the dream tale will perhaps prove of use. My aim is not to conduct an exhaustive survey, nor to pinpoint one definitive tale tradition in a contest for literary parentage. The relentless eclecticism of *KUM* itself reduces the value of such a quest. On the other hand, considering the range of the dream tale's possible origins may help us to identify *KUM*'s various strands of meaning.

Origins of the Dream Adventure Tale

A couple of theories have been advanced to explain the origin of the dream adventure tale in China. One view looks to the Taoist text known as the *Liezi*, composed roughly in the fourth century of this era. The *Liezi* is replete with tales concerning dreams, but the tale of King Mu of Zhou is particularly prominent and has been singled out as the matrix of the dream tale.[47] It is a story of a magician from the West who comes to the court of King Mu and is received with great hospitality as a result of his formidable powers of transformation. One day, the magician invites the king on an excursion. They soar up into the skies until they reach a heavenly palace. The king passes twenty or thirty years there, enjoying its unearthly pleasures without giving thought to his own realm. The magician invites him on another trip, this time to a place where the moon and sun above, and the rivers and seas below are obscured, and where the light and shadows are so terrifying that the king begs to go back. The magician pushes him, and the king awakes to find himself sitting in his own palace surrounded by his attendants. Apparently, the many years of his absence had passed in only a moment of self-absorbed thought. Questioning the magician, the king receives the reply,

> Your Majesty has been with me on a journey of the spirit. Why should your body have moved? . . . Your Majesty feels at home with the permanent, is suspicious of the sudden and temporary. But can one always measure how far and how fast a scene may alter and turn into something else?[48]

The magician's explanation seems to allude to common Chinese lore that dreams were actual journeys undertaken by the ethereal soul (*hun*) during sleep. The moral thrust of the tale, in any case, diverges somewhat from the lesson of the Tang tales examined above. First, there is little to suggest here that one should view the dream adventure as nothing but a pedagogical illusion. The "reality" of the adventure is open to interpretation. Nor is the moral that life itself is illusion implied at the end. Indeed, the magician's speech quoted above chides the king for making distinctions between illusion and reality. Thus the story of King Mu suggests a greater complexity in the relationship between illusion and reality than the Tang tales allowed for. I will eventually demonstrate the presence of this tale's perspective in *KUM*.

An opposing theory of the origins of the dream adventure tale looks outside of China to Indian sources—specifically to Indian Buddhism—and the translation of these sources into Chinese. A variety of Chinese and Korean scholars have proposed that the story of Śaranapiku, which is found in the *Sūtralamkāra* attributed to Aśvaghosa,[49] and the *Samyuktaratnapitakasūtra*,[50] is the paradigm for the Chinese tales.[51] The story concerns Śarana, son of the king of Udayana, who resolves to enter the life of religion. When his father dies, he renounces the throne to study under Katyāyana, a disciple of the Buddha Śākyamuni. One day Śarana sits in meditation under a tree in an area where the king of Ujjayini is out on an excursion with his wives. Śarana preaches to them while the king is asleep. Upon awakening, the king is furious and beats the monk nearly to death. In anger,

Śarana vows revenge and informs his instructor of his intentions to take up his position as king and to raise an army.
Persuaded to remain one night longer, Śarana that evening
dreams that he has regained the crown and raises a large army
against the king of Ujjayini. He is defeated, however, and at the
point of his execution, Katyāyana reappears and Śarana is
shocked awake. Regretting his desire for revenge, Śarana devotes
himself completely to the Buddhist path.

Knechtges rejects the inclusion of the tale of Śarana in his
category of the dream adventure for the reason that it fulfills
none of his three structural criteria: Śarana is not successful in
his adventure, there is only a brief lapse of time in the dream,
and there is no time measuring device. The tale does, however,
fit into my own definition of the dream tale as a frame story
with didactic intentions. The present case demonstrates the deficiency of overly formal criteria in the classification of fluid and
evolutionary traditions. Whereas Knechtges stipulates a static
diagnostic tool for pinpointing the occurrence of a certain phenomenon where and whenever it occurs, I am more interested
in tracing a specific line of narrative development which crosses
the boundaries between two cultures. With this in mind, it is
possible to allow for differences in cultural clothing without
permitting them to obscure the similarities.

Although the dream in the Chinese and Korean tales seems
to offer a greater degree of satisfaction to the hero (with *KUM*
offering perhaps the most extravagant degree), I believe our
focus should not be on the balance of the hero's success or
failure, but rather on the cultural language in which such evaluations are cast. The dream sequences invariably demonstrate a
Confucian coloring in their quests, as critics have noted, and the
lessons learned are equally relentless in their contrary Buddhist
sentiments. The antithetical structuring of the Confucian dream
and the Buddhist lesson gives artistic sense to the very real
historical and political contention that long embroiled these two
communities. The artistic resolution utilizes a cultural reality
that was obviously unknown in India.

If the Chinese coloration of the dream tale makes use of
some indigenous situations, it nevertheless does not eclipse its

common didactic thrust. Here it is interesting to note that the moral as such does not depend on the hero's unqualified worldly success. The bulk of the Tang tales, in any case, narrate reversals in the protagonist's fortunes. The larger point is, however, that whether the dream experience is happy or sad, "[t]he story demonstrates," in the words of Wendy Doniger O'Flaherty, "the illusory nature of apparent happiness and the enlightening power of apparent sorrows."[52] The pervasiveness of this lesson is displayed in a large variety of Indian dream/transformation tales discussed by O'Flaherty. I will consider some of these tales in relation to *KUM* at a later point. I bring up the Indian variants now in order to save myself a point-by-point refutation of Knechtges' narrative criteria and to counterpose a different agenda. Rather than establishing the historical link between Indian and Chinese narrative traditions, I confine my concerns to similarities in their ideological use of the dream—similarities that derive from a common fund of Hindu/Buddhist, or rather, Indian, metaphysical traditions.[53]

The Meaning of the Dream

Of course, the danger of considering too broad a spectrum of dream narrative traditions—the Taoist tales of the *Liezi*, the Buddhist story of Śaranapiku, and the Indian tales—is that any comprehensive formulation of the meaning of the dream may be too diffuse and undiscriminating. Roberto Ong notes that there is an affinity between the Buddhist and Taoist views of the dream and adds, "small wonder that, in the Chinese popular mind, the cliche 'Life is but a dream' is indifferently attributed to Buddhist or Taoist origin."[54] Chŏng Kyubok, who takes great pains to argue for the dominance of Buddhist thought in *KUM*, does not go far beyond the formulaic account of this thought as the message that all of life's glories are nothing but a spring dream.

   In a more detailed consideration, Anthony Yu examines the Tang dream tales and characterizes them as "cautionary devices," which are capable of teaching their lessons without forcing the reader to personally undergo the experiences. This observation can be extended to the nature of fiction itself, which parallels the function of dream in its potential to constitute a vicarious experience.[55] When it comes to the content of the lesson, however, most depictions are rather uniform. C. T. Hsia's analysis of Tang Xianzu's corpus of plays, which includes the *Tale of the Southern Branch* and the *Tale of Handan*, volunteers a sophisticated version of such depiction. Hsia rallies around the theme of time and its inexorability in catching up to the individual. Of the heroes of Tang's tales, he states,

> They have . . . grown aware of the treachery of time and they adopt one of the traditional religious systems to enable them to escape from time. The dream-device has foreshortened time, and each is brought face to face with the contemptible nature of human bonds because they appear ever so much more transient in the brief time-space of a dream.[56]

The effect of Hsia's analysis of the dream is to generalize maximally its philosophical thrust. Certainly whether there is meaning in the face of mortality is a question that all cultures ask, including Buddhism, but to ask it at this level or through this kind of formulation hardly distinguishes the dream from the screenplay of, say, Woody Allen's *Love and Death*.

In order to negotiate our way out of overly generalized views of the dream in narrative, it is helpful to distinguish the separate strands of meaning that coexist in *KUM*. Thus my own response to the debate over the origins of the dream adventure tale is that by the time we reach seventeenth-century Korea, *both* the elements of Taoist thought as reflected in the tale of King Mu of Zhou, and Buddhist structures which reach back to Indian tale traditions are clearly embedded. Neither of these two religious traditions, however, should bear the disservice of reduction into the maxim that life is but an illusion. Although this kind of observation may serve adequately in summarizing the moral of a fable, the metaphysical suggestions of the highly discursive traditions that back the tale are left largely untouched.

We must shift our focus of analysis, then, from the literary origins of the dream tale to philosophical origins. A second look into the dream motif in *KUM* readily reveals its ontological dimensions. Specifically, it asks through the mouth of the Master Liuguan that if the sensual world is an illusion, whether or not one must assume that there is a reality behind it. The query is made in direct confrontation with Xingzhen's conclusion that "My teacher knew of my wrong thoughts, and made me dream this dream so that I should understand the emptiness of riches and honor and the love between the sexes." (此必師傅知吾一念之差, 俾著人間之夢，要令性貞，知富貴繁華，男女情慾，皆妄幻也．)[57] Liuguan aptly invokes the Taoist philosopher Zhuangzi's famous anecdote of the butterfly dream: Zhuangzi dreamt he was a butterfly, but in the end he could not tell whether he was dreaming of the butterfly, or if the butterfly was dreaming he was Zhuangzi.[58] The whimsical tone of this story has assured its frequent recitation as an example of Taoist discourse. It harmonizes readily, however, with the larger corpus of Taoist vignettes (including the story of King Mu) which attempt to say something about the fluidity of reality.

A lesser known tale from the *Liezi* recounts the story of Laochengzi, a student of magic whose master tells him, "It is when you realize that the illusions and transformations of magic are no different from birth and death that it becomes worthwhile to study magic with you. You and I are also illusion; what is there to study?"[59] This is a relatively direct statement of the Taoist view of phenomenal reality as a constant process of change, or transformation (*hua*). The primacy of cosmic flux disintegrates any presumed hierarchy amongst phenomenal events. If we apply this back to Zhuangzi's butterfly dream, our tendency to privilege the dreamer over the dream commits the mistake of conferring greater ontological solidity on one transformational event over another. One can perhaps claim that the crusade against such metaphysical prejudice is the Taoist's greatest call to arms. The battle is fought against emotional fronts as well as the ontological, as displayed by Zhuangzi's frequent exhortations not to privilege life over death.[60]

To ask what is ultimately real, as Xingzhen does, shows that one has missed the point altogether. This wisdom comes to

a discursive climax at the end of the novel in the conversation
between master and disciple. Liuguan queries:

> Who knows what is dream and what is reality? Now you
> suppose Xingzhen to be your true self and the dream to
> be the dream of that self, and you also suppose that the
> self and the dream are not the same thing. But when it
> comes to Xingzhen and Shaoyou, who is the dream? Who is
> not the dream? (孰知何事之爲夢? 何事之爲貞耶? 今汝以
> 性貞爲汝身，以夢爲汝身之夢，則汝亦以身與夢，謂非一
> 物也，性貞小遊，孰是夢也? 孰非夢也?)[61]

The message of this passage is a perspective that is narratively rendered throughout the novel's pages. This is indicated
by the frequent use of deceptions by the nine main characters of
KUM. Primarily taking the form of identity-switching, these deceptions present frequent opportunities for the characters to play
with notions of what is real and unreal. The most extended
narrative instance of the theme of deception comes in the episode of Qiongbei's revenge on Shaoyou. Qiongbei had been de-
ceived by Shaoyou, who disguised himself as a Taoist priestess
in order to gain access to the women's quarters of the Zheng
household. The purpose of this had been to confirm for himself
the reputed beauty of the minister's daughter before making a
proposal of marriage. Qiongbei is more than miffed by this ruse,
which violates her Confucian sensibilities of female modesty.
Thus when the proposal is affirmed, she decides to return deception for deception through the aid of her maid Cloudlet.
Through the complicity of a cousin, Shaoyou is led to a pavilion
in a clearing in the mountains. Chunyun introduces herself as a
fairy who was once a lady-in-waiting in the court of the Queen
Mother of the Western Paradise, where Shaoyou himself was a
courtier. A flirtation between them led to Shaoyou's present
incarnation and her demotion, but the karmic destiny between
them would allow their love to be presently fulfilled. They make
love, and their pleasure is coyly described thus: "It was like a
dream, but it was not a dream. It seemed to be real, but it was
not." (似夢而非夢，似貞而非貞也.)[62]

The narrative unceasingly hammers on the theme of reality
and illusion, directly through its language and structurally by

piling on multiple frameworks of deceptions. After the pavilion episode, Qiongbei's deception is further spun out when Cloudlet reveals to Shaoyou that she is not a fairy after all, but rather the ghost of a dead woman. Asked if he is still willing to make love to her, knowing that she is a ghost, Shaoyou invokes the Buddhist view of the unreality of the body in a self-serving logic that justifies the intermingling of ghostly and fleshly forms.

Although the term "deception" implies a deliberate intent to trick or mislead, the narrative of *KUM* seems more intent on emphasizing the fluidity of all individual entities within the novel. Further on in the plot Shaoyou is duped once more when he is told that Qiongbei is dead because of the heartbreak caused by their broken engagement. In "reality," she has been elevated to the status of Princess Orchid's sister, and is simultaneously married off to Shaoyou as the elder princess. Finally stumbling upon this identity-switching game, the royal son-in-law exacts his own revenge by pretending to fall grievously ill in mourning for Qiongbei, knowing that this will force her to reveal her true identity.

The identity-switching maneuver is already familiar to us through Shaoyou's own disguise as a woman in order to gain access to Qiongbei. The motif recurs throughout other episodes. When Wildgoose is first introduced into the narrative, she comes disguised as a boy in whom Shaoyou takes instant delight. Her self-revelation is accomplished through another switching game when she substitutes herself for Moonlight in Shaoyou's bed during the night. Qiongbei's transformation into a princess, although viewed as "real" on the narrative level, only pushes the point of each character's existential fluidity. The observation is made in an inverse fashion with Cloudlet's disguises as a fairy and a ghost. Although the narrative views them as "false" identities, the episode still serves to disorder any sense of final realities.

The parade of identity masquerades in *KUM* develops the title motif of clouds as a metaphor or analogy for the nine main characters. The cloud image suggests a wispy, mutating insubstantiality which is fully explored in the novel's main frame. The episodes of *KUM* I have recounted thus far present many

opportunities for informal disquisitions on the distinction between illusion and reality. The strategy these episodes employ
is the compounding of illusion in a manner that deliberately
poses the question of whose identity should be considered "real,"
and on what basis such a judgment should be made.

When Shaoyou justifies making love to Cloudlet, whom he
believes is a ghost, he claims, "The Buddha said that man's
body is like foam thrashing about on the water and flowers
tossed by the wind, nothing but vanity. Who dare say whether
it is real or whether it does not exist at all?" (佛語云，人之身體，
以水漚風花，假成者也，孰知其貞也，孰知其假也?)[63] Although
the hasty reader might judge Shaoyou to avail himself of this
piece of Buddhist reflection as a rationalization of his pleasure-
seeking, this episode can also be used to argue that the use of
identity-switches has a definite metaphysical point of view. The
compounding of illusion within the narrative invites reflection
upon the nature of illusion, and more importantly, projects such
reflections outside of the narrative.

This process is demonstrated within the novel when
Liuguan provokes Xingzhen into applying the lesson of illusion beyond his dream to himself: "The difference between the
disciple and the dream person is a matter of transmigration.
And yet you take the dream and the world to be two separate
things, which proves that you have not yet woken from
the dream." (弟子夢人間輪回之事，此汝以夢與人世，分而二之也，
汝夢猶未盡覺也.)[64] The exploration of illusion is made to spill
over from the dream realm into the outside frame by posing the
question of whether or not there is a concluding reality or a
final dreamer. At this point, it is clear that the outward trajectory of this reflection upon illusion does not stop at the boundaries of the novel. It projects itself to the next frame, the one that
the reader occupies. Wendy O'Flaherty suggests a succinct formulation of this process in her examination of the tale of Gadhi
in the *Yogavāsistha*. Gadhi is a Brahmin who dreamt he was an
untouchable who believed he was a king. He is discovered to be
an untouchable but then wakes up to find that he is a Brahmin
once more.[65] O'Flaherty points out that the receding frames of

reality questions our own certainty that we are the final dreamer—"It is impossible to verify the reality of the scientist verifying the test."[66] Whereas the Taoists generally refrained from debating the question of metaphysical finalities,[67] the Yogācāra (Consciousness only) school of Buddhism resolutely affirms that nothing exists except in a limited sense, or as the temporary projection of our own minds. O'Flaherty dubs this view an extreme form of idealism which trespasses beyond the limits of the most radical Hindu thought. O'Flaherty also points out an important distinction between two Indian senses of illusion, both of which are readily perceptible in *KUM*. The first is a particular but simple mistake (*bhrama*) that confuses one object (which exists) for another object (which does not exist). The classical Indian example of this is the rope that is mistaken for a snake. In *KUM*, the identity deceptions we have just discussed often fit into this category. The aggressive and deliberate manner in which these deceptions are deployed, however, also supposes a second and more pungent form of illusion (*māyā*)—"the illusion that there is anything there at all."[68] O'Flaherty offers these two senses of illusion as separate categories that differ considerably in their philosophical implications. *Bhrama* merely states the fallibility of our perceptions, whereas *māyā* makes a far more extreme metaphysical claim: that the perception of anything at all is illusory. O'Flaherty points out that both forms of illusion can be present in a single tale, as they are in *KUM*. The two forms of illusion are conceptually related and easily allied. They are still, however, narratively distinguishable.

As in Indian tale traditions, the concept of *māyā* is implicated in another variety of dream tales in China. The strategy of these stories is to suggest that if nothing is more real than anything else, then nothing can be said to be false. If life is illusion, then illusion can also be "real." The concept is narratively formulated by a plot denouement in which the dreamer awakens to find out that his dream is true. There is the Indian tale of King Lavana, for example, who is visited by a magician and made to dream that he has become an untouchable. When he wakes up, the king goes in search of the place he dreamed of and not only discovers the village where he lived, but also meets the people that he knew there.[69]

This story bears a considerable resemblance to that of King Mu, whose dream excursion was also wrought by a powerful magician as the king sat on his throne. Both tales employ the magician to emphasize the purely created, illusory nature of the royal adventures. The story of King Mu, however, pointedly asks why the dream experience should be any less phenomenally real because of its relative brevity. All experiences, after all, are temporary resting points in the ever constant process of transformation. Although the ontological implications of the query run deep, the Taoist tradition poses it matter-of-factly rather than philosophically. This tone is evident in the tale which teaches that the belabored slave who dreams every night that he is a rich man leads a life that is equivalent to the rich man who dreams every night that he toils in labor as a slave.[70] Each dreamer's sleeping experience cancels out his waking condition, hence implying the convertibility of dream and reality. The Taoist anecdotes share the moral of King Lavana's dream, which surpasses the stop-gap conclusion that life is merely illusion. Let us explore some further cases of Chinese tales.

Bai Xingjian's "The Record of the Three Dreams" (*Sanmengji*), which was also composed during the Tang, claims:

> Some dreams are more unusual than others. A man might dream of going to a certain place, and another might see him there in flesh; a man might perform an act in reality and another might see that act in his dreams; or two men might dream of the same thing simultaneously.[71]

The three dreams recorded here are all presented as factual events. The first concerns a young bureaucrat who is returning home from a business trip. Passing by a Buddhist temple, he hears people laughing and singing. Looking over the crumbling wall, he is shocked to see his wife in the midst of the group. Unable to gain entry, he throws a tile at the people, whereupon everything disappears. He continues home and finds his wife, who awakes from a nap and relates her dream to him. It coincides exactly with his encounter at the Buddhist temple.[72] The second story provides more of an anecdote about the author and his brother, the noted poet Bo Zhuyi, and an incident when they were traveling together. Bo Zhuyi writes a poem about his friend Weizhi on a temple wall. Ten days later a letter arrives from the friend who describes having seen the brothers on their trip in a dream. The author informs us that all the facts, including dates, coincided exactly. In the last story, a traveler dreams of going to a temple where he meets a shaman priestess who tells him her name. The next day, he arrives at the temple and finds the same priestess, who tells him that she too dreamt of his arrival.

Like the story of King Lavana, the "Record of the Three Dreams" structures its episodes in a manner which blurs the distinction between the real and dream worlds. Thematically, there is a mixture of the motif of the shared dream (also frequent in India) and the dream that turns out to be true.

There is little doubt of Sŏp'o's acquaintance with this variant of the dream tale when we look at the episode of the Dragon King's daughter Whitecap. Whitecap and Shaoyou's first meeting occurs when the latter is on campaign against the Tibetans. Shaoyou falls asleep and dreams that he is led to the princess in her underwater palace. He defends her virtue against the Prince of the South Sea and wins her love. Ironically, it is in this dream within a dream that Shaoyou meets up with his Buddhist master, who informs him, "This is not the time when you are to come here for good" (今番非元帥永來之日)[73] and causes him to wake up. It seems that the dream within the dream cancels itself out and enables the protagonist to leap back into the "reality" of Lotus Peak for a brief encounter with his master. Here ontology is translated into the contiguity of dream and reality as physical spaces between which one can easily travel back and forth.

The proximity of dream and waking space is pushed into a perfect overlap when Shaoyou discovers not only that his men have shared his dream of the underwater battle, but that the evidence of this clash can be readily found at the lake. There are crushed fish scales, cracked turtle shells, and streams of blood. Most importantly, the water which was poisoning the soldiers has turned sweet, now that the Dragon Princess no longer needs its forbidding protection. The soldiers recover and win their battle against the Tibetans. The ultimate reality of this dream episode is not proven, however, until the very end of the novel when Whitecap materializes to join her scuba armored knight in his own palace.

The strategy of this subnarrative is all too clear: It pushes the contiguous realms of dream and reality closer together until they are completely isomorphic—somewhat like an actual size map of the world. What was depicted as a sequence of events occurring in a dream turns out, upon waking, to have been real and determinative of the outcome of events. This tactic devises a narrative version of the philosophy that if all events are devoid of reality, then the distinction between the illusory and the real also converges into a perfect correspondence.

As all the episodes recounted from *KUM* testify, the narrative influences on the novel include Indian, Buddhist, and Taoist dream tale traditions. From the vicarious lessons imparted by the dream about the emptiness of worldly pursuits to the disquisitions on the indeterminacy of the distinction between illusion and reality, Sŏp'o's novel functions as a repository of all variants of the dream adventure genre. Despite *KUM*'s broad display of narrative traditions, the conceptual agent which binds the novel together, as I will demonstrate in the next chapter, is decidedly Buddhist in tone. As a preliminary illustration, one might turn to a passage from one of the most important Buddhist texts of Chosŏn dynasty Korea, the *Mirror for Meditation Students* by Hyujŏng:

> Transcending illusion is like the moon appearing after clouds are cleared. It does not mean that the absence of clouds can be called the moon; instead, where there are no clouds, one can see the moon. It does not mean that nonillusion is the real and unchanging truth; instead, where there is no illusion, one can find the truth. In general, arising mind and moving thought (speaking falsehood and speaking the truth) are all illusions . . . [74]

This passage speaks of the need to lift the clouds of illusion in order to see the moon; but it paradoxically asserts that the moon itself does not represent a real and unchanging truth. Both clouds and moon are interchangeable illusions, but it is still possible to speak of finding truth. The episodes of *KUM* that have been recounted may be seen as narrative renditions of what in straight expository delivery sounds like Buddhist doublespeak. Indeed, as we shall see, the narrative of *KUM* responds to an enduring problematic in the Buddhist attempt to convey truth through words.

The Destiny of Illusion

Let us conclude this chapter with a final consideration of the device of karma and the way it imparts religious meaning into narrative. This point dovetailed with our initial observations about *KUM*'s lack of realism. This observation was made in conjunction with Kim Kidong's classification of *KUM* as an "idealistic" novel that unrealistically and perhaps wistfully depicts an idyllic household of multiple wives and concubines. I offered the power of karma as an explanation of this harmony, which is mandated by the inexorability of erotic destiny. Understandably, literary critics have not favored karma as a literary device. The infraction it is most cited for is this very sin of unrealism which makes it impossible to render the story's characters with a compelling sense of pathos.[75]

It is perhaps a measure of compensation that the Tang tales which deal with the matter of dreams are quite insistent on their factuality. Bai Xingjian's exactness in providing dates and place names, as well as personal assurances about his sources, is representative of the majority of compositions. Scholars have often attributed this to the tyranny of history even in the realm of fiction, which prompts the latter to cloak itself in the aura of facticity. Anthony Yu points out that the Ming novels *Shuihuzhuan* and *Jinpingmei* abound with historical references and duplicate history's aim to morally edify—"The implied status of art in this view is unmistakable: fiction is but repetition of history."[76]

These observations, however, raise an interesting question: If creations of the fictive imagination must be clothed in the language of history in order to make them respectable, then why choose the realm of fantasy for one's compositions? The query takes more than the unrealism of karmic schemes into account; it ensues from Kenneth DeWoskin's notation that Chinese fictive narratives originate from a subgenre of history which exhibits "fascination with the strange and remote, with supernatural happenings, and with the potential of individual effort."[77] There is, of course, the historiographical desire to record the furthest reaches of human experience which is revealed in Bai Xingjian's comment, "I put down these events that they not be forgotten." The sentiment is reminiscent of the *zhiguai* tradition which believed in the full historicity of the tales of the strange that it recorded.

This explanation, however, hardly applies to the fantasy elements of *KUM*. Sŏp'o wrote at a time when clear alternative models in the writing of fiction were available to him. Therefore it is significant that he followed the example of the *Journey to the West* rather than the other Ming classics in his decision to incorporate fantasy as well as pseudo-historical prose into his novel.[78] The choice bespeaks Sŏp'o's countercultural use of fiction, a use which DeWoskin credits with "a celebration of eccentricity in the context of a literate culture that generally venerates tradition and a conservative social order"; a use which "often illustrate[s] moral and ethical behavior contrary to what is officially sanctioned."[79] Sŏp'o's point, in fact, is to compose a narrative with an alternative interpretation of reality—one which does not have to claim that its events are real in order to say something about life. The choice of fantasy over historicity, however, amounts to more than a literary division of labor in which history represents Confucian viewpoints and fiction champions unorthodox traditions. Like the use of the dream, the deliberate conjuring of the fantastic also makes a substantive and methodological point about ultimate reality.

In searching for the possible meaning that karma offers as a literary device (or otherwise), it is perhaps useful to exacerbate the verdict of karma's unrealism by the observation that where karma functions to its fullest extent, a fantasy element is often present. An episode from the *Journey to the West* illustrates this point. Chapter ten initiates a series of events which terminate two chapters later in the Emperor Taizong's decision to sponsor a pilgrimage to India (through the agent of the monk Tripitaka, or Xuanzang) for the purpose of collecting scriptures. The episode is pivotal in the structure of the whole plot, and it is hinted that the Bodhisattva Guanyin played a deliberate hand in its denouement. The pilgrimage, I have argued, is fully invested with religious meaning which hangs upon the momentum of karma. The operations of karma are given a particularly fantastic setting in this episode. An evolution of events leads to the Dragon King's condemnation to death by the Jade Emperor for disobedience. In terror, the Dragon King appeals in a dream to Taizong, whose minister Weizheng is slated as the executioner. The emperor promises reprieve and attempts to distract his minister by engaging him in a game of chess at the appointed hour of execution. The minister falls asleep during the game, and in his dream commits the execution. Here too the events that occur in dreams are indistinguishable from reality, for the execution is successful. In anger, the beheaded Dragon King brings suit against the emperor in the underworld for breaking his pledge. The emperor is brought to the underworld, where a bureaucratic fast hand grants him another twenty years of life—but not without his first making a tour of the hells of the underworld.

The entire episode constitutes a minor disquisition on karma. All the events are stated to have been karmically determined: "Even before that dragon was born, it was already written on the Book of Death held by the Star of South Pole that he should be slain by a human judge."[80] More importantly, it is through the fulfillment of karma that religious goals, such as the investiture of the scripture pilgrimage, are attained. The unshakable designs of karma are best illustrated and aided by the incorporation of the fantastic, such as Weizheng's recourse to a dream in order to fulfill the Dragon King's destiny. It is tempting, of course, to dwell on the frequent use of dreams in the operations of karma. It suffices here, however, to lump dreams with any number of "unrealistic" ploys—the appeal to the underworld and the court of King Yama, the decrees of the heavenly court of the Jade Emperor, reincarnation through the hells and rebirth into life from death, the ceaseless travel between and betwixt worlds of fantasy and reality—which are associated with the operation of karma.

If we broaden our perspective beyond the purely structural use of karma, is it not possible to see that the use of fantasy demonstrates the inexorability of Buddhist destiny rather than its unrealism?[81] The religious urgency of this destiny does not merely disregard the ordinary physical boundaries and limitations of the universe. It is capable of bending nature to its will and of conjuring worlds that will do its bidding, just as the historical world of Tang China was created for Shaoyou in order to forge his mind in true understanding. The force of karma drives that forging process; it is that which creates the impetus for experience, and it is experience itself which constitutes the religious journey.

Buddhas—both celestial and historical—have always been invested with magical powers; powers which are exhibited for the religious edification of others. This practice looks deceptively like a concession to the undisciplined, thrill-seeking demands of the religiously shallow. This apparent corruption must be reconsidered, however, in light of Buddhism's metaphysical claim that *all* the world is an illusory, fantastical creation. Victor Mair deftly highlights this point in his study of the precursors of fiction in China—the *bianwen,* or "transformation texts." Mair relates the term *bianwen* to the Chinese Buddhist term *shenbian,* defining it as follows:

> Basically, it is a miraculous transformation (that is, appearance or manifestation) performed by a Buddha or Bodhisattva for the edification of sentient beings. Not only is the transformation in and of itself an impressive display of the abilities of the enlightened one who performs it and hence an effective device to encourage those who witness it to be receptive to his teachings, but, for those whose wisdom

is sufficiently advanced, it is also a none-too-subtle affirmation of the illusory nature of all existence. If the enlightened
one can so effortlessly produce such marvelous—but
insubstantial—entities, there are profound ontological
implications which, being directly perceived, need not be
expressed verbally.[82]

The effect of this ontology is to shift one's focus away from
demands of "realism." When it comes to the mandates of karma,
a lack of ontological firmness is not an obstacle. In the literary
world, it is on the contrary a vehicle. The absoluteness with
which karma is given priority suggests that ultimately, questions of reality do not matter. The import of this view surpasses
the original claim of Sakyamuni that metaphysical questions
"tend not towards edification." For it does not proclaim the
irrelevance of metaphysics to salvation as much as it assumes
that ontology itself provides a malleable stage in which the religiously purposive functions of karma have full play. When
Xingzhen awakens from his dream, he concludes that his dream
has no reality, that it was merely a device of his master. Presumably, when Liuguan answers by preaching the *Diamond
Sūtra*, the ontological discourse of that text is sufficient to take
Xingzhen beyond the lesson that life is illusory, to the perception that illusion is liberating.

Unlike the novelists who strove for historical realism,
Sŏp'o's choice to employ the dream metaphor counterposes an
alternative model of truth. History's concern with verification is
overthrown in favor of the author's ability to conjure his own
world—hence fiction's glorification of the creative imagination.
The criterion of truth shifts away from What Really Happened
to the construction of an internal, hermetically sealed system
which exposes the mechanism of the Way Things Are, specifically, of the religiously charged cosmos.

Pei-yi Wu notes that "one of the reasons why so many
dreams have been recorded in China is that the authority of
the dreamer is seldom assailable."[83] Dreams, in other words,
offer a safe haven of discourse. The dreamer cannot be held
liable for his dreams. In Sŏp'o's politically charged environment,

composing a novel (which is as private as one's dreams) betrays a pragmatic desire to stay outside the boundaries of political accountability. The safety of dreams result from the fact that the events of one's dreams, unlike the events of history, cannot be disputed. Dreams and novels are one's own creation, exempt from the strictures of official, rule-governed discourse.

Sŏp'o's defiant ingenuity, however, has yet to be thoroughly displayed. It is not enough to relegate his fiction to a purely private act. Sŏp'o's declaration of the way the world is—like all such declarations—claims on its behalf the backing of truth, of a validity that all must acknowledge. Sŏp'o traverses the polarity of private act to public declaration within the single discourse of his fiction by virtue of its double disposition: If fiction is free from the rules of public discourse, the creative imagination must nonetheless be restrained by tradition in order to have more than a solipsistic meaning. Sŏp'o avails himself of the dream, which is a culturally patterned symbol, to make his sentiments immediately recognizable to his reader. Although Sŏp'o took refuge in the narrative form, which seems to relinquish all claims to historical veracity, a proper understanding of its philosophical message makes clear how he managed to deliberately analogize the internal meaning of *KUM* to the real world, thus forcing its claims outside itself.

We have in this chapter examined two important facts about the philosophical activities of *KUM*. The first has been its basic metaphysical—specifically ontological—perspective on the world. As referenced by the dream, this perspective can be summarized as a desire to question the distinction between illusion and reality, ultimately suggesting that the dualism is invalid. This metaphysical attitude has been accounted for primarily through the historical religious traditions of Buddhism and Taoism and the discrete metaphysical speculations that they engaged in.

The second philosophical activity of *KUM*, which I have only begun to examine, is the desire of Sŏp'o to assert the symmetry of illusion and reality as his public truth claim through the narrative of *KUM*. His use of the fantasy/dream narrative for this purpose takes pragmatic advantage of its exemption from orthodox political agendas. Quite importantly, the elements of traditional Chinese fantasy literature—particularly the element of karma—themselves imply a specific cosmic reality. Briefly put, this reality is one that is not concerned with realism in a historiographical sense but rather with cosmic possibilities, even necessities, as indexed to religious goals.

The wedding of *KUM*'s metaphysical assertions with its narrative strategies will form the crux of the discussion to come. The initial foray of this chapter into this area of consideration offers a paradigm case of the general problematic that needs to be examined: *KUM*'s abolition of the reality/illusion distinction is an ontological assertion that is hard to actually articulate. Sŏp'o's decision to utilize fantasy narrative disencumbered him from the demands of verisimilitude in the making of his truth claims, and also allowed him to posit the supremacy of religious liberation as a normative goal. As we have seen, however, this narrative conjures and structures its own world. The dominant example of this is the agency of karma in fantasy narrative, a cosmic force which presumes quite definite ideas about how the world operates. One must ask, then, how the world presumed by the narrative of *KUM* can be made exempt from its own critique. In other words, the articulation of a truth claim always assumes a view of reality which is problematic when, as in the case of *KUM*, the truth claim is that assertions of reality are not possible. The manner in which *KUM* dodges and resolves this paradox comprises what I call its metapractice and is our next topic of concern.

Chapter 4

A Metaphysics in Search of Expression

Western intellectual musings on the question of meaning in art, as Andrew Plaks comments, "serve[s] only to point up the recurrent dualism of the perception of reality and the conception of meaning."[1] Two implicit issues drive this observation: First, there is the assumption that the mimesis of human action—i.e., all art—and what it purports to represent are two separate things. Given this situation, a second issue is raised that questions the manner in which mimetic action can successfully represent reality.

In arguing for the success of Chinese fiction in modeling the world, Plaks affirms that "the existential universe does in fact bear within itself—or does at least project—an orderly structure of meaning that is in the final analysis susceptible to human comprehension. . . ."[2] The patterns of cosmic alternation and periodicity perceptible in the world of experience are replicated in narrative. The result is a form of allegory which bears its meaning in itself, as opposed to the Western allegorical function which projects the reader to another level of reality that is inherently evasive of mimetic representation.

Wendy O'Flaherty offers another tack in understanding the use of narrative in the representation of ontological structures. In this instance, the initial perception of reality (which art attempts to reproduce) is not as transparent as in the Chinese universe. It is in fact the very impenetrability of the world which orders narrative into action—"The attempt to approach infinity, to produce the illusion that one has described infinity, drives us inevitably into narrative, into parable and metaphor."[3]

Narrative, parable, and metaphor admit of a broad range of applications. For example, the receding frames of reality which structure *The Dream of the Nine Clouds* are similar to Indian narratives which used this format to parallel artistically geographical conceptions of the universe. Hindu geography, which pictures concentric worlds within worlds, is narratively replicated by the constantly awakening dreamer who finds himself within ever-broadening worlds. O'Flaherty notes, "It is not surprising that there should be an analogy between cosmology and the concentric loops of narrative structure, since both geography and mythology map the world and thus, either implicitly or explicitly, order it."[4]

This systematic geography and narrative patterning substitute for direct explanations of a world which is by definition beyond intellectual apprehension. In this sense, O'Flaherty's suggestion that narrative philosophizes does not present narrative as an option for discourse as much as a necessary strategy. In the absence of a perspicuous universe, fictive discourse can no longer be held to be direct patterning of reality. It is instead its own form of systematic speculation and ordering.

The consideration of these two views of the meaning of fiction greatly complicates our consideration of *KUM*. The central question concerns how we are finally to assess the fiction of *KUM* in relation to the ontically real, regarding which it has much to articulate. I have adhered to Victor Mair's theory of the meaning of the rise of fiction in China— the philosophical recognition that the world is created and illusory in the same way that fiction is. *KUM* seems to articulate this understanding of the world through the receding frame motif, which questions the possibility of a final awakening that distinguishes between illusion and ultimate reality. If we persist in applying this ontology to the theory of fiction, the only course seems to be to affirm fiction as a direct embodiment of the world rather than a mimetic or symbolic representation of it.

The nondualism of fiction and truth suggested here diverges radically from Plaks' version. *KUM* offers a universe that is far from transparent; it is, in fact, treacherously illusionary. The manner in which *KUM* embodies this vision goes beyond merely replicating and reproducing it. Through its self-awareness as a work of fiction, and hence as ontically equivalent to the world it seeks to disclose, it uses itself instrumentally as a vehicle of revelation.

At this point, the function of fiction must be considered beyond its world-ordering or representative mode. While it is clear that the philosophical views expressed by *KUM* are patently derived from specific Buddhist strains, what is more subtle in such expressions is the implicit discourse on the problem of discourse, or the attempt to express this view of reality. Here O'Flaherty's reference to the pragmatic philosophical utility of narrative as a *form* of expression, apart from the views it chooses to contain, holds greater possibility. The emphasis here falls on the question of philosophical discourse; that is, the way in which views of reality get expressed, apart from the actual views themselves. To the extent that *KUM* also participates in and embodies a philosophical discourse, we must affirm that a full understanding of this discourse does not become apparent upon a reading of the text alone. This is where the historical level of perspective becomes critical and proof of the fact that a text's metapractice, as opposed to its metaphysics, does not always bear its meaning in itself.

The central problematic which fuels *KUM*'s metapractice can nevertheless be demonstrated relative to itself. It is my thesis that Sŏp'o chose the dream metaphor for his novel in order to embrace both emotionally and philosophically a vision of reality which comprised the most historically cogent alternative to the structures that bound his own embittered life. The articulation of this alternative vision, however, is fraught with inherent dangers—the dangers posed by discourse itself, which often creates a distraction from the truth that it attempts to signify.

KUM's profound self-referential message of the thoroughly created and illusory nature of existence is ultimately non-referential in its articulation of this truth. By *KUM*'s self-referentiality, I mean the fact that its view of the world—its ontology of illusion—is applicable to itself as a medium of expression; that is, to itself as fictive discourse. By *KUM*'s non-referentiality, I mean that as a form of truth discourse, the fiction of *KUM* does not actually represent a reality physically or metaphysically existing outside of itself. In the act of conceiving meaning which is attributed to reality, however, structures must be created. In the creation of that structure—in this case, the frame motif—the deliberate manipulation of form can often start to look like a symbol. The nested realities look like a direct representation of cosmology, as O'Flaherty suggests. Given *KUM*'s situatedness in a broader history of metapractical arguments, however, I contend that the receding frames of reality are more a manner of representation—a part of the artistry—than an ontic structure. The point is not to keep waking up until we reach the outermost frame, but rather to acknowledge the equivalence of all frames of reality.

The complexity of the meaning of fiction in the current context ensues from an apparent contradiction: fiction is more than mimetic representation because it is ontically real, or of the same ontic status as the reality it portrays. On the other hand, the structures within that fiction should not be consumed literally as a picture of reality. This degrades the literary structures into symbols, into representations of something outside of themselves. One might characterize the struggle against this tendency as the struggle against the implicit *referentiality* of all articulated truth claims. Indexed by such terms as symbol, representation, and mimesis in my discussions, the supposed referentiality of language is an illusion that comes under direct scrutiny in *KUM*.

But how is it possible to exempt this novel's philosophical purpose from the sabotaging effects of its own discourse? The effect of the receding frames of reality is to point outside of its narrative boundaries, to suggest a trajectory outside of its artistic creation to some final resolution. This effect must be constantly neutralized by the self-referentiality of *KUM*'s ontology of illusion; that is, the fact that fiction is an instantiation rather than representation of reality, and thus cannot point to a reality outside of itself. The act of pointing that the novel's structure suggests does not attempt to lead the reader to a metaphysical disclosure. Instead, the act of pointing jabs into the reader's own reference frame to challenge his or her greater fixity on this supposed final reality. Proper emphasis should fall not on what the pointing points to, but on the soteriological implications of the act of pointing itself.

This interpretation justly underscores the dominant function of *KUM* as philosophical practice over metaphysical expression. Historically, *KUM* inherits a long tradition of Buddhist stipulations about discourse which are concerned more with its pragmatic effects than with what it says. Thus the theme of recurrent dreams and awakenings must be plumbed beyond what it suggests about the nature of life, to what it demands of the reader.

As the author of this work, Sŏp'o also made pragmatic use of his fictive discourse. Recognizing the outward thrust of the dream, he elevated his private musings to the level of public truth claims which assert that no one is immune from this vision. Sŏp'o is an example of one man who used culturally evolved paradigms to instantiate his personal declarations. The cultural resources that were available to him in this act comprise their own history, a history of the development of Buddhist philosophical discourse. It will be necessary to look directly at this history in order to locate Sŏp'o on the cultural map. The act of situating *KUM* in the broader context of Buddhist discussion—specifically its concern with the problems of textual discourse—should make the most tangible contribution to the question of art and meaning. The philosophical nature of this last question requires us to consider the kind of philosophizing the Buddhists themselves were apt to engage in. For a fair assessment of what Buddhist philosophical practice was able to achieve requires that we hold it up to its own standards—standards that may ultimately impinge on broader, cross-cultural practices.

The Problem of Language

To claim that *KUM* sits within an historical tradition of Buddhist religious discourse means that it seeks to reveal something significant about the nature of reality. This act is a necessary part of its soteriological mission. Its attempt to communicate such information, however, must take into account the Buddhist dictum that words are incapable of referring to the real. This non-symbolist stance in Buddhism goes all the way back to its *anātman* ("selflessness") theory and the stipulation that language does not express ontological entities. This problem of language can be conceptually distinguished as a concern for religious practice which ensues from Buddhism's actual view of reality.

It has been pointed out that the Western philosophical discipline has traditionally focused on metaphysics over questions of metapractice.[5] In its quest for theories about reality and justifications for how that reality can be perceived, philosophy has overlooked the equally important question of how a conception of reality is instantiated by religious and other communal practices, and how those practices may be justified.

Buddhist philosophy in East Asia, on the other hand, reveals a relentless metapractical obsession with the utility (or lack thereof) of speech and discourse in the realization of Buddhist enlightenment. The depth of this issue in East Asia resulted in much literary-critical consideration of the nature and function of not only scholastic texts, but of creative literature in the pursuit of religious goals. This metapractical tradition was conceived at the very beginning of Buddhism when the Buddha was recorded in the *Majjhima-Nikāya* (the "middle-length sayings") of the Pāli Canon as refusing to respond to metaphysical questions. The Buddha stated, "Whether the dogma obtain . . . that the world is eternal, or that the world is not eternal, there still remain birth, old age, death, sorrow, lamentation, misery, grief, and despair, for the extinction of which in the present life I am prescribing."[6]

If the Buddha's refusal to engage in metaphysical speculation is considered in light of his historical and intellectual background, one can argue that this act amounts to a deliberate privileging of praxis over metaphysics. The Indian traditions of his day offered a wealth of philosophical argumentation and distinctions regarding the nature of ultimate reality. The Buddha rejected these traditions of speculation, and instead issued an urgent call for immediate action in order to alleviate the suffering of the world. This call for action over theory was revived and sounded most loudly in East Asia through the Chan sects, who built their reputation on the denunciation of texts. In the modern era, the primacy of praxis has been championed most vocally by D. T. Suzuki, perhaps the foremost representative of Zen Buddhism to the West, who ceaselessly reiterates the impotence of intellectual knowledge and understanding in attaining the primary value of soteriological transformation.[7]

The rhetoric of anti-intellectualism cannot succeed in obscuring the record of Buddhism's rich metaphysical ventures. I do not wish to pose a dualism of metaphysics and metapractice as much as to distinguish them conceptually in order to perceive better their interaction. Specifically, I posit that in the East Asian Buddhist tradition, metaphysical pronouncements set metapractical problems and solutions into motion. Thus conceptually, metaphysics, or beliefs about reality, come first.[8] Metapractical resolutions make sense only in relation to the beliefs about reality that they attempt to accommodate. Therefore, although anti-intellectual and iconoclastic gestures fashion a strategy for achieving religious goals, one must not forget that the metapractical justifications for these acts are solidly grounded in intellectual positions.

The Buddha's stance against metaphysical discourse must be reexamined, then, in terms of its intellectual foundations. The Buddha's injunction to stop the suffering of the world implicates an explicit view of reality—of its impermanence and egolessness, or the lack of an absolute reality behind changing phenomena.[9] In the early Theravāda tradition, the Buddhist mistrust of words focused on the tendency of words to lead to epistemological error. To wit, words are conventional designations of meaning which tend to take on the aura of metaphysical reality—

a reality that cannot exist according to the Buddhist assertion of impermanence.[10]

In the *Prajñāpāramitā* literature of Mahāyāna Buddhism, a somewhat different mistrust of discourse is articulated which views the conditioned and discriminating function of speech as inherently incapable of encompassing an unconditioned, non-discriminated perception of reality. The futility of all discourse ensues from the fact that a pure experience of the world must by definition leave the distinctions of speech behind. The Mahāyāna objection to language is not that words themselves tend to get absolutized, but that they are inadequate to describe the absolute.[11] The praxis which this position gives rise to, however, can often look the same as the Buddha's original strategy. In the *Vimalakīrtinirdeśa Sūtra*, Vimalakīrti's applauded "discourse" on the "dharma-door of nonduality" is to maintain silence.[12] To speak would only be to violate the precept of nondualism.

My purpose in this present chapter is to situate *The Dream of the Nine Clouds* within an historical context of metapractical strategies for overcoming the limitations of discourse. Although many East Asian Buddhists were serious students of the lessons of Indian Mahāyāna Buddhism on the nature of speech, they also engendered a history of theoretically justified practices. *KUM* stands within this tradition of metapractical solutions. In order to understand the nature of the solution, however, one must begin with an examination of the East Asian appropriation of Buddhism. This path of appropriation took its cue from the divergent voices within the Indian tradition. What is notable about the development within the East Asian setting, however, is the degree of consensus it reached within itself based on the synthetic reworking of diverse Indian texts.

It is perhaps best to state at the outset that despite East Asia's earnest consideration of the speech problem, it ultimately and unequivocally affirmed the utility of language as an instrument of religious soteriology. Indeed, as we shall see below, many Buddhist articulations of literary theory went so far as to confirm language's referential powers as well as its pragmatic religious uses. The beginnings of this rather heretical view are visible within the Indian Mādhyamika school, the tradition which most audibly asserted the impotence of language. Within this school, the Prāsangikas practiced the negative dialectic (*prasaṅga*), whose sole purpose was to refute all linguistic assertions with the claim to assert finally nothing at all. The Svātantrikas, however, seemed to recognize the Prāsangika's instrumental use of speech (even if only to refute) and claimed that the role of language must be admitted—that the use of language soteriologically rather than referentially still constituted a constructive use.[13]

The distinction in linguistic usage that the Svātantrikas pointed to was perhaps most famously formulated by Dahui Zonggau (1089–1163), a Chinese monk who stressed the "live-word/dead-word" distinction. As a well-known representative of Song dynasty Chan Buddhism, Dahui vouches for Chan's understanding that the emptiness of words does not prohibit them from becoming instrumental tools of religious practice. The trick is in understanding the praxeological use of words without falling under the illusion of their ontological substantialism. Thus, "any type of theoretical description, whether found in Chan or in scholastic writings, would be considered a 'dead-word,' while any teaching that is intended not to explain but to enlighten would be a 'live-word.' "[14] Although the specific terminology of the "live-word" arises from the Chan context, its general sense of soteriologically enabling words or discourse is present in most of the mainstream Mahāyāna traditions that had significant impact on East Asia. I refer specifically to the Prajñāpāramitā literature, the Mādhyamika school, and of course, to Chan itself. A consistent characteristic of this "live-word" practice is the strategy of employing words against themselves— a strategy in which words are rendered useful by using them to thwart their seeming reality.

Certain Chan practices offer the most direct embodiment of this "live-word" tactic. Chan Buddhism's boycott on words never went to the extent of maintaining total silence. The "recorded sayings" or *yulu* of Chan masters, and the well-known "public cases" or *gongan* (Japanese: *koan*), made up a literary genre which practiced an inverse praxeology of words that was used not to sustain intellectual understanding, but to subvert it. D. T. Suzuki's explanations of the Zen *koan* has capitalized on its anti-intellectual, paradoxical use of words to break down the illusion of ontological reference frames. The absurdity of such responses as "Three catties of flax" to the question "What is the Buddha?" is aimed at snapping one's implicit trust in the existence of a coherent, contoured reality. In Chung-ying Cheng's explanation, " . . . the language of the Zen paradoxes has a surface semantic structure which is not embedded in or correlated with any common-sensical ontological structure which is its framework of reference."[15] One is encouraged, in other words, to abandon all ontological categories through a realization of emptiness. This act, however, does not disallow the use of words. The proper use of language can render it "so that it is *expressive* of the Enlightenment without being *assertive* of it."[16]

It is possible to sustain the distinction between the two uses of language without violating Buddhism's basic suspicion of language's ontological properties. One can reject the view that language refers to real metaphysical entities but nevertheless embrace it as a praxeological tool. The Chinese Buddhists affirmed this path by relegating the Mādhyamika (which was identified closely with the Prāsangika school) to the category of relative and interpretive (Sanskrit: *neyārtha*) teachings in its classification of doctrines (*panjiao*). The prominent Huayan school was particularly consistent in this regard. Representing a significant school in the mature period of Chinese doctrinal understanding,[17] the Huayan led the movement beyond negative discourse. In regard to Chinese Buddhists generally, Robert Gimello states that:

> All are able to acknowledge Nāgārjuna's caution—that uncritical use of the constructive language of philosophical views is a species of intellectual bondage—but they acknowledge it only as a caution, a corrective to false views. They insist, however, that the way of denial and negation, the unremitting distrust of positive language, is necessary but

not sufficient unto enlightenment. . . . [They] took it upon themselves to reassert the salvific value of kataphasis, the spiritual utility of positive and affirmative language. They chose, in short, eloquence over silence.[18]

Although the conceptual distinction between metaphysical and metapractical categories allowed for the final affirmation of language, it is not clear that in this act of affirmation the conceptual distinction was in fact historically maintained. In its greatest departure from early Indian Buddhist doctrine, the Chinese tradition's final return to kataphatic discourse did not stop with praising the utilitarian values of positive language. It also lauded its representative powers. Again, this course was suggested, or at least hinted at, within the Indian tradition. Nathan Katz points out that at issue between the Prāsangika and Svātantrika debate about language was the fundamental methodological problem of how ultimate reality could be revealed. The methodological consideration, however, could not be resolved without impinging on ontological issues. Katz formulates the problem succinctly with the question, "Is the absolute to be found only in the negation of the relative, or is the stuff of the relative somehow contiguous to the absolute, allowing one to attain cognition of the absolute by means of the relative?"[19]

The problem of the "two truths" (relative and absolute) and their relationship was perhaps initiated by the philosopher Nāgārjuna's own ambiguity in his *Mūlamadhyamakākarikās* (*Fundamentals of the Middle Way*) 24: 8–9, in which he affirmed the separateness of relative and absolute truths, and yet also stated that "Without relying upon convention, the ultimate fruit is not taught. Without understanding the ultimate fruit, wisdom is not attained."[20] Positing the instrumentality of relative truth in the revelation of absolute truth created a connection between the two realms which could be interpreted ontologically as well as pragmatically. Chinese Buddhism maximized this logical conclusion by collapsing the dualism of relative and absolute truth and asserting their unity. This move represents a significant development in Buddhism's theory of reality which violated some fundamental tenets of the early tradition. Understanding this development is not only essential in appreciating the Chinese synthesis of Indian philosophical schools, but also in understanding the basis of the East Asian Buddhist literary tradition.

In the previous chapter, I identified the teaching of emptiness, or *śūnyatā*, as the most pertinent metaphysical perspective operative in *KUM*, with its use of the dream. The doctrine of emptiness is the hallmark of the Mādhyamika school of Indian Buddhism. Although we have been using the term emptiness in this chapter to refer to the negative dialectic of Nāgārjuna which pronounces that language is "empty" of real meaning, we must also recognize the negative *emotional* value of the term which proclaims that all things in the world are found wanting. The emptiness doctrine ontologized this psychological perception to make definitive comments on the nature of reality, which is often analogized to the dream as something that is ultimately empty and unreal.

The extent of Mādhyamika influence in China, Korea, and Japan can be concretely gauged by the cultural artifacts of these societies. Edward Conze states that "while some European scholars may regard Yogācāra as 'the most important school of the Mahāyāna,' their views have never stirred the East to the extent that the Emptiness doctrine has moved it."[21] It is important, however, not to overemphasize the sectarian purity of the emptiness doctrine in East Asia. The dominant language of "emptiness" (*kong*) in Chinese Buddhism does not suggest a strict doctrinal adherence to the Mādhyamika, and even less the philosophical practice of *prasaṅga* as established by Nāgārjuna.

Repeated claims by current scholars that the *śūnyatā* doctrine forms the core of Mahāyāna Buddhism[22] are often and justly tempered by recognition of the extent to which Yogācāra elements also figure in Chinese Buddhist philosophy. The Yogācāra factor is recognized in the prevalent theories of mind, or "mind only," which allude to the Indian school's portrayal of the world as a projection of consciousness. The claim that Bodhidharma (ca. 530?), the first patriarch of Chan, emphasized the teachings of the *Laṅkāvatāra Sūtra* (which is accounted a

Yogācāra text) points to the high regard in which this school was held.

Like the Chinese appropriation of the emptiness doctrine, however, the theory of mind was digested in limited ways which ultimately served to fill in stages of the Chinese classificational system. Although the *panjiao* schema differed somewhat according to schools (particularly Huayan and Tiantai), and even according to individuals, they were united in their principle of establishing a hierarchy of relative (Sanskrit: *neyārtha*) to absolute (Sanskrit: *nītārtha*) teachings.[23] All the classification schemes were unanimous in placing the "Hīnayāna" teachings—defined primarily as the doctrine of *anātman* and the principle of causality and dependent origination—on the lowest rung. This teaching was given to the most deluded individuals who lacked all spiritual insight. For Guifeng Zongmi (780-841), a patriarch of both Huayan and Chan Buddhism, this level of teaching also represented an inferior phase of positive, or kataphatic, doctrine.

The selective appropriation of Indian philosophy is evident in the next phase of Zongmi's classification—the middle one which places the negative, or apophatic discourse of the *śūnyavāda* as the highest of the relative Buddhist teachings. This categorization tilts the balance of the Mādhyamika tradition to its Prāsaṅgika side, but it rejects that tradition's own understanding of itself and its attitude toward language as definitive. The third and last phase of the Buddha's teaching is characterized as the "revelation of the nature," or the "direct revelation that the mind is the nature."[24] Before assessing what this revelation means, the important item to note here is Zongmi's movement back to positive, kataphatic discourse. This kataphatic discourse is not only positive in its embrace of language, but also in its belief that it can substantively describe reality. As Gregory puts it:

> Only after one has recognized the emptiness of words, their provisional and arbitrary character as dependent upon convention, can religious language take on a new and potent function. When words are no longer mistaken for essences, they no longer provide a basis upon which an imaginary

reality can be constructed and are thus free to reveal the essence directly.[25]

The pointing function of words as described here and in the textuality of *KUM* admittedly goes beyond a naive realist's view of language and its relationship to reality. And well it should, for on the East Asian Buddhist map, such a progression of understanding about language represents spiritual advancement. But the very possibility of such progress is predicated on a substantialist and affirmative view of reality, most often indexed by the language of "essence," "nature," and "mind." Here the Chinese tradition betrays its inability to sustain the game of linguistic chicken instigated by the Prāsangikas. It openly abandoned the collision-track into the void by veering off into a realm of renewed ontic discourse.

Buddhist Ontology Renewed

In the late Tang period, Zongmi excoriated Confucianism for its lack of cosmogonic sophistication. In his *Inquiry into the Origins of Man*, Zongmi charged that the teachings of Confucius and the Taoists were not up to even the most basic Buddhist concept—that of karma—in their ability to explain fundamental problems of theodicy.[26] Zongmi's fighting words came in the wake of neo-Confucian attacks on Buddhism, particularly those launched by Han Yu (768–824), Buddhism's most famous nemesis of the era.[27] Zongmi's own polemics presaged much of the discourse that neo-Confucians themselves would engage in during the Ming, but it is critical to note that the momentum of Buddhist ontology in China was initially gained by its encounter with indigenous views.

Most problematic in this encounter was the clash of Buddhist cosmogony, which rooted the origins of the world in the timeless and unexplained ignorance of human beings, with the basic optimism of Chinese thought, which equated man with heaven and all its goodness.[28] The most constructive aspect of the Chinese appropriation of Buddhism, one may argue, was its attempt to fuse an affirmative view of the world with the Buddhist soteriological path. The attempt is evident in the detailed exegetical works of Buddhist scholastics. Dushun (557–640), the first patriarch of Huayan Buddhism, is noted for replacing the terms "form" and "emptiness"—an equation made famous in the *Heart Sūtra*—with the native philosophical terms of "principle" (*li*) and "phenomena" (*shi*). The substitution initiated a school of thought which eventually affirmed the numinous nature of all phenomena, on the grounds of the mutual penetration of phenomena and principle. Thus Dushun's work signalled an "important shift toward an affirmation of the phenomenal world."[29]

Perhaps the most direct evidence of this affirmative attitude cashes out in the theory of original enlightenment—a position defined well before the establishment of Chan Buddhism. In Zongmi's *Inquiry into the Origins of Man*, the highest revelation of the Buddha is characterized as the teaching that reveals the true nature; the teaching which explains that

> . . . all sentient beings have been endowed with the true mind of original enlightenment. From the beginningless beginning this mind has been constant, pure, luminous, and unobscured; it has always been characterized by bright cognition; it is also called the Buddha Nature or the Womb of Tathāgata.[30]

The terminology which forms the aegis for this viewpoint is the concept of *tathāgatagarbha*, which eventually outdistanced the language of *kong* as the emblem of East Asian Buddhism. *Garbha* indicates the "embryo" or "womb" of *tathatā*, which is commonly translated as "suchness," or "thusness." Although *tathatā* was often used synonymously with *śūnyatā* as a more positive yet corollary rendition of the void, scholastic circles actively shifted away from the nihilistic idiom of emptiness in favor of the theory of the immanence of enlightenment in all beings.[31] *Tathāgatagarbha* theory, then, resolutely affirmed the principle of original purity by virtue of all beings' possession of Buddha-nature.

Tathāgatagarbha theory is Indian in origin. Its development suggests an awareness of the contradictory views of the mind that were arising within the Indian tradition. The conflict was most visible in the Yogācāra, or "Mind-only" school. In the *Trimśikā* (*Thirty Verses*) of Vasubandhu, one of the most important texts of the Chinese "consciousness-only" (*weishi*) school, two views of the mind co-exist. The first conforms with classic *anātman* theory which views the mind as merely one component of the so-called "self" which is actually comprised as ever-changing aggregates of *dharmas*. From this perspective, mind contributes to our experience of the world as suffering and should ideally be extinguished. The other view characterizes the mind as the true nature of reality and equal to suchness, with its essence as immutable. Here the mind is elevated into a principle far beyond what was allowed in early *anātman* theory.[32]

The conflict between the two notions of mind expressed by this text points to an inherent lack in Buddhist doctrine—a lack of an ontic analysis of what, if anything, lies behind the deluded and conditioned phenomena of the world as projected by the mind. Further scrutiny into the nature of mind—most notably the concept of *ālayavijñāna*, or the "storehouse consciousness," which formed the basis of all phenomena arising in the mind—merely served to press the question of the mind's original nature. The *Lankāvatāra Sūtra* suggested the innate purity of mind by equating the *ālayavijñāna* with the *tathāgatagarbha*, but also held out for the mind's all-encompassing nature by stating that "the Tathāgata-garbha holds within it the cause for both good and evil, and by it all the forms of existence are produced."[33]

The establishment of the Yogācāra school in China in the sixth century revolved around this very question of the mind's original nature. The school's inherited division between an emphasis on purity and impurity soon gave way to the vision articulated by the *Lankāvatāra*,[34] and fundamentally sought to create an ontological basis for understanding the mind.[35]

The essential components of this preoccupation were laid out as early as the fifth or sixth century with the appearance of the *Awakening of Faith*. This text, reconstructed in Sanskrit as the *Mahāyānaśraddhotpādaśastra*, is attributed to Aśvaghosa and is said to have been translated by Paramārtha into Chinese.

The internal and external evidence of the work suggest, however, that it is of Chinese composition.[36] Within the text, a theory of "one mind" with "two aspects"—absolute and phenomenal—is presented, which is said to "embrace all states of existence. . . . Because these two aspects are mutually inclusive."[37] The "two aspects" of the mind elaborated here point to the text's synthetic amalgamation of the mind's original nature interpreted both as pure and impure. The apparent dualism, however, is resolved through an ontological affirmation of innate purity. Robert Buswell points out that in this respect, the *tathāgatagarbha* takes on more significant meaning than its namesake in Indian texts:

> Tathāgatagarbha, as seen previously, would typically be construed as more concerned with soteriological issues—the possibility of enlightenment. The *Awakening of Faith*, however, gives it more of an ontological bent: tathāgatagarbha is the singular reality of absolute existence as seen by both the deluded individual . . . and the enlightened saint. . . .[38]

The "one mind/dual aspect" formula of the *Awakening of Faith* can be justly accused of betraying the Buddhist theory of causality which steadfastly denied the possibility of positing a ground or substratum for phenomena. The idea of innate purity, often characterized as the "substance" (*ti*) of mind which manifests phenomena as its "function" (*yong*), posited just such a support in the Chinese push for a theory of "nature origination," as Zongmi put it, or a cosmogonic basis for the world. Although this development smacks of Vedantin heresy in classical Buddhist eyes, its suggestions, as we have seen, were implicit within the Indian tradition itself.

One can perhaps begin to gauge the impact of the *Awakening of Faith* in East Asia by the fact that over 170 commentaries have been written on it, including an authoritative version by the Korean monk Wŏnhyo (617–686).[39] The unifying efforts of the *Awakening of Faith* were given a warm reception in Korean Buddhism, which has been noted for its ecumenical strivings toward a "comprehensive Buddhism."[40] Wŏnhyo's intellectual pursuits focused on the *Awakening of Faith* as a synthetic perspective that was therefore superior to the rivalry between the Mādhyamika and Yogācāra sects of his day. Wŏnhyo's own efforts to champion such a synthesis between the two Mahāyāna camps reflect the dominant trends which eventually emerged as the "indigenous" school of Chan Buddhism.

The Problem of Language Renewed

Some influential scholars such as Hu Shih and D. T. Suzuki have argued that Chan/Zen Buddhism represents the first complete break from Indian philosophical traditions, and the triumph of the pragmatic Chinese, or Japanese (respectively), spirit.[41] Claiming a special transmission of teaching outside the canon and directly from the first patriarch Bodhidharma, Chan touted the primacy of a direct experience of Buddhist illumination attained by sundry, sometimes rather startling methods. Based on my own principle of distinguishing between metaphysical and metapractical elements of a tradition, however, it is my conclusion that the polemical observations of these scholars (which are still routinely perpetrated from time to time) fail to distinguish the fact that the aggressively deconstructive thrusts of Chan are not aimed at the metaphysical tradition that it inherits, but rather form a metapractical strategy.[42]

As for the question regarding which East Asian nation can claim greatest ownership of the practical "spirit" of Chan Buddhism, we need not be detained by matters of cultural chauvanism but there is an historical point that is relevant to our present study: Given the realities of area studies, most scholarly and popular investigations of this topic have focused on Japan and China, giving currency to the terms "Zen" and "Chan," respectively. Although the Korean scene has enjoyed less attention, the studies that do exist attest to the active participation of Korean Buddhists in the rise of Chan, or Sŏn. Robert Buswell's investigation of *The Formation of Ch'an Ideology in China and Korea* not only explores the intimate connections between the Chinese and Korean Buddhist scenes, but specifically attributes Korean authorship to the *Vajrasamādhi Sūtra*, an apocryphal and highly influential text which voices the major doctrines and controversies of Chan in nascent form and which predates the earliest extant writings of the Chinese Northern Chan schools by three decades. The close interaction between Chinese and Korean Buddhists underscores Buswell's caution regarding the "splendid isolation" of area studies. It also demonstrates how useful a knowledge of the Chinese scene is in understanding the particularities of the Korean one.

Chan Buddhism's supposed revelry in heterodoxy has been put in proper perspective by recent scholars who demonstrate that Chan repeatedly sought "legitimation through integration with the inherited tradition," especially through reference to prior Buddhist scriptures.[43] Chan Buddhism's inevitable deference to and acknowledgement of an orthodox tradition resulted from the fact that its own inception followed the period of translation, study, and systematization of major Buddhist texts from India—a process which was completed by the end of the sixth century and which centered on the *Perfection of Wisdom* tradition of texts as authoritative.[44]

Chan's acceptance of this prior tradition is an important step in understanding the crux of its metapractical dilemma. This dilemma is based on the metaphysical contention that the mind of all sentient beings is originally pure. The ensuing problem for the logic of religious practice was repeatedly posed in Sŏn discourse throughout the East Asian region. In late twelfth-century Korea, the Koryŏ dynasty's most famous monk, Chinul (1158–1210), put it this way:

> If we take it for granted that our own true nature is originally complete in itself, we need only to let the mind act freely on its own and conform with the ancient principle [of all the saints]. What need is there to contemplate and thereby bind ourselves without ropes?[45]

Half a century later, the Japanese monk Dōgen (1200–1253), dedicated his career to the resolution of the same question:

> As I study both the exoteric and the esoteric schools of buddhism, they maintain that man is endowed with the Dharma-nature by birth. If this is the case, why had the

buddhas of all ages—undoubtedly in possession of enlightenment—to seek enlightenment and engage in spiritual
practice?[46]

The Sŏn tradition's best efforts to answer these questions
pivoted around updating the Buddha's original pragmatism in
refusing to engage in metaphysical discourse: the efficacy of this
strategy of non-discourse was ontologized in understanding as
the only method by which one could attain an immediate, existential experience of one's original nature. The act of discoursing
would only objectify and therefore externalize the realization of
one's original purity as a goal outside of one's self.

Hence we come full circle in the Buddhist affair with words.
What began in our analysis with the Buddhist metaphysical
distrust of language—that is, the assertion that words do not
point to ontological entities—is completed here with doubts expressed about its praxeological utility as well. But the debates
are essentially the same. While all Buddhists generally deny the
referential quality of words, the use of language (and logic) as
an expedient means in the revelation of truth has been a topic of
recurrent contention.

The Sŏn context is contiguous with these prior debates and
neatly summarizes them. The "live-word/dead-word" distinction examined above constitutes a significant marker in Buddhist philosophy which is simultaneously deconstructive *and*
reconstructive in its use of discourse. The deconstructive phase
is embodied in methodological and psychological strategies designed to break down existing attachments to views of reality.
The reconstructive aspect is carried out by praxeological uses of
language which are grounded in the metaphysical understanding that the emptiness of words itself participates in the greater
emptiness of reality. Hence the degradation of words as symbols of a non-existent reality only shows up the unenlightened
nature of the one who persistently holds to this view. The logic
of emptiness ultimately dictates that words are included in the
all-inclusive beyond of nondualism.

Although Chan on the whole exhibits both deconstructive
and reconstructive attitudes towards religious discourse, inter-

nal conflicts between individual Chan lineages often centered on the competing tendency to emphasize one at the expense of the other. The famous split between the so-called "Northern" and "Southern" schools can be viewed as one prominent example of this. If we look at Korean Sŏn in the context of this broad Chan evolution, this is where the particular characteristics of Korean Sŏn make themselves felt.

The strategy of reinstating the utility of words and discourse through both metaphysical and metapractical justifications found one of its fuller expressions through the thought of Chinul. Credited with consolidating and fathering the orthodox Korean Sŏn school, Chinul exemplified the Korean tendency to unify the rifts between Buddhist thought and practice. Acting more as a reformer than founder, Chinul reinvigorated the twelfth-century Buddhist world by mending its institutional divisions as well as by attempting to restore the purity and discipline of the *sangha*.

The Sŏn school had been established in Korea since the eighth century in the so-called Nine Mountains sects (*kusan*). Most of these schools traced their lineage to the Southern Chan master Mazu Daoyi (709–788). Daoyi, along with the master Linji Yixuan (d.866/67), represents the most radical outpost of Chan, whose adherence to the "sudden enlightenment" teaching announced its dismissal of all conceptual and intellectual modes of training. This influential lineage of Chinese Chan has been the most pivotal in perpetuating the rhetoric of religious deconstruction. The radical orientation of Nine Mountain Sŏn quickly alienated the established scholastic—particularly Hwaŏm—schools of Silla dynasty Buddhism. Chinul and others before him labored much to bring together the doctrinal (*kyo*) schools, which emphasized scriptural study, with the Sŏn schools, which emphasized meditation. This division within Korean Buddhism indicated not only an institutional split, but replicated the fundamental Chan debate about the logic of religious practice.[47]

The issue was given greater clarity and focus in the debate over "sudden enlightenment" and "gradual cultivation," a dualism that Chinul also sought to fuse. The controversy emerged from the sectarian rifts of Chinese Chan lineages and quite explicitly evoked the debate on the utility of discourse. The principle of sudden enlightenment drew upon the idea of every being's originally pure and perfected buddha-nature to assert that true understanding went beyond intellectual discrimination and the conceptual distinctions of language. Gradual cultivation, on the other hand, asserted that given the obstinacy of our defilements, a discipline of sustained religious practice (which for Chinul included textual and philosophical study as well as meditation) was necessary to uncover our original nature.

Although there was no inherent metaphysical contradiction between the principle of sudden enlightenment and gradual cultivation, the historical opposition of these two Chan schools points to a praxeological feud: Our original natures are pure, but which spiritual practice succeeds in restoring this essential purity?[48] Chinul's resolution, following the lead of the Chinese master Zongmi, was to combine the two in a linear progression—one must begin with a sudden enlightenment to one's true noumenal nature, but follow up with gradual cultivation in order to reform one's phenomenal and worldly self.

The significance of Chinul's synthetic, reconciliatory attitude towards the sudden/gradual debate lies in his metapractical affirmation of metaphysical discourse—a solution that became normative in the Korean context. Chinese Chan in large part turned away from the conciliatory efforts of Zongmi and embraced the radical iconoclasm of Linji Yixuan, whose lineage became one of the most influential Buddhist schools of the Chinese Song dynasty. It is to Linji that we owe the peculiar Chan practice of shouting and beating enlightenment into bewildered seekers. This "practice" was constituted in the mode of an antipractice designed to disabuse the adherent of the notion that he had anything to gain. The major problem with texts, discourse, and any form of religious practice, after all, was that they created the illusory goal of spiritual progress. The original purity of our being, according to Linji, demands instead that we simply let our natures be:

> Followers of the Way, the Dharma of the buddhas calls for
> no special undertakings. Just act ordinary, without trying
> to do anything particular. Move your bowels, piss, get
> dressed, eat your rice, and if you get tired, then lie down.
> Fools may laugh at me, but wise men will know what I
> mean.[49]

In addressing the utility of his own discourse, Linji cannot
but deny the ultimate use and meaning of it: "Followers of the
Way, don't be too taken up with my pronouncements either.
Why? Because pronouncements are without basis or underpin-
ning, something painted for a time on the empty sky . . ."[50]

In contrast, Chinul's actions turned towards affirming
Nāgārjuna's suggestion that there is an interdependency between
the realms of absolute truth and relative practices.[51] In one instance, he explicitly states this belief:

> What has been discussed here about the mind-nature being
> originally pure and the defilements being originally void
> corresponds, of course, to supreme vehicle Sŏn. Neverthe-
> less, beginners who are involved in earnest application can-
> not do without the help of the counteractive measures of
> the provisional vehicle. Consequently, in the text of this
> *Encouragement to Practice* you must be aware that the pro-
> visional and the real are displayed together.[52]

Chinul offers a metapractical justification of "provisional" religious practices that was bound to and supported by his ontological understanding of the dual nature of one's original mind.

Korean Sŏn's synthetic outlook, which ultimately validated
linguistic practices, continued beyond Chinul's own era to the
Chosŏn dynasty. About a century before Sŏp'o's time, Hyujŏng
consolidated the mountain tradition of Chosŏn Buddhism.
Hyujŏng is particularly noted for forming a band of warrior
monks that helped to ward off the Japanese invasions of
Hideyoshi Toyotomi at the end of the sixteenth century. By
rendering this service to the state, Hyujŏng made a case for
Buddhism's utility to national interests, but court sympathy towards the former state religion varied with the personal inclina-
tions of each monarch. The greater and more lasting contribution

of Hyujŏng to Chosŏn Buddhism was in his internal organization of the tradition. In accomplishing this task, Hyujŏng is
credited with transmitting Chinul's vision of Buddhism into the
seventeenth century.[53] Like Chinul, Hyujŏng favored Sŏn
Buddhism but at the same time asserted the necessity of *kyo*, or
doctrinal study, and also encouraged the Pure Land practice
of reciting the Buddha's name (*yŏnbul*).

After Hyujŏng's death, his disciple P'yŏngyang Ŏngi seeded
a descent line of monks who identified themselves with Sŏn but
also actively participated in scriptural study. This entailed publication of Buddhist literature, eventually establishing a standard curriculum of texts for the monastic schools (*kangwon*).
This curriculum was primarily composed of the Four Collected
Works (*sajip*) which included commentaries by Zongmi and
Dahui, as well as Chinul; and the Four Teachings, which were
comprised of the *Śūrangama Sūtra*, the *Sūtra of Perfect Enlightenment, the Awakening of Faith*, and the *Diamond Sūtra*.[54]

The aspects of Buddhist ontology that dominated the East
Asian setting sanctioned a peculiar understanding of words,
which in turn urged its enthusiastic cultivation in the religious
arena. In Chosŏn Korea, the continuing valuation of scriptural
study as a practice that was consonant with Sŏn principles not
only ensured the continuing production of Buddhist texts, but
also allowed for the expansion of Buddhist literary practices. To
be sure, Sŏp'o's novelistic composition was not the product of
institutional Buddhist practices. Although both Sŏp'o and Chosŏn
Buddhists created their literary labors in political exile, they
outwardly represented two opposing models of social identity.
To the extent to which they both endeavored in the Buddhist
vein, however, parallels can be drawn between them.[55] In the
Sŏp'o manp'il, the author states,

> Although Buddhist texts are numerous, their essence does
> not exceed the phrase, 'true emptiness, marvelous exist-
> ence.' Guifeng Zongmi was an expounder of true empti-
> ness and he did not violate the emptiness of existence. As
> an expounder of marvelous existence, he did not violate the
> existence of emptiness.[56]

Sŏp'o's reference to Zongmi reveals the strength of Chinul's legacy in Korean Buddhist thought. In identifying Zongmi as an authority, Sŏp'o follows in the footsteps of the twelfth-century Sŏn master and his concern with falling into the trap of "emptiness only." The doctrine of emptiness is a speculation on the nature of reality with an inherently dual structure. To end with the assertion that all is empty courts the danger of overlooking the equivalent fact that emptiness is the reality of all. Although the two assertions say the same thing, they encourage opposing epistemological attitudes. The statement that all is empty seems to banish the apprehension of truth to some nether realm beyond our reach; the statement that emptiness is all, however, retrieves truth into a realm of paradoxical immediacy. Sŏp'o's novel is the definitive proof of his desire to maintain the balance between the two formulations.

Our brief survey of the Sŏn theater in Korea has suggested that its major campaign was to reconstruct the function and utility of religious discourse in light of the metaphysics of original enlightenment. The reconstructive agenda is clearly visible in the syncretic strategies that seek the union of sudden and gradual enlightenment, and of Sŏn and scriptural study. What this reconstruction amounted to was a major concession to the point that in spite of the doctrine of original enlightenment, a regimen of religious practice was nevertheless necessary. Hence Chinul answered for himself his own question, "What need is there to contemplate and thereby bind ourselves without ropes?"

It is the trajectory of this contemplative practice—rather than its enactment per se—that is of supreme concern in *KUM*. As its own trajectory admonishes, religious practice creates the illusion of somewhere to go, just like the receding frames of reality in the novel create the illusion of the final dreamer. Our dilemma is that the equivalence of all frames of reality, and, similarly, the immanence of spiritual perfection within oneself, by no means dispenses with the need to set off on the religious journey. The trajectory of this journey, however, is not linear but rather traces a full circle in which one ends where one began.

The circularity of the Buddhist path is traced by scholastic texts predating Sŏp'o's novel. If we look back to the early Sŏn text, the *Vajrasamādhi Sūtra*, for example, the teaching of the "two accesses," the access of principle and the access of practice, is expounded.[57] The access of principle involves a direct, implicit realization of one's original buddha-nature, whereas the access of practice involves a series of graduated steps towards soteriological liberation. Written before these two approaches were factionalized into the "sudden" and "gradual" schools of Chan, the *Vajrasamādhi* assumes the eventual convergence of the two techniques. Buswell notes in his study of the "two access" theory that this convergence creates a circularity; that there is a

> ... tendency for graduated programs to culminate in a final stage of insight that verifies the understanding that first catalyzed the process. The inspiration for this convergence of the beginning and end of training is the *Avataṃsaka Sūtra*'s renowned statement that the culmination of the path is identical to its inception.[58]

These converging programs, as Buswell points out, were repeatedly instantiated in Chinese/Korean Buddhist thought. The *panjiao* schemes of the Tiantai and Huayan schools manifested this in their chronological ordering of the Buddha's revelations. The Buddha's career would be depicted as launching with an initial revelation of ultimate principle—embodied in various sūtras such as the *Avataṃsaka* or *Nirvāna*—which proved too difficult to understand. The Buddha then resorts to much simpler teachings which progressively move towards enabling an understanding of the initial revelation. The gradations of teachings not only represent a hermeneutical scheme for classifying varying Buddhist doctrines relative to each other, but a soteriological progression that culminates in the apprehension of ultimate principle.

The final convergence between where one begins and where one ends is an organizational principle that is embedded within the frame tale of *KUM*. Here we have an example of how a religious path can be duplicated by narrative structure. Thus, the Buddhist ontological views that sanctioned scholastic literary practices were perhaps even better served by fictive narrative. I have suggested so far that sinitic Buddhism's embrace of positive, kataphatic discourse was instinctively married to an equally affirmative and rather substantialist ontological doctrine. I will continue this principle of coupling metaphysical and metapractical perspectives in the next task of this chapter, which is to flesh out the implications of the Buddhist perspectives on language and reality for an explicit literary theory. Specifically, given that the Buddhist tradition allows for the pragmatic use of words and texts, the next necessary move is to ask the question of what kind of relative discourse is most effective in conveying Buddhist truth. This task too must be guided by the criteria of substantive views about reality—or the truth that one wants to convey. The representation of Buddhist truth in literary traditions must be determined, in particular, by what Buddhist ontology itself might have to say in regard to the notion of artistic mimesis.

Literary Solutions

In the beginning of this chapter, we considered *KUM*'s desire to paint a Buddhist picture of reality without becoming a symbol of it. This effort was required because *KUM* operates within a metaphysics which assumes that language, as symbol, is irrevocably cut off from the expression of truth. In this context, Plaks' assumption of the dualism between the perception and the representation of meaning is problematic. If a gap between perception and representation does truly exist, then Buddhist ontology offers no artistic avenue for bridging that gap. Even an optimistic view of the world which insists on its immanent purity does nothing, in and of itself, to explain how language is capable of functioning in that world. In order to resolve this issue, let us turn to some examples of how Buddhist language and literature operate within their own philosophical boundaries. Let us turn in particular to the dream trope and examine how its appearance in an indisputably philosophical text offers a precedent for the mating of language and meaning.

Our examination of the sources of dream tales in the last chapter did not focus at all on the treatment of dreams in Chan Buddhist literature. Bernard Faure's handy survey in his *Rhetoric of Immediacy* points out that dreams were popular *topoi* of Chan literature but, Faure concludes, were not systematically discussed—probably in large part due to the unwanted association of dreams with popular religious Taoism. Faure summarizes the significance of the dream as a negative metaphor for the emptiness of existence—a lesson that is drawn when the distinction between dream and reality is collapsed to undermine the ontic status of both. Faure insists, however, that the Chan fixation on dreams as a symbol (and therefore an intermediary world) demonstrates even the Chan tradition's inability to give up the possibility of mediation in the communication of ineffable truth. Hence, Faure points to the largely symbolic nature of Chan's negation of the symbolic.[59]

The possibility and logic of symbolic mediation, particularly through the dream, is an issue that one can find explored within the pages of much earlier Buddhist texts. We can, for example, look at the consideration of dreams by the "Mind-only," or *weishi,* scholastic tradition. Specifically, we can turn to Vasubandhu's *Vimśatikā* (*Twenty Verses*), which was familiar to Chinese Buddhists through Paramārtha's sixth-century translation.[60] I have reserved the examination of this text's use of the dream for this chapter in order to dwell on its philosophical, as well as its literary import. Although the *Vimśatikā's* use of the dream hardly fits into the category of literary narrative treatment, we clearly have a Buddhist instance in which life is declared to be nothing but a dream.

The assertion, to be sure, is not made in the context of moral fable but as part of an arsenal of argumentative debate seeking to prove the school's primary thesis: That all reality (the "triple world") is nothing but representation, or the projection of mind. The example of dreams is adduced when this Yogācāra claim about reality is attacked by the objection that if the world is nothing but representation, it would not conform to the laws of space and time, nor would it have functional efficacy. Dreams,

Vasubandhu counters, are clear examples of representation which in fact do observe the limits of space and time and bear functional fruit (the case of wet dreams being the paradigmatic example). Thus dreams are used to prove the viability of the "representation-only" thesis by demonstrating that even a world that is purely a projection of mind can possess certain characteristics that often deceive us into the belief that this world has external reality. The dream, one might say, serves as Vasubandhu's logical ammunition to the extent that it functions as an analogy of what he wants to prove. Once this analogical function is admitted, its literary qualities take on significance.

One prominent aspect of the dream as Vasubandhu uses it is its metaphorical nature. In an extension of such usage, dreaming is also used to analogize the condition of spiritual delusion. The *Vimśatikā* states, "When dreaming, one who has not yet awoken does not understand that the objects of his visual perception do not exist".[61] In other words, the dreamer does not know that he or she is dreaming and therefore does not know that the dream is unreal. Awakening from the dream results in correct knowledge of the unreality of the dream, and this realization is akin to the Yogācāra's assertion that all of life, like the dream, is a projection of mind which has no ultimate ontic reality. Life, one might say, amounts to nothing but a dream.

Although Vasubandhu uses the dream as logical ammunition in the refutation of his opponent's objections, the metaphorical impact of positing life as a dream is potent. This analogy was certainly not overlooked by East Asians. Observe Zhuangzi's own statement:

> He who dreams of drinking wine may weep when morning comes; he who dreams of weeping may in the morning go off to hunt. While he is dreaming he does not know it is a dream, and in his dream he may even try to interpret a dream. Only after he wakes does he know it was a dream. And someday there will be a great awakening when we know that this is all a great dream. Yet the stupid believe they are awake, busily and brightly assuming they understand things, calling this man ruler, that one herdsman—how dense![62]

Here the metaphor of dreaming and waking to analogize levels of spiritual understanding seems patently clear. But we must ask if it is sufficient to stop here—if the concept of metaphor exhausts each text's philosophical meaning. In both the case of Zhuangzi and Vasubandhu, it is in fact possible to push their use of metaphor and argue that analogy ultimately converges into identity. That is, reality is not only *like* a dream, it is ontically no different from it. Zhuangzi's tale of the butterfly already makes this point within the Chinese setting. In the case of Vasubandhu, this final step is essential to his philosophical position. Vasubandhu's whole point in using dreams, as we have seen, is to offer an example of representation which functions in the same way as our mind-projected consciousness of reality. In producing dreams as such an example, Vasubandhu makes his philosophical point through a particular instance of what he is trying to claim broadly and absolutely.

Rather than characterizing Vasubandhu's use of the dream as an analogy, Victor Mair's notion of "localized intensification" is far more appropriate.[63] The import of this terminology is to reject the notion of mimesis, which conceives of literary instruments as an imitation or symbolization of meaning, to favor instead the notion of condensed ontological replication. Buddhists are perfectly capable, of course, of making epistemological and practical distinctions between dreams, or between those events that occur while in the state of sleep and the "reality" we understand ourselves to be in when awake. It is the ontological perspective, however, which asserts that there is no difference: Dream and reality are equally projections of consciousness.

The Yogācāra philosophy of ontic equivalence has been noted for its epistemological consequences—particularly its abolition of the subject/object dualism implicit in most philosophies of knowledge. The philosophy of Mind-only which eliminates external objects of knowledge effectively eliminates the gap between the knower and the known. This consequence is most relevant to our consideration of the meaning of art, which also assumes a dualism between knowing and that which is to be known. Here too the significant question focuses on how the knowing subject can use various means—philosophical or artistic—to traverse the space between itself and meaning.

Given this concern, Yogācāra's dismantling of the subject/ object dualism has profound implications for Buddhist literary theory. The impact may be phrased by reversing Plaks' observation about art: There is, in fact, no disjunction between one's perception of meaning and its representation. Rather, the perception of meaning is equivalent to its representation. The disappearance of the gap between truth and its representation in turn forces a revised understanding of how words impart meaning. Just as Vasubandhu used the dream as an illustration of the truth he wanted to convey, literary illustrations can be made equivalent to, and not just a means to, their message. This conclusion gives philosophical teeth to Victor Mair's thesis that the sanctioning of fiction in China arose out of an ontic awareness of the sameness of literary and world-phenomenal creation. Both are alike projections of mind. Fiction's desire to express truth non-symbolically, then, is not so much a desire as a fact. But this fact demands a self-conscious praxis, or else a text's truth-provoking function may very well be mistaken as signalling an external reality.

The mechanics of this self-conscious praxis is evident in other Buddhist contexts. William LaFleur brilliantly documents Medieval Japan's reconciliation of Buddhist soteriology with the literary arts, which affirmed through the words of the Chinese poet Bo Zhuyi that even "floating phrases and fictive utterances" were capable of preaching the *dharma*.[64] This assertion nuanced the native Japanese view of symbols as more than "merely" the vehicles of hierophany. Based on the Buddhist assertion of original purity, or original enlightenment (Japanese: *hongaku*), the non-symbolic understanding of symbols ensued from the ontic observation of emptiness, which when applied to all phenomena leveled them to equal metaphysical status. The emptiness of all phenomena not only renders them originally pure (before being defiled by the attribution of substantiality), it renders all phenomena equal to each other.

Here the assertion of Mādhyamika elements, as referenced by the language of emptiness, is crucial. On the one hand, Vasubandhu's implicit assertion of the equality of dreams and reality is founded upon a negative ontological mission—that of proving that external objects of reality do not exist. In this sense, one might posit that both dreams and reality are empty of ultimate reality. There is within this assertion, however, a positive gloss on emptiness which successfully evades a substantialist understanding of the "pure mind" as the ground of all illusory phenomena. This is the observation consequent to the analysis of emptiness that because all elements of existence are empty, there is in fact no ontic difference between them. This is the kind of observation which leads Nāgārjuna to aver that *nirvāna* and *samsāra* are the same. His disciple Candrakīrti offers an exegetical explanation of this position: ". . . all the putative elements of existence are of the same nature because in not being produced, in not being born in any sense at all, they are the same nature."[65] The focus on the emptiness and hence equality of all phenomena is critical in mitigating the ontic hierarchy of events implied by such categories as pure and deluded minds.

Back in the literary context, the equality of all phenomena in their emptiness make them impervious to the very definition of a symbol as a pointer to something else. In the pursuit of meaning, one need not look beyond phenomena:

> It requires the return of a poet's perceptions and mind to the simple recognition of phenomena. This recognition is powerful because it represents a *renewed* simplicity rather than a naive simplicity. This aesthetic mode lives off the way it *redirects* our focused attention to phenomena for their own sake. It does so with stunning effect by reversing the symbolizing habit of the mind.[66]

The renewed affirmation of phenomena as bearers of rather than pointers to reality justifies Buddhists in their use of words, both poetic and discursive. LaFleur's analysis of the *Lotus Sūtra*, which exerted tremendous exegetical and literary influence on East Asian Buddhism, illustrates the mechanics of such use, a mechanics that LaFleur calls a "self-reflexive allegory."

The *Lotus Sūtra* is best known for its exposition of *upāya*, or "skillful means." Its second chapter is dedicated to expounding this principle, which is used as an instrument for resolving the problem of the multiplicity of Buddhist paths. In this process, the chapter simultaneously demonstrates the profound wisdom of the Buddha as a teacher. It states that the apparent plurality of the Buddha's teachings is an expedient concession to the differing abilities of mortal beings. The Buddha's wisdom lies in knowing the best method of engaging the diverse abilities of individuals for their own benefit. True to the pragmatism of the historical Buddha recorded in the *Majjhima-nikāya*, the goal of *upāya* is to find the most expedient and quickest means for bringing deluded beings to religious realization. This often means that the Buddha will resort to trickery, as demonstrated in the fifteenth chapter of the *Lotus Sūtra*. Here the Buddha reveals that the duration of his life is eternal, and that he only makes a pretense of dying in order to galvanize mortals into turning toward the path of liberation. As illustration, a parable is offered of the compassionate physician whose sons refuse, in their delusion, to take their father's medicinal remedy. The physician feigns death so that his sons, in their remorse, drink the potion and are healed.

Many of the chapters of the *Lotus Sūtra* both illustrate and embody the notion of *upāya* through their parables. It is these demonstrative tales which LaFleur points to as "self-reflexive" allegories, in contradistinction to the Western allegoric use of parables. Rather than understanding the parables of the *Lotus* as allegorical vehicles which point beyond themselves to the principle of *upāya*, these narratives are recognized as fundamentally identical with what they illustrate: "Thus the illustration is in no way subordinate to what it illustrates."[67] LaFleur thereby draws out the manner in which the *Lotus* collapses the dualism of meaning and its representation. This literary feat also parallels and fulfills the demands of *hongaku* metaphysics, which dissolves the gap between deluded and enlightened minds. The fact of original purity means that the perception of truth does not lie outside of us; the dualism of religious means and ends must be extinguished. The *Lotus Sūtra*'s method of pointing to religious truth is accordingly faithful in not externalizing truth outside of its own act of illustration. In meeting the demand for a non-dualistic, non-symbolic discourse, the *Lotus Sūtra*'s exposition of the principle of *upāya* fills the bill with praxeological finesse—with a self-referential discourse that might be described as the use of *upāya* to discourse on *upāya*.

We began with a consideration of the general problem of language instigated by the Mahāyāna Buddhist emphasis on the non-referential quality of language. The Sŏn tradition latched on to this philosophical observation through its own declaration that intellectual discourse is not a means to truth because truth is extra-linguistic. But it is also the case that this uniform degradation of language did not result in Buddhist silence. The *Vimśatikā* and *Lotus Sūtra* are two canonical examples of how to get around the language problem. *KUM* is yet another. Although its "canonicity" may be debated, its artistry demonstrates a cogent understanding of one of Buddhism's most significant praxeological dilemmas.

From within the generality of these observations, let us venture a more determinative assertion particularized to the historical field of *KUM*. This is a point that I have already made regarding the final objective of this novel's literary practice. To wit, the goal of the texts I have examined is the ultimate one of spiritual liberation. The manner in which one serves this aim, however, must be determined by a tradition's understanding of its metaphysics. This is where the East Asian ontological attitude that the world is substantial, immanent, originally pure, and all pervasive becomes determinative of its literary practice. As we saw above, the Sŏn affirmation of the use of language is inextricably tied to an affirmative cosmology that believes in both the expedient and face value of the world. This optimistic stance often veers into heterodox language about the ultimate ground of phenomena in such terms as the "one mind" (*yixin*), the "truly existing" (*zhenyou*), the "marvelously existing" (*miaoyou*), and "substance and function" (*tiyong*). Both the affirmation of language and the given world are grounded in the

Buddhist ontology of illusion which deems that to reject them exhibits an inferior understanding. Given this view of ultimate reality, and the presumed soteriological purpose of linguistic discourse, we may conclude that the importance of the texts we examined above is that they demonstrate how, once words are empowered with value, they may actually carry out their religious function.

We have examined the extent to which *KUM* features the ontology of illusion as its literary theme. We can now move on to see how this theme is converted into a direct philosophical declaration by the novel's literary structure.

Chapter 5

Philosophy in
Narrative Action

The Praxis of Fiction

It is highly unlikely that any reader of *KUM* would mistake it
for a veiled history, or be so drawn in by its realism as to confuse it with reality. As the discussion at the end of chapter three
indicated, Sŏp'o's choice of fantasy over historical fiction—particularly as embodied through the dream—afforded him a
politically non-assertive form of discourse. Sŏp'o's fantasy fiction removed him from the realm of neo-Confucian values, which
historiographical and pseudo-historical prose was programmed
to assert. On the other hand, although fantasy fiction was non-
assertive in respect to orthodox political views, we have also
seen that it nevertheless is capable of making truth claims of its
own. One may go so far as to say that *KUM* offers a purposive
examination of philosophical questions through the medium of
art. The fact that the philosophical question asked in the novel
is greatly concerned with the distinction between illusion and
reality sets the work on a parabolic, self-implicating trajectory.
The primary dynamic within the novel itself, however, is not so
much a self-conscious examination of its own artistry as the
fictive construction of a philosophical debate.

We must fully appreciate the philosophical significance of
KUM's artistry apart from and in distinction to the question of
how it embeds the patterns of Buddhist philosophical argumen-

tation. The choice of fantasy fiction as a way of making truth claims inherently recognizes that the truth-value of fiction does not lie in its referentiality to external realities. This is a statement that is generalizable to all fiction. As Michael Riffaterre asserts in his notion of "fictional truth," this oxymoronic concept requires a redefinition of referentiality:

> ... truth in fiction is not based on an actual experience of factuality, nor does the interpretation or aesthetic evaluation of fictional narrative require that it be verified against reality. Rather, truth in fiction rests on verisimilitude, a system of representations that seems to reflect a reality external to the text, but only because it conforms to a grammar. Narrative truth is an idea of truth created in accordance with the rules of that grammar.[1]

If fictional truth releases itself from the need of reality verification, then its very mode or process of making truth claims coincides perfectly with the Buddhist truth claim that there are no metaphysical realities that correspond to conceptual and philosophical terms. The substance of this lesson, which I call the ontology of illusion, was made by *KUM*'s desire to challenge the notion of awakening—that is, the awakening to some greater reality. The greatest ontological lesson that the dream offered was to question the very existence of this greater reality. The literary mechanics of the *Vimśatikā* and the *Lotus Sūtra*, as we have seen, embody this larger metaphysical lesson. In subverting the referential function of their own literary expression, they verify that there can be no awakening or pointing to an external truth. Everything exists within the field of representation. The persisting relevance of the metaphor of awakening, however, can be justified by the fact that one must still awaken *to* the dream. Realizing the fact of the dream constitutes spiritual progress.

The dream, then, is symbolically significant. I use the term "symbol" here through the eyes of William LaFleur's "renewed affirmation" of words. Having traversed the negation of language and its metaphysical pretensions, one can turn to analyzing the dream as something that stands for itself; a symbol which constitutes both the means and end of its own expression. In this function, the dream serves as a simple homology or further localized intensification of fictional discourse, which also asserts the ontology of illusion through its very refusal to operate within the realm of metaphysically assertive discourse.

The artistry of Sŏp'o's fiction does not stop at the boundaries of its literary form as a way of making truth claims. The structure of his fiction is also molded into the content or substance of that truth claim. This is where both Sŏp'o's artistry and his Buddhist agenda are most evident. An examination of the literary structure of *KUM* reveals Sŏp'o's intent to embody and recapitulate the patterns of Buddhist philosophical debate. This debate, as indicated in the last chapter, is a long-standing one which carries within itself an acute awareness of its linguistic medium of expression. The direct precedent for *KUM* is actually incorporated into its own narrative framework: the *Diamond Sūtra*. An investigation of *KUM*'s internal praxis requires that we first consider this philosophical and canonical antecedent. Here Korean scholarship provides a solid framework on which to build. Most scholars of *KUM* who have engaged in any protracted analysis of the text have made a case for the structural similarity between the novel and the sūtra. Sŏl Sŏnggyŏng offers one of the most extensive comparisons, focusing on each text's temporal sequence and making point-by-point correlations.[2] Some of the correspondences are quite general in nature, pointing to some literary conventions that apply not only to *KUM* and the *Diamond Sūtra*, but many other canonical texts as well. Their endings, for example, are argued to be identical in character: In the *Diamond Sūtra*, we are told that the Buddha's sermon has resulted in the weal and edification of countless monks, nuns, lay followers, as well as superhuman beings. Similarly, the enlightenment of Xingjen at the end of *KUM*'s narrative (through the preaching of the *Diamond Sūtra*, incidentally) has the same broad effect of leading to the salvation of all mortal and super-mortal beings on Lotus Peak. Xingzhen's own realization, which was effected by living through the events embodied in the novel, in turn makes it possible for him to liberate others.[3]

Sŏl's study helps to make the general point that the conventions of canonical literature often find their way into the
practices of secular literature. Here, the theme of religious words
and actions leading to the spiritual emancipation of the whole
hierarchy of beings is a common theme in Buddhist texts and
recognizable in many popular narratives. Sŏl's comprehensive
attempt to offer a point-by-point structural correlation, however, argues for more than an incidental diffusion of religious
culture to popular levels. The detailed analysis settles for nothing less than an explicit, self-conscious analogy on the part of
Sŏp'o. Based on this argument, various interpreters of Sŏp'o's
novel have made very specific analyses of the structural parallelism between *KUM* and the *Diamond Sūtra*. Some of these
will be invoked in my own analysis to come. I take advantage
of Sŏl's (and others') claim of deliberate analogizing to make
my own argument for the similarity of philosophical strategies
between the two texts.

To turn, then, to the *Diamond Sūtra*, the first notable characteristic of this text is its peculiar and consistent use of language, a use that might be described as the employment of
negation as a form of assertion. The repeated instances of this
expression can be rendered in formulaic terms: "*X* is not *X*; it is
called/named *X*." (X 者則非 X. 是名 X.) This formula is best
broken down into two parts. The incidence of negation comes at
the beginning, with the assertion that "*X* is not *X*." The rhythm
of this discourse begins almost immediately in the sūtra when
the primary dialoguer, Subhūti, is queried by the Buddha as to
whether or not the Tathāgata can be recognized by his material
attributes. Subhūti answers in the negative, forming the imprint
for the string of negations to follow. He answers, "No, World-
honored One; the Tathāgata cannot be recognized by any material characteristic. Wherefore? Because the Tathāgata has said that
material characteristics are not, in fact, material characteristics."[4]
(不也世傳. 不可以身相得見如來. 何以故. 如來所說身相即非身相.
749a.)

The most distinctive feature of these negations pertain to
the apparent orthodoxy of the principles which are denied. The

most cherished and standard tenets of Buddhist doctrine are subjected to this process, as above with the negation of the standard belief that the Buddha can be recognized by various minor and major physical characteristics which are a sign of his religious attainment. The notion of merit, which most Mahāyāna sūtras claim will accrue to the reader of the self-same texts, is also negated, although it is reasserted in other sections. This process is applied to the notion of perfect liberation, the concept of *dharma*, and to the Buddha's teaching itself.

This strategy of negation stems from an awareness of the dangers of language in its ordinary usage. All positive assertions tend toward erecting the false idol of concepts—of forms and categories—as a refuge for truth-seekers. The Chan master Hanshan Deqing (1546–1623) of the Ming dynasty declared: "As all living things are deluded and upset by their views of forms and since their grasp is very hard to break, the Buddha used the Diamond-mind wisdom to demolish these views one by one. . . ."[5] In his commentary on the *Diamond Sūtra*, Hanshan repeatedly asserts that the purpose of its teaching is to forsake all "forms." In addition, the Mahāyāna tradition recognizes that negative or nihilistic beliefs fall into the same trap. The classic formulation of this is the category of "Non-being" in opposition to "Being," which represents all positively formulated propositions. Although the choice between Being and Non-being would seem to offer the limit of philosophical possibilities, the Buddhist desire to assert nothing at all leads to the double-negation in Mādhyamika philosophy of "neither Being nor non-Being" that is reiterated in our present text: "Subhūti, those to whom you refer are *neither living beings nor not-living beings* [emphasis mine]. Wherefore? Because 'living beings,' Subhūti, these 'living beings' are not really such; they are just called by that name."[6] (彼非眾生非不眾生．何以故．眾生眾生者．如來說非眾生．是名眾生．751c.)

The *Diamond Sūtra* is aware that the seductiveness of language works both ways. It can assert the presence of certain characteristics in the world or deny them. Both ways are, however, "assertive" in claiming facts about the world.[7] The text's sensitivity to this problem is demonstrated by its awareness that even the assertion of emptiness, which attempts to absolve itself of all assertions, can lead one to forget the emptiness of emptiness. As the Buddha states,

> ... if [men] grasped and held on to the notion of things as having intrinsic qualities they would be cherishing the idea of an ego-entity, a personality, a being, or a separated individuality. Likewise if they grasped and held on to the notion of things as devoid of intrinsic qualities they would be cherishing the idea of an ego-entity, a personality, a being, or a separated individuality. So you should not be attached to things as being possessed of, or devoid of, intrinsic qualities.[8]

The *Diamond Sūtra*'s negative use of language barely manages to avoid constructing its own snare of assertions by sticking to the simple negation of orthodox concepts— "*X* is not *X*"—rather than stating a negative principle. With this strategy, the text can invoke the lesson of emptiness without employing the kind of language that will lead one astray from the substance of the lesson. The impact of the tactic is as emotional as it is intellectual. It is imparted by the shock of denying the most hallowed terms in Buddhism. In this respect, the *Diamond Sūtra*'s use of language has much in common with Chan *gongan*, or *koans*.

Still, it is difficult to avoid the irony and contradiction involved in using words to denigrate words, suggesting a form of self-compromise here that many Buddhists themselves have taken to heart in their avowal to refrain from speaking. It is too hasty, however, to conclude that the metaphysical denigration of words automatically entails the uselessness of words. The *Diamond Sūtra*'s formulaic use of language against itself, in fact, is eventually completed with a positive affirmation of words. This is where we must consider the second half of the *Diamond Sūtra*'s formula, the final comment which follows "*X* is not *X*" with the statement that "It is called *X*."

Consequent to the *Diamond Sūtra*'s strategy of negation, the follow-up assertion that "It is called *X*" would seem to offer a summary philosophy of language. In a majority of the text's statements, the assertion that something is "called" or "named" (名) X can be interpreted as a metaphysically pejorative description. That is, it implies that the object in question, X, is *only* or *merely* called X, but, as the first part of the formula argues, does not exist as a real metaphysical entity. Whereas iterating "X is not X" is a negative strategy for avoiding the assertive use of language, the statement "It is called X" is a straightforward declaration which denigrates the status of words.[9] An example should suffice.

The Buddha and Subhūti's discussion of Pure Lands renders the judgment that "The establishment of a Pure Land is not an establishment; it is called an establishment [my translation]." (莊嚴佛土者則非莊嚴. 是名莊嚴. 749c.) In contrast to my neutrally rendered translation, A. F. Price's stresses the pejorative sense. He translates the same passage as "Because setting forth majestic Buddha-lands is not a majestic setting forth; this is *merely a name* [emphasis mine]."[10] Edward Conze's commentary to this particular passage explains that, "A Buddhafield (Pure Land) is no material or perceptible fact, and its harmony is not an objective arrangement. It has a quasi-sensory appearance as the by-product of a Buddha's meditative gnosis, but in reality it is no more than a mental construction."[11] The semantic content of the formula "It is called X" seems to suggest categories which are nominal and illusory constructs.

At first glance, then, the summation that "It is called X" seems to simply reinforce the idea that words have little philosophical value. A closer consideration, however, suggests that more is going on. The semantic openness of the Chinese (as well as English) formulation of "It is called X" (是名 X) allows for more than one interpretation of this code. In considering any interpretation, however, one must keep in mind the indubitable importance of this code as an integral part of the overall formula of "X is not X; it is called X." The most immediate significance of the second half of this design—relative to its first half—is its break away from the strategy of negation to that of assertion. Within the boundaries of its own discourse, the formula's norm of negation is contradicted. Sŏl Sŏnggyŏng maintains that a critical feature of emptiness thought is the structuring of its own discourse into what he calls the double negation.[12] His description of this process, wherein through the act of negation, negation itself is negated, is implied although not explicit in the *Diamond Sūtra*'s choice to conclude with a self-contradicting assertion. If we characterize the practice of the formula's discourse in this manner, it also becomes possible to render the semantic content of "It is called *X*" in more positive terms as well.

If asserting that something "is called *X*" comprises a positive use of words, the message—as well as the act—of the assertion might possibly imply the normativity of such a use. This is clearly suggested in cases when the text inserts the term *gu* (故), meaning "therefore," in order to arrive at the altered designation of "*X* is not *X; therefore* it is called *X.*"[13] Consider the following statement about the realm of *dharmas:* "That which is said to be all dharmas are no-dharmas. It is therefore called all dharmas" [my translation]. (所言一切法者即非一切法. 是故名一切法. 751b.) In other cases, the text abandons the formulaic expression to offer a more exegetical explanation of the formula's meaning. Let us take the case of merit. Subhūti is made to claim, "Because merit partakes of the character of no-merit, the Tathāgata characterized the merit as great."[14] (是福得即非得福性. 是故如徠說福德多.749b.) The initial negation of merit, followed by its reconstitution, enfleshes the patterned discourse of "*X* is not *X,* therefore it is called *X.*" Conze's translation emphasizes the affirmative sense of "Therefore it is called *X*" in a slightly different way. His translation reads: "Great, O Lord, great, O Well-gone, would that heap of merit be! And why? Because the Tathāgata spoke of the 'heap of merit' as a non-heap. That is how the Tathagata speaks of 'heap of merit'."[15] The explanation "That is how the Tathagata speaks of 'heap of merit' "—that is, as a "non-heap"—amounts to a direct exposition of the meaning of the Buddha's negations which nevertheless assumes the necessity of language.[16]

The initial message of the formula has been completely turned on its head. Rather than the rejection of language, we are confronted with the idea that the *use* of language does not necessarily conflict with a correct understanding of language's meta-physical properties (or lack thereof). Indeed, the import of *"X is not X;* therefore it is called *X"* would seem to posit the necessity of language in the process of understanding it. In this sense, the formula cannot help but evoke the seminal and oft-noted doctrine in the sister text of the *Heart Sūtra* that "Form is emptiness and emptiness is form." (色即是空. 空即是色) The parallelism of the *Diamond* and *Heart* sūtras is explicit. *"X* is not *X"* is analogous to the negation of form as empty. It follows next that the closure of "it is therefore called *X"* is equal to the *Heart Sūtra's* paradoxical logic that if form is empty, then emptiness is form. Hanshan is attuned to this config-uration when he reverses the forsaking of all forms with the observation: "However, these four forms (of an ego, a personality, a being and a life) are themselves fundamentally absolute and if this can be understood, the Dharma-kāya can be perceived."[17]

The loop back to form, or language, does not upgrade its metaphysical status but rather reinstalls it into the metaphysi-cally egalitarian world of emptiness. In this sense, the reinvest-ment of language doesn't imply a change in its own status as much as a breakthrough in the wisdom of its user. In the case of the *Diamond Sūtra*, despite the initial appearance given by its use of negation, its purpose is not to use language to demean itself as much as to use it as a tool to get beyond the dualism of all conceptions of reality. Going beyond this dualism is for-mulaically rendered by the double negation of "neither Being nor non-Being." More suggestive, however, is the *Diamond Sūtra's* frequent substitution of the parallel terms "reality" and "illusion" in expressing this dualism. It states, for example, "The Dharma to which the Tathāgata has attained is neither real and neither illusion" [my translation]. 如來所得法此法無實無虛. 750b.) There is also the line that the perfect, incomparable En-lightenment of the Buddha "is neither real nor illusion. There-fore the Tathāgata says that all dharmas are Buddha dharmas." (方是中無實無虛. 是故如來說一切法皆是佛法. 751b.)

The point of this language is to go beyond the inherently dichotomizing process that any statement about the Buddhist teaching activates. This point is sometimes made in more explicit terms. In going back to the case of merit, which is constantly redressed in the *Diamond Sūtra*, it is stated that belief in the reality of merit would fall into just this trap: "Subhūti, if such merit was Real, the Tathāgata would not have declared it to be great, but because it is without foundation the Tathāgata characterized it as 'great.'"[18] (若福德有實如來不說得福德多. 以福德無故如來說得福德多. 751c.) The greatness of this merit, it would seem, is that it is beyond reality and non-reality. It is only in the beyond which transcends dualism that such positive affirmations can be made. The final affirmation of merit in the *Diamond* is not long in coming, for several sections later the sūtra declares in recognizable, intertextual terms that any being who reads and memorizes even four lines of this teaching reaps greater merit than one who donates as alms a mass of seven treasures equal in quantity to the Mount Sumerus contained in three thousand galaxies of worlds.[19]

The sūtra's general message that "the cosmos cannot be explained through words" (一合者則不可說 752b.) does not imply that words must be discarded nor that there is nothing to be explained. In Hanshan's own words, "The Buddha's meaning was that prajñā has no written words but that written words are prajñā."[20] The *Diamond Sūtra's* use of words suggests the utilization of a vehicle to drive beyond the dual metaphysical realms of Being and Non-being, of Reality and Illusion. The final affirmation of language in the formula *"X is not X, therefore is called X"* suggests the constructive nature of this exercise. The final *"X,"* whether encoded as Dharma, merit, enlightenment, universe, or the Buddha himself, may be declared a mere figure of speech, name, or designation, but it is one which points to a desirable condition—the realm beyond all distinctions.

As noted above, Korean scholars have already noticed the parallelism between the discourse structure of the *Diamond Sūtra* and the literary structure of *KUM*. Chŏng Kyubok offers another interpretation of this parallelism by suggesting that both texts embody the structure and recursive motion of emptiness thought. In Chŏng's view, the doctrine of emptiness states that ultimately, there is no difference between awakening and illusion. Or rather, the difference can be stated as the distinction between the location of zero and 360 degrees on a circle. They occupy the same space, but one must travel full circle in order to get from the first point to the other.[21] Although Chŏng is more metaphorical than explicit in his use of the circle diagram, the reference is highly suggestive. The *Diamond Sūtra*'s movement from assertion to negation to assertion can be fruitfully grafted on to this circular space. Through the medium of language, a journey is undertaken that does not lead to a new ontic place but rather reveals a whole new vista on where one originally began. Similarly, the young novice's journey from reality to dream to reality in *KUM* plots his spiritual awakening from the belief in the reality of appearances to realize the futility of distinctions between illusion and reality. This realization does not take him to a new place but rather back to the old one. In Chŏng's assessment, the deluded Xingzhen and the awakened Xingzhen are the same and are also completely different.[22]

Let us attempt to map the emplotment of the *Diamond Sūtra*'s use of language in the tale of *KUM* a little bit more closely. Let us begin by positing that the formula of "*X* is not *X*, therefore it is called *X*," or "Form is emptiness; emptiness is form," is represented by the frame sequence of the initial reality on Lotus Peak (form), to the dream sequence in Tang China (emptiness), followed by the awakening back to the reality of Lotus Peak (form). This can also be formulated as the sequence of identities given to the main protagonist, first known as Xingzhen, then as Shaoyou, and then back to Xingzhen. As noted in chapter two, *KUM*'s tripartite structure emplots Xingzhen's religious quest into "before" and "after" identities. The initial Xingzhen, just like the initial assertion of form, represents an untried and unenlightened understanding of the world. This Xingzhen's contraction of karma forces him to undergo his incarnation as Shaoyou, which represents the forging process of experience. This process in turn triggers the insights which allow him to emerge as the final Xingzhen, the truly awakened identity.

The threefold structure of *KUM* details a progression of spiritual understanding that is parallel to the *Diamond Sūtra*'s negation and final affirmation of form. The novel's movement through reality-dream-reality is functionally equivalent to the sūtra's progression of form-emptiness-form. The parallelism of these two sequences is evinced by the fact that *KUM*'s alternate settings in waking and dreaming states novelistically enfleshes the sūtra's language of truth and illusion. Hence the polarity of dream and reality, as well as that of emptiness and form, can be reduced to analogical variants of the unifying concepts of truth and illusion. This understanding helps us to pare down the proliferation of terms and see that both the fictive and canonical texts illustrate a dynamic process in which conventional and inadequate notions of truth are traded for more satisfying versions. This is accomplished through the pathway of illusion.

A closer look at this shared process must scrutinize the center portion of each text's framework: *KUM*'s dream sequence and the *Diamond*'s assertion of emptiness, an assertion that is rendered by its negation of form through the formula "*X* is not *X*." Our analysis of *KUM* up until this point has already highlighted the conventional rendering of dream as illusion. This is reinforced by the common interpretation of *KUM* as suggesting that all of life itself is an illusion. Superimposed on the abstract discourse of the *Diamond Sūtra*, we may read the illusion sequence as a correlate to "*X* is not *X*." The justification for this is that the dream sequence plays a vital role in the progression of philosophical logic which must travel the pathway of negation—as represented by the dream—before emerging on the other side.

Let us look first at where these respective journeys in the Land of Illusion are designed to lead. Clearly, the *Diamond Sūtra*'s final affirmation of form, just like Xingzhen's final awakening on Lotus Peak, represents a qualitatively different state from its initial incarnation. As our investigation of the *Diamond Sūtra* revealed, the final affirmation of form is an affirmation that goes beyond the dualism of form and emptiness. The inevitability of this route comes from the correct understanding of emptiness, which expressly is not an absolute and alternative principle to form, but rather the vehicle for travel beyond all forms.

Similarly, the danger of installing illusion as the final principle is demonstrated by Xingzhen's initial thoughts upon awakening back at Lotus Peak. When he meditates, "My teacher knew of my wrong thoughts and made me dream this dream so that I should understand the emptiness of riches and honor and the love between the sexes,"[23] Xingzhen exemplifies the wrongheaded propensity to seek a substantive principle of truth in a signifier that is intended to dispose of truth claims altogether. At least one interpreter of the novel as a whole has fallen into the same trap as the protagonist. Kim Iryŏl has criticized *KUM* as offering only the most elemental of Buddhist thought—the conclusion that everything is transient—while ignoring the *Diamond Sūtra*'s desire to breach the division between form and illusion.[24] But surely, Kim is mistaken in his interpretation of the message of *KUM*. In response to Xingzhen's thought quoted above, Liuguan tells the anecdote of Zhuangzi and the butterfly, which, in questioning the reality of the dreamer, parallels the Buddhist move of exposing the emptiness of emptiness. Both moves indicate that we must go beyond the quest for the final and ultimate reality; indeed, we must go beyond the distinction between truth and illusion altogether.

The urgency of this mandate warrants the return to "reality," or form. In the final reality of the novel, the realm in which Xingzhen attains his definitive awakening, the justification of form is offered through an understanding of the expedient nature of illusion. The pivotal factor in the attainment of Xingzhen's final awakening is the vital lesson imparted by Liuguan which questions the separation between truth and illusion. Indeed, the ambiguity between truth and illusion is the novel's most consistent theme. Although the protagonist of the waking state—Xingzhen—is initially assumed to be more real for being awake, from the narrative point of view, it is Shaoyou who assumes the greater degree of mundane, historical realism.[25] This paradox already sets the fluidity of dream and reality in motion, which is endlessly explored within the dream sequence itself.[26]

In order for Xingzhen's realization to take place, however, he has to travel the path of illusion, just as the *Diamond Sūtra* must utilize words as a vehicle to journey to the realm beyond dualism. The dream sequence first prompts Xingzhen to consider the dichotomy of truth and illusion so that he can ultimately banish it. Thus to go beyond dualism necessarily assumes the initial illusion of dualism.

The *Diamond Sūtra*'s formula that "*X* is not *X*" is a shorthand notation of the problem of the dichotomy created by language, which is then superseded by the creative use of language. *KUM*'s fictive emplotment of the *Diamond Sūtra*'s strategy through the dichotomy of dream and illusion offers a fuller use of form—of words fully crafted into narrative rather than limited to philosophical propositions—for working through this intellectual and soteriological process. There is a difference, of course, between positing that fiction can convey philosophical meaning and positing that it constitutes philosophical discourse. My analysis of *KUM* in chapter three did not travel beyond the first contention. In that chapter, I attempted to convey what the use of the dream usually intends to say about the meaning of life. This perhaps utilizes Riffaterre's notion of grammar, which is a key factor in the creation of narrative truth. In order to be grammatically correct, each component of a narrative structure "must conform to a consensus about reality, a consensus already encoded in language."[27] The dream is encoded within a cultural grammar that is designed to immediately and automatically evoke an evaluation of life as vain and illusory.

My primary effort here, however, has been to argue for the second position—that *KUM* comprises philosophical discourse—through a structural analysis of the novel. This analysis reveals the presence of the *Diamond Sūtra* as a subtext; that is, a text within a text which serves as the larger text's heuristic model.[28] The extent to which *KUM* is modeled on a sacred and discursive text reveals something of its own self-conceptualization. The patterns of philosophical reasoning identified within *KUM* can also be recognized within broader historical practices. Although Sŏp'o composed his dream within fiction long after the climax of Buddhist scholastic traditions in East Asia, his version of Buddhist talk could not have materialized without these prior traditions. Their most significant legacy was a self-conscious examination of the question of justified discourse on Buddhist truth.

Perhaps the most obvious historical parallel, already alluded to in the previous chapter, is the Huayan classification of Buddhist teachings as exemplified by Zongmi. This *panjiao* system also instantiates a dynamic which moves from the *kataphatiche* of the so-called Hīnayāna teachings, to the *apophatiche* of the teaching of emptiness, and finally back to a renewed kataphatic discourse which purports to be the ultimate Buddhist revelation. The movement from assertion to negation to assertion replicates the circle of emptiness that was discovered by countless Buddhist philosophers who puzzled over the question of philosophical and religious expression.

To the extent that *KUM* recapitulates this progression of discourse, we can see how its own message far exceeds the gloomy adage that life is nothing but an illusion. The point about illusion in fact indicates a much larger problem of religious perception and the role that artistic and linguistic representations are allowed to play within it. By affirming the positive value of linguistic assertions by means of an artistic (fictive) one, *KUM* also offers a collapsed means-end discourse that is reminiscent of the *Lotus Sūtra*. *KUM*'s philosophical value inheres as much in this self-referential quality as in its reiteration of the *Diamond Sūtra*.

The fact that the dream motif of *KUM* labors within a continuum of Buddhist philosophical speculation offers the occasion to make one further observation about the sinitic tradition. My choice of novelistic discourse to highlight philosophical issues is perhaps more representative of the East Asian tradition than has been recognized. This assertion is best made in contrast to the paucity, within East Asian Buddhism, of the kind of logical discourse more commonly associated with philosophical thinking. The contrast is further underscored when one considers the flourishing of Buddhist logic in India from the fifth and sixth centuries onward. With the notable exception of Xuanzang (596–664) and his disciple Kuiji (636–682), little of these materials were imported into the Chinese setting, which was already engaged in the ontological speculations that would emerge in the Chan tradition of the eighth century.[29]

It is perhaps no accident that the *Lotus Sūtra*, which is particularly generous with its metaphors and parables, vaulted to an almost unparalleled popularity in the East Asian context. The interesting question is to what extent the sūtra's success in embodying Buddhist philosophical principles was achieved by its willingness to abandon discursive language. The answer to this question must be contextualized within the specific notion of reality proffered by the Buddhist ontology of illusion. The nullified distinction between truth and illusion, which liberates discourse, still demands a form of expression that is equal to its subject.

The hazards of creating such a vehicle through discursive philosophical conversation had been long established. Take, for example, the Indian Mādhyamika's concern with the two truths problem, which offers yet another schema for sorting out the relative merits of affirmative and negative accounts of ultimate truth. Here it is recognized that affirmative statements of conventional truth can be justified and judged according to their soteriological benefits—another consistently pan-Buddhist criterion. Its subsequent negation of conventional truth in silent reference to a greater, ineffable truth was itself superseded by the realization that from that ultimate point of view, negation is also relative.

These points are salient to and summarize the philosophy of emptiness that we have flushed out of *KUM*. These insights, however, are perhaps more traditionally made in the kind of philosophical discourse offered by Nāgārjuna in the *Vigrahavyāvartanī* (*Averting the Arguments*). The immediate cause of Nāgārjuna's defensiveness in this text centers directly on the problem of assertion and negation. In verse 1, which voices the objection of an opponent, it is stated:

If self-existence (svabhāva) does not exist anywhere in any existing thing, your statement, itself being without self-existence, is not able to discard self-existence.[30]

The objection is simple: the assertion of non-existence (emptiness) is self-contradictory because if everything is non-existent, so is the assertion of this fact. This objection admirably summarizes the problem that the teaching of emptiness creates for its own propagation. The Mādhyamika theory of śūnyatā asserts that all things arise in causal dependency and that therefore entities do not possess self-nature or self-existence. But since all philosophical assertions assume the real existence of entities—indeed, the assertions posit them through the very act of assertion, then the assertion of the theory of śūnyatā falls into self-contradiction. As Bimal Matilal explains, "It may be that everything lacks its own-being or essence, that is to say, everything is empty, but this cannot be *stated* as a thesis. For a thesis that lacks essence or own-being is unstatable."[31]

The resolution of this problem is familiar to us by now: It is the very emptiness of words that justifies Nāgārjuna's use of them. He does not use words to refer to substances, but to point to the emptiness of everything. In absolute emptiness, language can be reestablished. In Matilal's words, "Such utterance of his is itself empty! Utterances of this type do not assert or state anything! This is what I have called before the problem of nonassertion."[32] The reestablishment of language, in other words, is founded upon its non-assertive use.

While the charge made by Nāgārjuna's opponent first seemed to reduce his assertion of emptiness into a non-assertion, from the operative field of emptiness, one has the freedom to make any statement one wishes. Nāgārjuna makes this point obliquely, however, from his own particular direction. Instead of arguing for the non-assertive use of positive language, he points out the fallacy in his opponent's use of negative language. His opponent has charged that Nāgārjuna's denial of essences leads to the denial of his own statement to that effect. Nāgārjuna reveals that his opponent is still bound by the wrong view of assuming essences within the object of denial. He claims in verse 63:

Since anything being denied does not exist, I do not deny anything; therefore, the statement: "You deny"— which was made by you—is a false accusation.[33]

Nāgārjuna does not deny anything, because the truth of emptiness means that there is nothing to deny. Nāgārjuna's focus on his opponent's use of the negative assertion highlights an important point. Despite the negative dialectic's preoccupation with denying assertions, it is shown that even negative statements can be used assertively. Both positive and negative statements can be used assertively or non-assertively. This opens the way to paradoxical uses of language that allow for the identity of opposites. Nāgārjuna concludes the *Vigrahavyāvartanī* with the statement that:

All things prevail for him for whom emptiness prevails; Nothing whatever prevails for him for whom emptiness prevails.[34]

The use of paradox is familiar to anyone who has perused Mādhyamika literature. Nāgārjuna's identification of *nirvāna* and *samsāra* immediately comes to mind, as well as the *Heart Sūtra's* formula that "form is emptiness and emptiness is form." Behind this paradox lies a dialectical succession of views that gives grounding to this use of language. It is a perspective which acts as a tremendous liberator of language in both its positive and negative modes. The claim that words are empty is a way of releasing words so that they may truly function, invoking again LaFleur's notion of "renewed affirmation."

This consideration of Nāgārjuna offers a parallel to Sŏp'o's own labors from within the cultural and semantic field of Indian philosophical traditions. Nāgārjuna agrees with and of course long precedes *KUM*'s own philosophical concerns about the nature of affirmative and negative discourse. *KUM*, however, also presents its fictive discourse as a non-assertive form of proposition. It is in this latter, metapractical respect that Nāgārjuna and Sŏp'o part company. Sŏp'o chose the vehicle of fiction rather than direct philosophical discourse. I believe Sŏp'o's choice reflects a greater historical direction taken by the sinitic Buddhist tradition which consciously discarded the example of Indian logical practices in favor of more poetic modes of expression.

To attempt to explain this divergence between Indian and East Asian Buddhism would probably require a prolonged examination of Chinese intellectual traditions. Confucian and Taoist conceptions of knowledge would figure prominently in such an investigation, keeping in mind the long-standing intellectual alliance between Taoism and Buddhism. Lisa Raphels has suggestively compared Taoist wisdom with the Greek notion of metic intelligence, a quality equivalent to what Confucian orthodoxy disparaged as cunning or cleverness, and which Raphels constrasts with the propositional knowledge of *epistēmē*. As Raphels points out, one's ideal of knowledge must be distinctly wedded to some sense of what there is to know. The relative invisibility of Taoist wisdom in East Asia (vis à vis Confucianism) is "... precisely because it cannot be formulated in terms of a definition or essence and because its 'objects' are changing, ambiguous situations that are not amenable to rigorous logical demonstration."[35] The demonstration of Taoist/Buddhist wisdom, then, explicitly questions the value of abstract, propositional discourse. One can also follow this up with historical observations about the prevalence of aesthetic and literary expressions as primary vehicles for embodying religious ideas.[36]

Historical context aside, the emergence of non-propositional discourse in Buddhism can be explained on the basis of philosophical considerations alone. The pertinent issue ensues from the liberation of language effected by Nāgārjuna's assertion of emptiness. The metaphysical moorings of this development hopefully have been made clear. As the explanations of Nāgārjuna demonstrate, it is possible to offer reasoned and theoretical accounts of why the liberation of language is mandated by the doctrine of emptiness. The difficulty, however, arises in the linguistic articulation of this fact. In other words, a problem arises not in the theory, but rather in the practice of the theory. Specifically, the use of language to proclaim the liberation of language is prone to make one forget the initial admonitions about the treachery of language. It is this danger which suggests that the *metapractical* considerations of a philosophical tradition— that is, an explicit evaluation of what practices best convey one's theories—might dictate that certain discourse practices are more suitable than others.

Let us demonstrate through the divergence in Nāgārjuna and Sŏp'o's respective discourses. According to Gadjin Nagao, in absolute emptiness, "language stands firm, logic stands firm, and the whole world stands firm for the first time."[37] Nagao makes it a point to affirm categorically the liberation of all words as referenced by the Sanskrit term *vyavahara*. Although this term is rendered by the Chinese as simply "word" or "speech," Nagao posits that "it really includes both meanings of language and logic."[38] Nagao's uniform approval of language and logic warrants both Sŏp'o's fictive and Nāgārjuna's rational practices. A broad historical view of the cycles of Buddhist philosophical endeavors, however, raises the evaluative question of whether or not this equal warrant is justified. Despite Nāgārjuna's protest that he holds no thesis (*pratijñā*), his manner of locution cannot help but look like an assertion, hence threatening to trigger another round trip in the Buddhist circle of emptiness. On the other hand, Sŏp'o's fictive idiom displays sufficient proof of the merits of his own choice in narrative practice. This is because discourse through dream and fiction claims no reference to reality through its very understanding of itself as illusion. It is a literal constitution of non-assertive discourse.

The Praxis of Reading

Malcolm David Eckel describes the Buddhist progression from relative to absolute back to relative truth as a paradoxical rather than dialectical movement.[39] The danger of paradox is that unlike a synthesis, which clearly terminates its prior phases of thesis and antithesis, one can never be sure what side of the paradox one is on. Eckel states, "Correct relative truth is the ordinary cognition of things *minus* the illusion that they are ultimately real."[40] The problem with this revisitation of relative truth is that it can easily slide into a relapse. As the dynamics and history of Buddhist philosophical discourse shows, the symbolizing habit of the mind insures a recidivistic and interminable passage around the two levels of truth.

The non-assertive parlance of *KUM* offers a trajectory out of this circuit by presenting its own means of expression as an embodiment rather than symbol of its truth claims. It can affirm the functional value of purely created and illusory words without allowing its own discourse to give rise to self-subverting ontological impressions. Is it feasible to judge, then, that as fictional discourse, *KUM* represents a kind of philosophical culmination? The criterion by which I have set the standards for philosophical discourse is the integration of metaphysics and metapractice so that the *expression* of a truth claim is conscious of and in conformity with the truth claim itself. In reading *KUM* as a virtuous example of philosophical discourse, I have attempted to illustrate a broad metaphysics/metapractice problematic of the Buddhist tradition: the paradoxical need to use words to get beyond words without getting entrapped within them. *KUM* is a fictive illusion that replicates within itself the echoes and rhythms of canonical truth discourse—a truth discourse which in and of itself leads to the justification of form/illusion/discourse as vehicles for the movement beyond. Thus the convergence of metaphysics and metapractice in *KUM* is notable not only because the metapractice (*KUM*'s discourse) conforms to the metaphysics (the ontology of illusion), but also because its metaphysics supplies a justification for discourse itself. We will explore this justification further in the next and last chapter.

But there is another problem to consider. If fiction presents a viable alternative in the composition of philosophical discourse, what about its soteriological mission? As much as one can appreciate *KUM*'s philosophical traits, its participation in the Buddhist tradition automatically brings it under another kind of scrutiny. This I have previously stipulated as a *religious* criterion; to wit, the proviso that the point of undertaking truth discourse at all is to lead individuals to spiritual transformation. It is from this religious perspective that *KUM*, as a work of fiction, seems prey to yet another form of circularity of discourse, which again threatens to entrap one in words. In order to characterize this brand of recursive motion, let us take the example of a classic Chinese novel.

Anthony Yu has given much attention to the unusual kind of reflexivity featured in *Dream of the Red Chamber* (*Hongloumeng*; hereafter *HLM*); that is, to its awareness of itself as a work of fiction. Referring to the author Cao Xueqin's practice of fiction, Yu states, "He will use illusion to discourse on illusion."[41] This literary strategy is inscribed into the opening chapter of *HLM* with an unusual self-accounting that purports to reveal to the reader the tale of its own origins. This opening is not an author's preface which rehearses an autobiographical account of the creative literary process. Rather, the novel's self-referentiality provides the outermost framework for the total narrative, which, in Yu's analysis, "engage[s] the reader in an unprecedented and continuous discussion on the nature of fiction itself and, simultaneously, on the nature of reading."[42]

As perhaps the most engaging and masterful of novels in the dream literature tradition, *HLM* is more than proficient in expounding its own fictional discourse on the ontology of illusion. Its strength as a work of fiction, however, leads Yu to conclude that "The profound paradox emerging from Cao Xueqin's masterpiece seems to be that the illusion of life, itself a painful avowal of the non-reality and untruth of reality, can only be grasped through the illusion of art, which is an affirmation of the truth of insubstantiality."[43] This tacit preference for the illusion of art in *HLM* is a built-in mechanism that ensues from the novel's speculations on its own origins. In being treated to an account of the protagonist's original incarnation as a stone, the reader is compelled to follow the karmic consequences of this figure's passionate transgressions—that is, to read the novel. The artistry of the novel exerts such a powerful influence, however, that the dramatized reader, represented by the figure of Vanitas, immediately rushes out to find a publisher for the story. The act of publication, scripted into *HLM*'s own narrative, suggests the author's confidence that the reader of his novel will not follow the example of its protagonist Baoyu, who abandons the world for religion. Instead, the act of publication signifies the novel's perpetual revisitation as fiction. The paradox of this situation is that the reader, "knowing something [life] as illusory, empty, and dreamlike as fiction, he nonetheless must live by the need of constant attachment to it."[44] The process of reading in this instance ends in an affirmation of form which spawns a perpetual return to it.

The scenario established by *HLM* suggests the final triumph of art over religion, crafted through the allure of form which renders the reader incapable of discarding it once it has served its function. Buddhism constantly warns against this seductive allure of words. Pondering whether or not art finally serves the cause of faith, Yu maintains his sight on the aesthetic discourse and merits of *HLM* to conclude that it eventually subverts the ontology of illusion: " . . . the cosmos may be regarded as illusory and dreamlike, but the world of fiction, its 'reality' and appeal far more resistant to such dismissal, remains paradoxically a more potent and permanent illusion."[45] The Buddhist domestication of the literary arts would seem here to have been surpassed by the engaging power of the art, thus subverting the final goal of religious detachment in favor of aesthetic addiction.

The persistence of illusion, of course, is an observation keenly felt by Buddhists. Here the final incongruity of art and the religious goal of worldly transcendence voice more than the conventional objection that literary pursuits are too secular or preoccupied with inappropriate topics such as love and sex. Rather, in the case of *HLM* the problem seems to rest on a fundamental gap between fictive discourse and religious goals. Although the author succeeds in conforming the structure of his novel to the metaphysics of emptiness, this conformity seems to be contradicted by the seemingly anti-soteriological effects of reading.

What remains to be seen, however, is whether or not some inherent quality of fiction necessitates the recursive motion that

is present in *HLM*. It might be possible, in other words, to identify other patterns of movement. In the case of *KUM* the motion
that its narrative course describes is in fact not circular or recursive, but ever recessive in its frameworks of recitation. This motion is evident not only in the movement from dream to
awakening, but is recapitulated in the dream sequence itself.
This is achieved through the fluid transformations of the characters, ever obfuscating the identification of "reality." What these
frameworks represent are receding and ever-elusive categories
of reality whose spectral quality is explicitly brought to bear on
Xingzhen's final enlightenment. The momentum of the novel's
recessive motion cannot be defused before landing in the lap of
the reader—the final frontier of reality—and thereby forcing the
question as to whether or not one can verify oneself to be the
final dreamer.

It is this final act of recession through which Sŏp'o infuses
this novel with soteriological import. By implicating the reader
in the metaphysical consideration of truth and illusion, the novel
implicates itself—in its status as illusory fiction—as the vehicle
by which the reader is personally confronted with the ontology
of illusion. The novel's status as fictional form is the necessary
ingredient for querying the nature of truth. This function exemplifies Buddhist philosophy's return to and reaffirmation of form
as a means of religious instruction.

In *KUM*, however, this final return is not narratively
represented by an invitation to read the novel over again.
When Xingzhen begs Liuguan, "I am confused: I can't tell
whether the dream was not true, or the truth was not a dream.
Please teach me the truth, and make me understand,"[46] the
master preaches the *Diamond Sūtra*, the canonical text that
KUM analogizes in elaborate and literary form. The success
of Liuguan's sermon testifies to the efficacy of this sūtra. The
advantage of this final return to the *Diamond Sūtra* in the
liberation of Xingzhen, however, is presumably predicated
on his prior experience, and the appropriation of the sūtra in
light of the more elaborate, fictionalized expression of the

teaching. The novel's reassertion of its charter text nonetheless emphasizes a movement away from self-perpetuation in favor of the direct, streamlined religious discourse of the *Diamond Sūtra*. Having served its purpose, the fictional form can now be discarded.

Chapter 6

Remythologizing the
Comparative Enterprise

I began this study with a brief discussion of the nature of comparisons. To summarize, I suggested that the comparative enterprise is always driven by a community's desire for self-definition. The constitution of an "other" creates ciphers against which we measure ourselves, in attempts to assimilate or differentiate. The comparativist brings an indelible focal point to the comparison, which largely determines how the object of comparison is to be constructed. For this reason, I have adhered to the point that comparisons are exercises of the self-interested imagination.

The present endeavor is no exception to this general description of the nature of comparisons. Up until this point, however, the comparison has been implicit, focusing primarily on the Korean Buddhist setting. The presence of the silent partner of this venture—the Western academic scene—has nevertheless been forceful in determining the contours of this whole study. Having come this far, it is appropriate, even necessary, to justify the manner in which I have constructed the subject of late seventeenth-century Korean Buddhist philosophical discourse in terms of what direct import such a study has for Western scholarly practices.

At the most general level of significance, my desire to credit fictive narratives with philosophical weight offers a useful tonic to those who would fashion the boundaries of philosophy too

177

narrowly. The advantage of this liberal attitude is that a broader range of social and cultural phenomena can be dignified with the adjective "philosophical." My point is not to place indiscriminately this label on all cultural discourses that ponder the meaning of life. I have sought to impose a specific definition of philosophical discourse keyed to the primary factors of metaphysics and metapractice. Although these criteria are specific in nature, their embodiment cuts across literary genre lines, as well as the distinctions between elite and popular cultures. A definition of philosophical discourse that allows for these possibilities offers a stronger and more viable heuristic tool for making sense of cultural systems.

In this context, the claim for the merits of fictional narrative is one that can be made cross-culturally. Martha Nussbaum reports that even in ancient Greece—the culture most credited with asserting the superiority of rational discourse—there was once a time when no distinction was made between poetry and prose in the examination of human concerns. Greek tragedies in particular amply fulfilled their role as observers of the human condition by portraying "the existence of conflict among our commitments" and the dramatic ends such conflict could bring about. Although Socrates decried such conflicts of value as a result of faulty logic, Nussbaum notes that tragedy was capable of keying in to the "practical intuition" of real lives in a way that the theoretical solutions of philosophers could not:

> But we can say provisionally that a whole tragic drama, unlike a schematic philosophical example making use of a similar story, is capable of tracing the history of a complex pattern of deliberation, showing its roots in a way of life and looking forward to its consequences in that life. As it does all of this, it lays open to view the complexity, the indeterminacy, the sheer difficulty of actual human deliberation.[1]

The applicability of these observations to Chinese and Korean traditions is almost seamless. Here too fiction operates very close to the ground, demonstrating the attempt of individuals to translate ideals into action, and more often than not, showing how such attempts can often collide. Sŏp'o's beloved *Romance of the Three Kingdoms* offers a perfect example of such dramatization. Liu Bei's determination to restore the Han contrasts the Five Phases theory of dynastic cycles, which dictates that all reigns must come to a determined end, with the ideal of the man of action who is capable of overcoming fate. The novel is littered with references to the inevitable fall of the Han, and yet it asserts the heroism of men like Liu Bei and Zhugeliang, the men whose ability to uphold personal virtue or strike with decisive action at the right moment are believed to be capable of determining history. The contradiction is not a sign of compositional deficiency. Rather, it is an accurate portrayal of "the complexity, the indeterminacy," as Nussbaum puts it, of cultural ideals.

One specific example from the *Three Kingdoms* recounts the experience of Dan Fu, a loyal adviser to Liu Bei who is forced to the enemy side when his mother is held for ransom by the cunning general Cao Cao. Torn by filial feelings, Dan Fu leaves the service of Liu Bei to rush to his mother's side, only to have her admonish him for abandoning his ruler. She hangs herself in abject protest. The poignant episode gives the lie to Confucian belief, directly affirmed in the *Great Learning*, that filiality can be literally homologized to political loyalty. If one's house is in order, the logic goes, one can put the state in order. The two actions are analogous, not antithetical. The *Three Kingdoms*, however, instantiates the wisdom of our "practical intuition," as well as practical experience, that duty to the family and duty to the state often clash.

Many episodes from the *Three Kingdoms* suggest perhaps that fiction is particularly suited for mimicking the complexities and contradictions of experienced reality in a way that the narrow rigor of theoretical argument is not. Following this point, it is possible to conclude that fiction is also better equipped for philosophical investigation as a result of its ability to engage one's lived experiences, of its "true to life" feeling. The recognition of one's self in the narrative, the engagement of emotions, the arousing of pathos are all a forceful arsenal in the task of

persuasion—which is the point of all metaphysical proclama-
tions. Hence Nussbaum's observations about the nature of tragedy, if generalized to cross-cultural contexts, seem to hold out
the option that fictive narratives constitute a viable form of philosophical metapractice.

This point about the persuasiveness and accessibility of
narrative allows us to come full circle by reengaging an earlier
chapter's assertion that it is these very same qualities of fiction
that bring it so close to autobiography. This theme was drawn
out by exploring Sŏp'o's creation of *The Southern Expedition* as
an internal theodicy which allowed him to reflect on and compose the meaning of his life as a statesman. *NJG* permitted Sŏp'o
to indulge his autobiographical impulse by using a standard
model to frame and flesh in the contours of his identity. These
strokes of self-definition represented an archetypal convention
of meaningful existence and perhaps only in the most diluted
sense can be designated as philosophical. The identity modeled
in *NJG* is a cultural paradigm which was historically, if somewhat obliquely, intertwined with the Confucian intellectual and
ethical system. The primary purpose of *NJG*, however, is not to
delineate or propagate this system as much as it is to find a
place of meaning for the author within it. Therefore, in serving
as Sŏp'o's autobiographical medium, the *NJG* demonstrates that
narrative's persuasive capacities need not always be utilized
towards espousing a particular philosophical point of view.

This observation confronts us squarely with the thesis on
fiction with which this study began: Martha Nussbaum's assertion that fiction is wedded to a particular view of life, one which
confirms its indeterminacy and the limited utility of universal
principles. I have attempted to demonstrate that the Buddhist
lessons of *KUM*—embodied both in its thematic content and
structural framing—present the same kind of reality. The metaphysics of emptiness informs us that spiritual progress is predicated on one's ability to become unfettered by absolutes. Its
hesitancy to apply words to life simply reflects its belief in a
world that refuses to be tamed by assertions about it. The illusions which make up our experience of life are momentary re-

alities that amount to both nothing and everything. The spiritual challenge posed by this world badgers the self—a being severely limited in perspicuity—to resist the defensive yearning for transcendence to some higher, more stable reality and to accept the ultimate solution of embracing illusion.

But the point of Nussbaum's thesis, of course, is to predicate this worldview of all fiction—not just Buddhist versions. In her study of the novels of Henry James, Nussbaum demonstrates how their narrative texture, their true-to-life quality, makes a claim on the nature of our own experiences. In the case of Asian fiction generally, however, its assumption about life is manifested neither through its narrative quality nor even, as in the case of *KUM*, its Buddhist content. It is demonstrated by the implicit understanding *behind* the writing process that narratives provide a way of creating life, and that that act of creation exposes the fallacy of the stable and autonomous self. The *NJG* shows us that even the symbols of an absolutist ideology, which poses the existence of clean, hard-edged selves, can be used to instigate a process that paradoxically divulges the malleability of being. Here the symbols may be Confucian but the lesson is strictly Buddhist.

Martha Nussbaum's work suggests the desirability of moving philosophical inquiry away from the pursuit of universality and certainty to the pursuit of "perceptive equilibrium" in our encounter with the world. *KUM*'s use of Buddhist content to explicitly render an inherently Buddhist process suggests one way in which this work of fiction offers a cross-cultural contribution. The contribution may be posed as a question: If the fictive narratives of Nussbaum's concern display a certain view of life, is there a virtue to articulating that view outside of its narrative mode? In other words, is there a philosophical point to articulating the metaphysics of fiction in non-fictive language? One might point out that within her own academic discourse, Nussbaum performs this act of metaphysical abstraction automatically in the course of probing the metapractice of fiction. In the case of *KUM*, the use of Buddhist symbols as the major theme of the novel transforms the metaphysics of its own metapractice into the object of scrutiny. We must consider the question as to whether or not there is particular merit in such reflection.

The assertion that the world is uncertain irresistibly invites scrutiny and contemplation. Despite the disclaimer that general principles and ideological absolutes can never clarify this world, we still want to know it, to confront and describe it, to ask why it is so. The metaphysics of emptiness is one attempt to give some contours to that which is ultimately contourless, and the repeated reminders that even emptiness is empty is an integral part of that descriptive endeavor. Hence even the assertion of uncertainty cries out for ontological grounding. In extolling the philosophical potency of fiction, it is worth making both its metaphysical and metapractical components as explicit as possible. Having done so, the next logical question is, So what? What does the metaphysics of fiction reveal that can be useful outside of the comparative construction?

The lessons of fiction are pertinent to my concern with comparative studies, which is the outermost framework of my own composition. The metaphysical observations of fiction impinge on the enterprise of cross-cultural studies, which must ultimately wrestle with the truth question. As a discipline, this field seeks a method for sorting, comparing, and ultimately, for some, assessing competing cultural truth claims. As a part of this task, the discipline is forced to wrestle with questions about how to justify its own scholarly claims. Admittedly, it is unclear how much fictive discourse, as delineated thus far, can contribute to this latter academic enterprise. Although fiction can be a valid mode of ethical and philosophical discourse, it is not academic discourse, per se, nor should it be. Reflections on the lessons of fiction, on the other hand, could prove immensely helpful in grounding the academic enterprise as a whole. It is this possibility that remains for me to pursue in this final chapter.

A Comparative Framework

Much of this study has been preoccupied with the virtue of fiction as philosophy. In the pages to come, I will attempt a broader comparative evaluation of the specific Buddhist ontology of illusion which renders fictive narrative a most laudable form of metaphysical expression. In other words, I will explore the possibility that the Buddhist ontology of illusion may have specific answers to some of the important questions that drive the academy today. One should not conclude, however, that by urging the merits of Buddhist ontology in our own academic context, I am suggesting that we all start composing novels. Sŏp'o's literary rendition of Buddhist philosophy through *KUM* was an historically determined strategy that achieved two major objectives: the desire to maintain a non-assertive discourse about Buddhist reality, and the need to create a viable Buddhist practice that both responded to and expressed the social and institutional contexts of the time. These philosophical objectives and structural considerations were historically rooted and therefore bear little relevance to our present concerns.

The Western academy is not so puzzled over what its intellectual practices should be—that is, what literary genres are best suited to its goals. It is, however, in some trouble as to how to justify them. This is particularly true of comparative endeavors which transgress into the sensitive area of making assertions about cultural others. The observation and study of human life in whatever form it is found has been the legitimate pursuit of all academic inquiry. Recent intellectual trends, however, have challenged our faith that the conclusions we draw are anchored to some notion of reality or truth. Our methodologies have evolved in a continuous direction but they have been implicitly undermined by the suspicion that the truth assertions that they are aiming at are mere illusions. Whereas Sŏp'o labored to create a practice that fit a particular theory and truth, we find ourselves with the more fundamental challenge to articulate the truth that charters our practices.

In drawing out this offset yet symmetrical comparison of the premodern Korean Buddhist setting and the modern Western intellectual one, I bring my own study to bear on the question of truth. What can the pursuit of comparisons add to the pursuit of truth? Philip Quinn has stated,

Comparisons are, to be sure, interesting in their own right, but it is not obvious that they help with the task of evaluating religious doctrine with respect to truth or warrant, coherence or plausibility. I take this task to be central to philosophy of religion as it is currently practiced in academic departments of philosophy in the anglophone world.[2]

Although there appears to be no intrinsic correspondence between the question of truth and the exercise of comparisons, the nature of my comparison suggests that the two concerns in fact historically and intellectually overlap. In the Buddhist case, the turn towards fictional narrative represents a particular strategy in the quest to convey that tradition's notions about truth. In applying this example to ourselves, I suggest that Buddhist ontology may be capable of grounding our own methods as justified and true. By paralleling the two contexts' search for viable truth discourses, I offer my foregoing study as a more general exploration of the nature of truth and warrant, coherence and plausibility.

If the insights gained by such an examination clarify the standards by which we practice our own discourses, could they not be justifiably applied to the discourse of others? If this act is justified, then the application of comparative questions is no longer purely descriptive. It implies the application of broad, even "universal" standards of discourse which are not so much demanded of the comparative context as they are posed as a holistic framework for understanding others.

Unlike past ignominious attempts to use the standard of Western rationalist thought to rate the wisdom traditions of other cultures, the present comparative framework desires to salvage the category of "philosophical" discourse without getting confused over questions of discourse styles. My focus on fiction makes this aim quite clear. Hence my argument that fiction is a form of philosophizing curtails the danger of interpreting the category of philosophy too narrowly. On the other hand, the question of what constitutes the parameters of the term is perhaps the more significant one. In my analysis of *KUM*, the most consequential consideration that emerged has been the

question of metapractice. Against the temptation to equate philosophy solely with metaphysical inquiry, the case of Buddhism
reveals that metapractical issues can and should play an equal
role.

The balance of metaphysics and metapractice is a cue that I
have taken from Thomas Kasulis' own injunctions for philosophy.[3] It is on the basis of this criterion that I have judged the
virtue of *KUM* and identify the ailment of the modern scholarly
community. For my present purpose of constructing a comparative framework, the ingredients of metaphysics and metapractice
must be bracketed by a larger process that this study, up until
now, has only implicitly alluded to. This is a tradition's tendency to experience moments of deconstruction and reconstruction—a progressive yet recursive movement of the sort displayed
in what I have called the Buddhist circle of emptiness. In this
particular instance, the cycles of deconstruction and reconstruction revolved around Buddhist linguistic practices. This dynamic
can be more broadly applied, however. Whatever the focus of
analysis, it will undoubtedly be bound up with a culture's perception of itself, and with its charter myths.

Philip Quinn, in examining Christianity's discourse on the
problem of evil, in fact uses the language of "demythologizing"
and "remythologizing." My present endeavor is very much fueled by his suggestion that this cycle might be paralleled in
other cultures. Quinn asks, "Is there . . . anything to the idea
that there is a propensity in cultures of a certain complexity or
even in all cultures to evolve in the direction of demythologization?"[4] Quinn submits that the only way of supporting such
speculation is through detailed comparative studies. I offer my
present study as a comparative endeavor that substantiates his
conjectures. The manner of substantiation, I hope, suggests a
further refinement of the theory in this manner: Specifically, I
posit that the mechanics of demythologization and remythologization is a function of the balance (or lack thereof) between a
culture's metaphysical and metapractical self-understanding.

Let us posit that societies can experience historical moments of rupture between the metaphysical and metapractical

aspects of their endeavors—endeavors that focus primarily on the pursuit of truth claims. The rupture heightens consciousness of these two aspects of being which, *in situ*, should ideally manifest a seamless harmony. When the rupture is made conscious, a phase of demythologization occurs. In the case of East Asian Buddhism, the rise of Chan sects represents this moment of rupture, a rupture that led to the demythologization of theoretical or metaphysical constructions in favor of the command to simply practice. The strident iconoclastic rhetoric of Chan Buddhism underscores its role in the demythologizing process. Although more recent scholarship makes the significant point that Chan practices and attitudes were not in fact so anti-traditional, the more interesting phenomenon is Chan's glorified ideal of heterodoxy. Within the present comparative framework, Chan antinomianism suggests a loud and clear indication—from within the depths of the Buddhist tradition— that the previous norm of scholastic exegesis had lost its credibility.

In order to understand the nature of this loss, we must explicitly turn to the structuring principle of metaphysics and metapractice. In Chan Buddhism, the sacrifice of metaphysical discourse was not a sacrifice of metaphysics per se. In truth, it was the *practice* of such discourse that was deconstructed as an invalid one, pointing to gaps and weaknesses in Buddhism's understanding of the nature of practice. One cannot understand the origins of this crisis without going back even further in the Buddhist tradition, back to the Buddha's original hostility towards philosophical conversation, coupled with substantive views about the ontological properties of language. In pointing to the elaborate overgrowth of exegetical literature, Chan indicted current Buddhist practices for being out of alignment with its own metaphysics. The revelation forced deeper speculation at the metapractical level, which ultimately drew upon its own metaphysical resources to overcome the crisis and fully revalorize discourse.

The bulk of this work, of course, has been an effort to demonstrate how the novel *KUM* enfleshed the latter process of revalorization. The phase of demythologization, which comprises the first stage of my comparative framework for examining cultural discourses, does not represent an inherently negative situation but rather a moment in a dynamic process. The phase of remythologization that follows must rebuild by repairing the ruptures of the prior stage. This reconstruction is based on the realization that success on the metapractical level, which explicitly formulates a theory of why our practices are important and why they work, cannot be achieved without the support structure of metaphysical theory. Here I return to my earlier assertion that in any philosophical system, the metaphysics comes first. It is not possible to judge the coherence of any practice without measuring it against some view of reality. Whether this view is pre-given or later derived as justification, the important point is the conceptual priority of metaphysics. Quinn's terminology of demythologization and remythologization—with its focus on myth—suggests the centrality of chartering discourses. Although myth and metaphysics are usually understood to comprise very different discourse styles, their more important commonality lies in their cultural function as licences to practice.

In my reading of *KUM*, I have perhaps given greater emphasis to Sŏp'o's *practice* of fiction, arguing that as a form of philosophical practice, the use of fiction represents a shift in Buddhist metapractice which admirably conforms to the demands of its metaphysics. It is equally important to emphasize, however, that while *KUM*, as a metapractice, conforms to Buddhist metaphysics, it is also chartered and vindicated by the metaphysics. Fiction may be easier to protect from reification into truth words, but only a metaphysical vision like the ontology of illusion can explain how fiction is still capable of expressing truth. In my discussions of the rise of fiction and its use and significance in China and Korea, I attempted to set the historical stage which made the rise of *KUM* as philosophical discourse possible. If the rise of fictive narrative in East Asia was wed to a specific metaphysical awareness of the ontic status and creativity of fiction—indeed of all illusion—then one can identify this historical development as the one that made possible the use of fiction to remythologize Buddhist philosophical practice.

There is an extremely normative attitude in this description of Buddhism's deconstructive and reconstructive processes. For I do not suggest, with this schema, some inexorable historical force which assures the eventual and successful completion of the stages. Nor can one presume the success with which each phase is accomplished. Therefore the comparativist finds him- or herself in the position of assessing the virtuosity with which a culture has enacted this process. The course of this judgment is guided by specific criteria. My comparative framework is specific about the need to look at how well a culture integrates its metaphysical and metapractical understandings of itself. On the other hand, this standard allows for a large degree of flexibility in evaluating a culture's truth claims. For the categories of metaphysics and metapractice are broad enough (compared to terms like "philosophy" and "reason" as they have been primarily used in the past) to include a broader range of expressions.

My investigation of *KUM* is meant to offer one instance in which the process has turned out rather admirably. But this assessment must also be conferred internally. That is, if this novelistic discourse represents a resolution to a particular problem, its accomplishments must also be measured relative to the historical situation it imposes itself upon. The merits of this novel must be determined from a grounded historical perspective that takes into account the institutional history of Buddhism, the development of literary genres, and Sŏp'o's personal history. The account that I have given of the coalescence of all three in *KUM* has questioned some prevailing views in the relevant disciplines. The supposed decline of Buddhism in Chosŏn Korea and the supposed meaninglessness of Buddhist symbols in East Asian fiction are some attitudes that I have attempted to redress.

The broader agenda of this study, that is, the desire to valorize fiction as philosophical discourse in a moment of historical time that fits within the schema of demythologized and remythologized cultural expression, has greatly determined my approach to my subject matter. Lest any objections be raised that my agenda has been too determining, let me offer this: It is my judgment that an interpretive framework capable of creating cultural wealth where once one saw little or nothing at all is a creation that invites further consideration. In applying the Buddhist concept of illusion and its criteria of validity to my own comparison which I have conjured for self-interested purposes, we must be consistent in upholding the primacy of the salvational properties of all created discourses. That is, the process of *informing* must become *transforming*. We ourselves and our theories must abide by the thesis of this study that it is only through the transformative process that self, reality, and truth can be maintained.

The Fear of Ontology

My emphasis on the priority of metaphysics within a philosophical system makes possible a further refinement of the demythologization-remythologization framework. The point of this is to enable the comparativist to evaluate the relative severity with which a given setting has undergone the demythologization process. As we have seen in the situation of *KUM*, its act of remythologizing Buddhist philosophical discourse entailed an affirmation of a priorly existing metaphysical tradition. One can say that *KUM* remythologized this tradition through a new kind of discourse practice—the metapractice of fictive discourse. The fact that the process of remythologization utilized and reinforced an inherited metaphysical perspective, however, renders the process into a relatively conservative one. The act of remythologization is really a reaffirmation and vindication of an existing metaphysical tradition through innovation in practice.

It is possible, of course, to imagine much greater upheavals in the demythologization process. If the retention of an existing metaphysical system through an evolution in practice represents a tame version of the process, then the obverse scenario— the rejection or dissolution of prior views of reality in order to invest existing practices with meaning—offers an even more significant point of development. It is this potential scenario that offers a nexus between this study of Buddhist discourse and Western academic practices.

Comparative scholars (specifically historians of religion) are notably conscientious about their practices, especially as they relate to academic methodology. Ironically, the examination of other cultures often leads historians of religion to expand notions about cultural discourse, but relatively strict limitations are posed on academic discourse about them. The limitations derive from an explicitly held ideal that the goal of the historian of religion is to describe, rather than normatively evaluate, the beliefs and practices of others. Any infiltration of normative goals are reined in by an implicit desire to demonstrate the virtues of other cultures. Let us take the work of the present volume as a case in point.

An evaluation of my study up until this point might conclude that my examination of fiction in seventeenth-century Korea has sought to increase respect for it; to argue that it is a way of philosophizing that demands our close attention. One might also expand the evaluation to say that I have sought to prove that contrary to our implicit expectations about philosophical discourse, there is a multiplicity of philosophical expressions and that the reasons for this are not arbitrary but intimately connected to substantive views of reality. This in turn seems to argue for diverging rationalities; the divergence not only of points of view, but of ways of making them, all of which, because of an internal consistency of form and expression, merit the label of "rational discourse."

Unfortunately, this evaluation only serves to exacerbate the problem of cultural multiplicity which is at the heart of comparative studies. Such terms as "diverging rationalities" suggest that efforts such as mine cannot go beyond the point of exposing divergent practices to actually *comparing* them, which is a normative and judgmental act. To many, descriptive practices are a virtue in and of themselves, and it would be inappropriate to attempt to do anything more. To underscore the complex practices of others has the laudable effect of decentering the

West's opinion of itself and teaching it how to appreciate the virtuosity of others.

I have hopefully contributed to this agenda, an agenda that is most commonly attributed to historians of religions. I aspire, however, to amble in thornier territory—that of the philosophy of religions, whose domain breaches the descriptive and embraces the normative. The disciplines of comparative religions and philosophy of religions have been content, for the most part, to leave each other to their own agendas. It is becoming increasingly clear, however, that the tradition of mutual unconcern is becoming harder to maintain in the field of religion, a field that envelops both disciplines. One can perhaps fault the general temper of the times, an era in which issues of multiculturalism pervade the academy and the general media. Much closer to the heart of the matter, however, lies the nature of our discipline itself, the study of religion, which has long presumed for itself a concern with that realm of human experience that pursues ultimate concerns and ultimate answers.

Witness the complaint of Huston Smith, who berates current trends in the study of religion and those who seek to obviate its pursuit of truth questions:

> So we pour our departmental energies into features of religion that have objective, empirical grounding—philology, archaeology, historical influences and textual parallels—and bracket the question of whether the beliefs that generated those fallouts were mistaken or true. Theology pursued systematically rather than historically seems a breach of academic protocol, and philosophy of religion backs away from talk that seeks to penetrate directly into God's nature, to talk about God-talk.[5]

Some might consider Smith and his implied directives as a bit bold: What earns us the charge, one might ask, to determine questions of truth just by virtue of the fact that we are scholars of religion? I myself do not venture such a bold stance. I am, however, acutely interested in the question of our own activities as scholars of religions and what they might possibly mean. In order to highlight the meaning of our practices, we must start with our own metaphysical grounding. As a part of this task, I seek to examine explicitly Buddhist ideas about the nature of reality because these ideas might prove of importance to us as modern academics. Indeed, this is where I see the actual convergence of the philosophy of religion with the history of religion to lie. The study of religion can no longer maintain its noncommittal stance towards the religious and philosophical ideas it examines because of the potential claims they can make on our own self-understanding. This potential is underscored by the fact that currently, we are impoverished from within of the kinds of ideas that can ground and justify our activities, particularly the attempt to describe (and sometimes even evaluate) the existence of others.

This assessment is different from Smith's directive that we concern ourselves with questions of truth, but it is related to it. We do not receive this charter by virtue of the subject we study—the "divine"—but rather through our scholarly conscientiousness about crafting methods for responsibly representing the meanings and truths of other cultures. At first blush, the quest for truth and the quest for the truths of others would seem to be separate concerns, concerns pursued by different professionals who call themselves, respectively, philosophers and historians of religions. But both professionals, as descendants of the Enlightenment and inhabitants of the university, share methodological assumptions about how to "get at" something, whether it is truth in the ultimate sense, or the true representation of the truth of others. This task has primarily centered on transcending our historical prejudices in the belief that the truth enterprise necessitates that we bracket our own cultural assumptions and predispositions in order to obtain the God's-eye view, or to get into the mind of others.

One need not prolong the requisite sniffs toward the naive version of objectivity here. I trust that no one will dispute that this assumption—at least in wholesale form—has fallen on hard times. But the reaction may prove to have been somewhat extreme. For many, the myth of objectivity has been superseded by the malaise of the modern intellectual world—that is, the belief that in the absence of certainty, we must commit to chaos, or at least render ourselves incapable of assenting to any belief or commitment at all. This is the kind of cultural temper that Huston Smith decries and justifiably accuses of having infected the university. It is odd that an institution that spends so much of its time dissecting truth discourse is so often loathe to engage in it. It retreats instead into the supposedly safe haven of methodology, which is parallel to philosophy's refuge in epistemology. Both are concerned with how one can know anything, and with understanding all ways of knowing in the world, but one hesitates to publicly embrace any form of knowledge.

It is peculiar that while many philosophers have long ceased to mourn for Plato's "real above," or the viewpoint outside of the human,[6] it is the dedicated descriptivist who most clings to the ideal of procedural rationality. In her conscientiousness about methodology, the descriptivist adheres to well-established canons of sufficiency in the presentation of evidence and argument. In lieu of the naive ideal of objectivity, she adheres to Clifford Geertz's injunction to refrain nonetheless from "conducting surgery in a sewer," a metaphor for gross subjectivity and scholarly irresponsibility.[7]

There is much wisdom in this course, a course that is endemic to the university. But the point is this: She imagines that by having retreated to the allegedly autonomous concern of methodology, she has succeeded in abandoning ontology. She imagines that methods can be expediently applied without having any truck with the ideology that spawned them. She imagines that she can obliterate her kinship with her siblings, the philosophers who are brazen about their truth enterprise, and whose shared strategies for getting at truth make blatant assumptions about the nature of truth. As much as the descriptivist would like to forget, however, both she and the philosopher are offspring of an intellectual tradition committed to the progress of knowledge based on human faculties alone, a tradition that relies not only on principles of procedure, but on a view of reality as well.

It is not my purpose to discredit the methods of the descriptivist by rubbing her nose in the rank evidence of her institutional and intellectual lineage. My complaint is that she does not embrace it enough. In describing the truth claims of others, she asks us to trust that we accept her representations as justified without committing to any substantive ideas about what makes her representations true. Before we undertake the task of describing others, we must make a commitment to the validity of our own actions. We have defaulted on this commitment through a determined (but ultimately misguided) ontological wimpiness.

To be sure, some scholars—rather consequential ones at that—have founded their careers on the right to thumb their noses at ontology. To them, methodology *is* commitment. Jonathan Z. Smith has discoursed long and engagingly on categories of the "sacred," all the while impishly parading the fact that these categories are all made up—by us.[8] Smith has done his convincing best to persuade us that counter to our cherished belief in the *sui generis* status of religion, religion is actually an arbitrary reduction of cultural possibilities in the creation of discrete traditions.[9] As Smith is fond of saying through a phrase borrowed from Arnold van Gennep's *The Rites of Passage*, the sacred "pivots." It is not a metaphysically real category which makes claims upon historical beings, it is something that we make up: "From such a point of view, there is nothing that is inherently sacred or profane. These are not substantive categories, but rather situational ones. Sacrality is, above all, a category of emplacement."[10]

In spite of the deconstuctivist glee with which J. Z. Smith seems to set about his task as an historian of religion, his insights and conclusions are fertile and illuminating. His insistence on his right to refrain from any commitments to the category of the sacred, on the other hand, underrates the highly creative processes that go into all cultural instantiations of it. We seem to assume that once we have "unmasked" religion, once we have exposed it to be "floating or undecided signification" which "is neither an ontological nor a substantive category [but rather] a linguistic one,"[11] religion has been discredited as a merely human foible. At the very least, religion no longer holds the grandeur and respect it once commanded. This is an implicit part of Huston Smith's lament.

The situation of the historian of religion becomes even clearer now. Not only is she suspicious of the truth enterprise as conducted by the philosophers, she is democratically wary of the truth enterprise of other cultures. And last but not least, she is egalitarian enough to be suspicious of herself. It might be possible, however, to dodge the corrosive effects of all this doubt if we came to terms with an understanding of our actions. Of course, many would contend that doubting is good, especially doubts that are applied to ourselves. I agree. A second naiveté may be neither possible nor desirable to obtain, but our self-examining, critical nature may in fact be our own salvation. But we still lack a constructive way of constituting this goal. We still have yet to remythologize our pursuits.

Let us draw graphically a picture of our current predicament according to the comparative framework I have been developing. One might aver that the origins of our situation reach back to the Enlightenment—an era when the faith in rational inquiry was empowered by a charter myth/metaphysics that pictured a world (both natural and human) completely accessible to the faculty of reason. The province of the divine—that is, the study of religion, was itself brought under rational scrutiny in the optimistic belief that the phenomenological and historical study of religion (as well as the study of nature) would constitute an act of faith, a testimonial to the greater glory of Christianity.

The symmetry of metaphysics and practice as instituted by the Enlightenment began to fall out of alignment, however, as scholars of religion began to recognize the invidious effects of their practices, particularly of the comparative variety. The supposed disinterested and systematic pursuit of knowledge by the defenders of reason was unmasked as an unmitigated power play in which restricted voices exercised the privilege of imposing their view of the world, not only for themselves, but over others. This revelation, wrought by countless scenarios in modern history, instituted an era of legitimate suspicion of our institutional and political moorings. The larger fallout of this self-examination, however, has been the erosion of our intellectual foundations through our recognition of the inextricable ties between power and knowledge.

We can perhaps define cultural relativism in the academy as a descriptivist approach to other cultures which affirms that they are worthy of study simply by virtue of being human. This stance rejects normative evaluations not only on the grounds that they are politically oppressive, but because of the more formidable suspicion that our operative notion of truth is no longer tenable. Without any concept of what constitutes truth, the whole idea of normative comparisons loses all meaning. Each culture and system represents a structure of meaning that makes sense only in relation to itself. The service that comparisons perform is to expand within our own consciousness the palette of human colors in order to facilitate mutual understanding and perhaps even expand personal options. These options, however, are between autonomous, self-contained systems whose appeal is based on historical and aesthetic preferences rather than on any criterion of truth.

The resulting changes in academic practice have consisted mostly of the kind of self-consciousness that I have already discussed. As in the Buddhist setting with *KUM*, the maturation of a system's metapractice is a critical step in reachieving the balance of metaphysics and metapractice. The difference here, however, is that in the present case the adjustment in practice is not enough. This is because we are unable to come to terms amongst ourselves about how to settle the metaphysical score. Against those who insist on maintaining the faith—of returning to Enlightenment optimism, the only remaining choice seems to be a default assumption that the loss of certainty necessitates the loss of truth altogether. Against this willful demythologization, a third option is possible. One can still uphold the historical legacy of the community and institution within which we operate. This time, however, this legacy must be formulated not as a commitment to a notion of truth as certainty, but rather to the possibility of constructing valid forms of truth.

It is toward this end that I have imagined my comparison of Buddhist philosophical discourse in the fiction of *KUM*. In full agreement with J. Z. Smith, I have imagined this religious tradition in order to serve the agenda of my present place and time. The fulfillment of this goal requires that I go beyond my examination of fiction as a *way* of philosophizing, that is, epistemologically, to looking at it *as* a philosophy, an ontology. As a respite from all the doubts cited above, Wendy Doniger O'Flaherty offers relief in the declaration that "Taking other peoples' myths seriously ultimately means recognizing that they are *our* myths, which means not only that they have a general meaning for us but that they narrate the stories of our own lives."[12] I believe that the Buddhist philosophy of illusion can narrate the story of our own scholarly activities, dignifying them in a way that we ourselves and the Western intellectual heritage have become too paralyzed to do.

The Redemption of Ontology

The task of revalorizing the truth enterprise requires a direct consideration of the nature of truth itself. In order to proceed with a comparative examination of this question, let us briefly revisit the Asian Buddhist setting. Here we see that the question of truth is best bracketed by the question of the nature of creation.

In our discussion of the rise of fiction in China, we adhered to the thesis that fiction represented a cultural turning point in which the creative imagination was liberated and extolled. This occurred against a background of Confucian literary practices, which, according to Victor Mair, were "so highly rationalistic in [their] . . . orientation and political in [their] . . . purpose that the utility of pure imagination (i.e., illusion) could not be accepted."[13] Mair includes the writings of Laozi in this assessment, despite that philosopher's reputation as a mystic. A close reading of the *Daodejing*, Mair points out, reveals the relentlessness of Laozi's political agenda. The only exception that Mair is willing to grant is to Zhuangzi, following A. C. Graham's insistence that he is not a philosopher but rather an anti-rationalist. Both note Zhuangzi's fanciful use of characters (often of the animal persuasion) and his construction of narrative and poetic forms of discourse. Mair contends that had Zhuangzi not been such a minority voice, he "might have served as the philosophical basis for the development of a Chinese theatre."[14]

As history would have it, it took the onslaught of Buddhism and Buddhist forms of discourse before the imaginative literary arts could take firm hold in China. The controversial boldness of this thesis must not allow us to overlook the most critical aspect of Mair's position. For my purposes, the central aspect of Mair's scenario about the rise of fiction in any culture is that the self-conscious participation in the literary imagination must be accompanied by a theory of creation in general. He assumes that there is a corollary between the way a culture views literary and cosmological production; that they are both included in a single theory of creation. To wit, the "literary and artistic *imagination* are intimately related to the ontological problem of *creation*."[15]

Although half of Mair's thesis is that Buddhist-derived narratives provided the materials out of which Chinese fiction arose, the other half of his effort, the half most pertinent to this study, is his contention that the Buddhist (and Indian) philosophy of illusion provides an ontological justification of fiction. Fictive literary practices, in other words, are backed by a full philosophical accounting. Beginning with the belief that the whole universe is an imaginative creation (*māyā*) brought into being by magic, transformation, play, and, importantly, the power of words, it is easy to see that fiction and drama are but "localized intensifications" of this same reality.

For Mair, the vital link between literature and ontology was created through theater. In his study of the picture-storytelling traditions of India and South Asia, which he believes formed the genesis of Chinese storytelling practices, Mair offers historical evidence of links between expository tale traditions (*pinghua*), and early religious practices.[16] Mair relies on E. T. Kirby's thesis that theater and drama were founded upon shamanistic practices which sought the manifestation of supernatural presences.[17] This presence is direct rather than symbolic. Thus each performance is more akin to a religious ritual in the sense that it seeks to establish a sacred space and moment, rather than a mimetic representation of events. To Mair, the sacred nature of narrative performance is intrinsic, for "[t]he natural corollary of attempts to *manifest* spiritual presence is the effort to *represent* it artistically or theatrically."[18]

In a sense, my study of *KUM* is an attempt to demonstrate Mair's ontological thesis. Specifically, I have suggested Sŏp'o's own awareness of the convergence of literary and cosmological creation in his use of fiction. The narrative of *KUM* exhibits its awareness of the ontological creativity of fiction through its theme that all of life is an illusory creation. This lesson's weak point is perhaps the emotional prejudices that we are apt to hold against this kind of reality, a reality that shifts and transforms like the illusions of a conjurer. These are the same prejudices that have been responsible for the decline of our own Enlightenment optimism. Our pursuit of truth and even the truth of others has been deflated by the suspicion that scholars can only generate a succession of timely paradigms of reality, but never really attain to Plato's "real above."

It is indeed striking to note the similarities between the Buddhist ontology of illusion, and the perceived crisis in our modern humanity's search for cultural reality. There is, however, a whopping *difference* between the two scenarios; and this difference appears at the level of ontological attitude. The Buddhist/Taoist sectors of East Asian culture have long appreciated the empowering value of transformative reality. They have believed that an ability to embrace this reality without imposing one's own will on it could confer enlightenment and immortality. *Our* modern prejudice against this reality is voiced clearly, however, through the magician of the *Liezi* addressing King Mu: "Your Majesty feels at home with the permanent, is suspicious of the sudden and temporary."[19]

The preference for the eternal is but a symptom of some peculiar views about reality. Contrary to our general understanding that this ontology has been discredited, its legacy still haunts us, phantom-like but unrelenting in its grasp. In the field of comparative studies, the legacy has been refracted into a doubt concerning the whole enterprise. It suggests that since we are incapable of seeing ourselves in a manner that is above ourselves, that we are also unable to understand others precisely because we are outside of their historicity. We are doubly limited as insiders who cannot get out, and as outsiders who cannot get in. The latter situation is personified by the comparativist who fears that as an outsider, a foreigner to the matrix of culture that is his object, he is incapable of representing or even understanding that self-sufficient and exotic entity.

The inconsistencies of what Stephen Toulmin has called the "myth of systems"—the relativist belief in autonomous, self-contained cultural units which share no bridgeheads of human commonality[20]—invites much philosophical scrutiny and opposition. What I wish to point out, however, is the extent to which the relativist's position still embodies the prejudice for the eternal despite its ostensible stance against it. To counter our growing historical consciousness with the claim that our lack of universal cultural truths means that we are trapped within cultural systems is to submit to a zero-sum game in which the old rules still dominate. Similarly, to feel threatened by Jonathan Z. Smith's revelation to scholars of religion that religion is an internal, self-made category is to reveal our own inability to let go fully of certain ontological prejudices long after we have renounced our faith in them.

Undoubtedly the biggest reason for our own inconsistencies stems from the fact that we have not yet moved out of our deconstructive phase. There is a considerable amount of energy that is required for implementing such turning points; but what is more significant is the fact that that energy must be generated from somewhere specific. I propose that it can only come from the imagining of comparisons; specifically, the examination of other ontologies and other literary examples which can be borrowed and internalized to constitute ourselves, in the same manner that Sŏp'o used various indigenized themes to constitute himself.

The ontology that is spoken for in *KUM* is one that embraces the processual and transformative nature of reality not only as a truth but as a situation full of potential. Taoists believed that if one studied the forces of nature, one could, like Laochengzi, "appear and disappear at will and turn around and exchange the four seasons, call up thunder in winter, create ice in summer, make flying things run and running things fly."[21] The larger point here is that the development of Buddhist ontological discourse squarely confronts us with a metaphor for the philosophical and hermeneutical dilemmas that we imagine we presently face. The crux of our problem does not lie in exactly the same place, but this is what renders the Buddhist case so instructive. The history of Buddhist concerns that I have traced out deals with how Buddhist discourse sought to justify itself in light of its own ontological assumptions. This was a primarily metapractical problem. The answer, I have proposed, was finally derived from the ontology itself, which valorizes all creation—even fictive ones—as valid. In our case, we continue our discourses unabated but lack an ontology to justify them. This is a metaphysical problem. The answer that I propose is that the needed ontology can be derived from the same one which validates the practices of Buddhist discourse. This ontology can affirm for us the fact that although our truths may be momentary and even fictive creations, they serve a mandatory function—the creation, rather than the mirroring, of a reality that will continue to transform and require redefinition.

The viability of this option is made clear by some of the incipient reconstructive thrusts that have already been made in the academic setting. Charles Taylor, who draws much from the hermeneutical efforts of Hans Georg Gadamer, talks about arriving at a de facto form of universality (the dream of philosophers) through the ideal of historical inclusiveness:

> The only possible ideal of objectivity in this domain is that of inclusiveness. The inclusive perspective is never attained

de jure. You only get there *de facto*, when everybody is on board. And even then the perspective is in principle limited in relation to another possible understanding which might have arisen. But all this doesn't mean that there is no gain, no overcoming of ethnocentrism. On the contrary; it is overcome in inclusiveness.[22]

The most important aspect of Taylor's statement is his move to reject the specter of two opposed realities—the human and the absolute—just as the Buddhist ontology of illusion invalidates the distinction between illusion and reality.[23] Taylor also confirms that within the historically determined contours that shape and make up our experience of the world, a "universal" perspective can be crafted by a careful representation and rigorous inclusiveness of those involved. This is an argument for the possibility of a new ideal of objectivity. But most importantly, by asserting the de facto, rather than de jure, nature of this universal understanding, Taylor assumes the necessity and inevitability of constantly renewing and advancing the process. This kind of universal understanding is one that requires ongoing readings and conversation as new participants are included; of reformulations which we can nevertheless affirm as universal for the moment and for the immediate purposes at hand.

Taylor's prescriptions exemplify our developing affirmation of the creative and ongoingly constitutive nature of all understanding. To backtrack, momentarily, to cultural relativism, my own disavowal of this position is not based on closely reasoned philosophical refutations but on a simple rejection of the inside view of the myth of cultural systems. Many have already focused on the fallacy that people outside of a cultural system are incapable of gaining entry. I reject the myth on the basis of its assumption that all those on the inside understand each other perfectly. Anyone who has struggled to overcome uncertainty in his or her most intimate relationships—including that with oneself—will recognize how deluded this perception is. Despite our relentless yearning to transcend the ambiguity of circumstances, to triumph over life rather than playing victim to it, the true art of living consists in perceptive equilibrium—a state

Martha Nussbaum describes " . . . in which concrete perceptions 'hang beautifully together,' both with one another and with the agent's general principles; an equilibrium that is always ready to reconstitute itself in response to the new."[24] The attempt to engender an equilibrium that is valid for all beings at all times is counterintuitive to this art of living. Hence nothing essential is lost by the impossibility of the static ideal of knowledge. The constitutive and creative acts behind all understanding are the same acts that substantiate our own realities and our own perceptions of ourselves.

To draw the analogy between the creation of fiction and the practices of ourselves as scholars to an explicit close, we may apply a central lesson taught by Buddhism. That lesson is that life may be an illusion, but it is illusion itself which makes life, meaning, and even deliverance, ultimately possible. I have chosen to call attention to this lesson in order to demonstrate Wendy Doniger O'Flaherty's assertion that there are scholarly ways of using other peoples' myths. The homely adage that life is but an illusion can be ontologically filled in to reveal, in O'Flaherty's most quotable words, that "The myth that we thought was just a window [into the other] turns out to be a mirror too."[25] Consequently, we find ourselves beholden to our primary text in a way that most academic studies of this kind attempt to skirt: Given the parallelism of the ontology of *KUM* and our emerging understanding of ourselves, we must indeed consider Sŏp'o's question of whether we are awake or whether we are also dreaming.

Notes

Foreword

1. See Hossein Ziai's "Beyond Philosophy: Suhrawardi's Illuminationist Path to Wisdom," in *Myth and Philosophy*, ed. Frank Reynolds and David Tracy (State University of New York Press, 1990), 215–243; Lee Yearley's *Mencius and Aquinas* (State University of New York Press, 1990); and Bantly's own "Buddhist Philosophy in the Art of Fiction," in *Discourse and Practice*, ed. Frank Reynolds and David Tracy (State University of New York Press, 1992), 83–107.

2. David Tracy, "On the Origins of Philosophy of Religion: The Need for a New Narrative of Its Founding," in *Myth and Philosophy*, ed. Frank Reynolds and David Tracy (State University of New York Press, 1990), 17.

3. See Martha Nussbaum, *Love's Knowledge: Essays on Philosophy and Literature* (New York: Oxford University Press, 1990); and Michael Riffaterre, *Fictional Truth* (Baltimore: Johns Hopkins University Press, 1990).

4. See Philip L. Quinn, "On Demythologizing Evil," in *Discourse and Practice*, 111–140. Full citation in footnote 1.

Chapter 1. Illusion and Imagination

1. Lee Yearley, *Mencius and Aquinas: Theories of Virtue and Conceptions of Courage* (Albany: State University of New York Press, 1990).

2. Ibid., 198.

3. Ibid., 197.

4. The title rendered by James Gale's translation is *The Cloud Dream of the Nine* (London: Small, Maynard & Company, 1922). The title of Richard Rutt's more recent translation is *A Nine Cloud Dream*, and appears in the volume *Virtuous Women: Three Classic Korean Novels*, trans. Richard Rutt and Kim Chong-un (Seoul: Royal Asiatic Society, 1974). My purpose in offering yet another variation on the English title is to bring this text explicitly into the tradition of Chinese and Korean tales with titles ending with the character for "dream" (Chinese: *meng*; Korean: *mong*). Because of the greater familiarity in the West with the Chinese classic *Hongloumeng*, which is rendered as *Dream of the Red Chamber* (with the variant title *Story of the Stone*), I will maintain this semantic convention in the translation of the Korean novel. The point here is more than to maintain stylistic consistency. The invocation of dreams in the title of these tales refers to philosophical viewpoints which also form a consistent association.

5. See Daniel Bouchez, "Buddhism and Neo-Confucianism in Kim Manjung's *Random Essays (Sŏp'o manp'il)*," in *The Rise of Neo-Confucianism in Korea*, ed. William Theodore de Bary and JaHyun Kim Haboush (New York: Columbia University Press, 1985), 445–72.

6. See Richard Robinson, *Early Mādhyamika in India and China* (Madison: University of Wisconsin, 1969) for an account of the problems of philosophical translation between India and China in the early period of Buddhist transmission, especially as centered around the efforts of Kumārajīva (344–413).

7. Nussbaum's thoughts on this matter are conveniently collected in the volume of essays under the title, *Love's Knowledge: Essays on Philosophy and Literature* (New York: Oxford University Press, 1990). Also of relevance is her title *The Fragility of Goodness: Luck and Ethics in Greek Tragedy and Philosophy* (Cambridge: Cambridge University Press, 1986).

8. Philip L. Quinn, "Tragic Dilemmas, Suffering Love, and Christian Life," *Journal of Religious Ethics* 17, no. 1 (Spring 1989): 151.

9. Nussbaum, "Fictions of the Soul," in *Love's Knowledge*, 255.

10. Ibid., 259.

11. Ibid., 258.

12. See Nussbaum's thoughts on transcendence in "Transcending Humanity," *Love's Knowledge*, 365–92.

13. Chung Chong-wha, "The Korean Classical Fiction and the Romance," in *Korean Classical Literature* (London: Kegan Paul International, 1989), 8.

14. Quinn, "Tragic Dilemmas," 182.

15. Robert E. Buswell, *Formation of Ch'an Ideology in China and Korea* (Princeton: Princeton University Press, 1989), 20.

16. See the body of evidence as given by Daniel Bouchez in "Le romain Namjŏng ki et l'affaire de la reine Min," *Journal asiatique* 264 (1976): 405–51. Bouchez is the only Western scholar that I know of who has focused on the works of Kim Manjung, particularly the present novel, which he renders as *Namjŏng Ki*.

17. For a discussion of this issue, see Richard Rutt's introduction in his translation of the novel that I cite in footnote 4.

18. See Andrew Plaks, "Towards a Critical Theory of Chinese Narrative," *Chinese Narrative: Critical and Theoretical Essays*, ed. Andrew H. Plaks (Princeton: Princeton University Press, 1977), 309–52.

19. I have made use of this aspect of Plaks' work in my article, "Buddhist Philosophy in the Art of Fiction" in *Discourse and Practice*, ed. Frank Reynolds and David Tracy (Albany: State University of New York Press, 1992), 83–107. For Andrew Plaks' discussion of allegories, see chapter five, "Allegory in Chinese and Western Literature" in *Archetype and Allegory in the Dream of the Red Chamber* (Princeton: Princeton University Press, 1976), 84–126. See also chapter three of the same title, "Complementary Bipolarity and Multiple Periodicity," 43–53, for his discussion of Yin/Yang and Five Phases theory.

20. Plaks, "Towards a Critical Theory of Chinese Narrative," 350.

21. Plaks, *Archetype and Allegory*, 223.

22. Plaks, "Towards a Critical Theory of Chinese Narrative," 349.

23. Francisca Cho Bantly, "Myth and Cosmology in *The Book of Poetry*" in *Myths and Fictions*, ed. Shlomo Biderman and Ben-ami Scharfstein (Leiden: Brill, 1993).

24. Anthony C. Yu, "The Quest of Brother Amor: Buddhist Intimations in the *Story of the Stone*," *Harvard Journal of Asiatic Studies* 49, no. 1 (June 1989): 55–92.

25. See Andrew Plaks' explicit justification of this choice in *Four Masterworks of the Ming Novel: Ssu ta ch'i-shu* (Princeton: Princeton University Press, 1987), 240–42.

26. Francisca Cho Bantly, "Buddhist Allegory in the *Journey to the West*" in *The Journal of Asian Studies* 48, no. 3 (August 1989): 512–24.

208	EMBRACING ILLUSION

27. The Ming dynasty monks Yunqi Zhuhong (1536–1615), Lin Zhaoen (1517–1598), and Hanshan Deqing (1546–1623) have received particular attention as leaders of Buddhist reform and syncretist movements. See Sung-peng Hsu, *A Buddhist Leader in Ming China* (University Park: Pennsylvania State University Press, 1979); Chun-fang Yu, *The Renewal of Buddhism in China* (New York: Columbia University Press, 1981); and Judith Berling, *The Syncretic Religion of Lin Chao-en* (New York: Columbia University Press, 1980).

On the Korean scene, the most prominent monk of the age, Sŏsan Hyujŏng (1520–1604), also espoused the unity of Buddhist teachings and its overall harmony with Confucianism and Taoism. Sŏsan is briefly discussed in Stephen Bachelor's introduction to Kusan Sunim's *The Way of Korean Zen* (New York: Weatherhill, 1985), 25–26.

28. Quite pertinent to the function of *The Awakening of Faith*, which is probably of Chinese composition, are Robert Buswell's comments on apocryphal Buddhist texts and their importance in the creation of a substantive, indigenous East Asian Buddhist tradition. See *Formation of Ch'an Ideology*, 14–19.

For a recent account of Chinese scholasticism in its use of *panjiao* classification in conjunction with the development of a specific East Asian Buddhist ontology and soteriology, see Peter Gregory's *Tsung-mi and the Sinification of Buddhism* (Princeton: Princeton University Press, 1991).

29. This term is taken from Kim Yŏngt'ae's study and refers primarily to the tradition and practices established by the monk Hyujŏng (1520–1604) which became normative for the dynasty. See "Chosŏn sidae ŭi pulgyo," in *Han'guk pulgyosa kaesŏl* (Seoul: Purok Han'guk Chongp'asa, 1986).

30. Stephen Teiser, *The Ghost Festival in Medieval China* (Princeton: Princeton University Press, 1988), 223.

31. James Huntley Grayson, *Korea: A Religious History* (New York: Oxford University Press, 1989), 154.

32. See John B. Duncan, "The Social Background to the Founding of the Chosŏn Dyansty: Change or Continuity?" *Journal of Korean Studies* 6 (1988–89). His conclusions are substantively confirmed by Martina Deuchler in *The Confucian Transformation of Korea: A Study of Society and Ideology* (Cambridge: Harvard University Press, 1992), 98.

33. The basic thrust of these criticisms were that Buddhist temples and monks posed an economic drain on the state due to their tax- and labor-exempt status; and that Buddhism's otherworldly orientation was detrimental to the creation of a moral society. See Deuchler, *The Confucian Transformation*, 89–128, for a detailed discussion.

34. For a good survey of the social and educational background of late Chosŏn dynasty monks, see Yi Kiyŏng, "Chosŏn sidae ŭi pulgyo," in *Han'guk ŭi pulgyo*, 159–219. A common thread that seems to run throughout the biographies of these monks is the death of one or both parents while still at a very young age. It can perhaps be surmised that such a traumatic event naturally persuaded the orphan to pursue a life of religious contemplation. It is perhaps more instructive, however, to consider this career route a standard social option for people in this predicament, contributing in turn to the repetitive, archetypal quality of the monastic biographies.

35. Quoted in Yu Pyŏnghwan's "Kuunmong ŭi pulgyo sasangŏjk yon'gu rŭl wihan chiban" [Foundations for research on the Buddhist thought of *Kuunmong*], in *Ch'oesin kungmunhak charyo nonmunjip (sokp'yŏn): Kojŏn munhak (sanmunp'yŏn)* (Seoul: Taejegak, 1990), 472.

Although the title of this article indicates *KUM* as its main object of concern, much of its time is devoted to an examination of *Sŏp'o manp'il* as an explicit source of Kim Manjung's Buddhist thought.

36. Ibid. Yu Pyŏnghwan's general argument is that the Buddhist concepts that are given literary representation in *KUM* are given theoretical form in the *Random Essays*. Much of his study consists of rendering point-for-point correlations between the two texts.

Sŏl Sŏnggyŏng also refers to Kim Manjung's use of the *Śūrangama* and contends that *KUM* tells the story of the personal mind experience of the young novice monk. The dream or incarnation is really a meditation journey which teaches the unity of all realities—waking, dream, dreams within the dream—as states of consciousness.

The corrolation between Buddhist theory and literary product is so explicit, according to Sŏl, that even the protagonist's name is taken from the *Śūrangama*. The novice monk is known as Xingzhen, composed of the two Chinese characters for "original nature." Although the concept of "original nature" is fundamental and pervasive in Chan/Sŏn Buddhism, Sŏl claims that Kim Manjung took it directly from the line in the *Śūrangama* which states, "Original nature is perfectly bright; all is tathāgatagarbha. Originally there is no birth, no extinction."

See the discussion of *KUM* in Sŏl Sŏnggyŏng, *Han'guk kojŏn sosŏl ŭi ponjil* [The essence of the Korean Classic Novel] (Seoul: Kukhak Charyown, 1991), 116–25.

37. Yu Pyŏnghwan, "Kuunmong ŭi pulgyo," 468–69.

38. Daniel Bouchez credits the overt Buddhist sympathies of the *Sŏp'o manp'il* as the reason why the text was never printed, despite the author's

posthumous fame. The scholarly legacy is that studies of this source have been thin, rarely going beyond random quotations, or more recently, article-length examinations such as Yu Pyŏnghwan's work referenced above and Bouchez's "Buddhism and Neo-Confucianism." This latter work is particularly useful in giving a summary of the text, although, as Bouchez himself points out, a comprehensive analysis of the text has yet to be made.

39. Yu Pyŏnghwan, "Kuunmong ŭi pulgyo," 479–80.

40. Bouchez takes up the question of dating the Sŏp'o manp'il, and concludes that it is of late date in Kim Manjung's life—most probably during his last exile between 1689 and his death in 1692. See Bouchez, "Buddhism and Neo-Confucianism," 465–466.

The dating of KUM poses an interesting question vis à vis its relationship to Sŏp'o manp'il. The consensus is that KUM was composed during the 1687 exile to Sŏnch'ŏn, which potentially puts the novel chronologically ahead of the collected essays. The dating of these works is an inexact science, however, and it suffices for the purposes of this study to put both sources at the end of Kim Manjung's life, when he was preoccupied with the task of reflection.

41. Bouchez, "Buddhism and Neo-Confucianism," 450.

42. Hong Kisam, "Han'guk pulgyo munhaknon" [Korean Buddhist literature], in Ch'oesin kungmunhak charyo nonmunjip (sokp'yŏn): Hyŏndae munhak (sanmun p'yŏn) (Seoul: Taejegak, 1990).

43. Bouchez, "Buddhism and Neo-Confucianism," 453.

44. Hong Kisam espouses the view that the term "Buddhist literature" should encompass all of the creative letters of Korea, including popular and mythical traditions that have no overt Buddhist elements. He includes the myth of Tangun, adapted in the Koryŏ dynasty as the founding myth of the Korean people, as an example of this broad interpretation of Buddhist literature. See Hong, "Han'guk pulgyo munhaknon" 723–25. Victor Mair contends that Buddhism was a dominant force in the rise of the vernacular as a significant literary medium in Korea. See "Buddhism and the Rise of Written Vernacular," in Journal of Asian Studies 53, no. 3 (August 1994): 707–51.

45. From Sŏnga kwigam [Mirror for meditation students], translated in Peter Lee, Sourcebook of Korean Civilization (New York: Columbia University Press, 1993), 662.

46. Edward Conze, Buddhist Meditation (New York: Harper & Row, 1969), 23.

47. The *Samguk Yusa*, which translates roughly as "the legends and anecdotes of the Three Kingdoms," was compiled in the Koryŏ dynasty and, along with the *Samguk Sagi* ("History of the Three Kingdoms"), represents the earliest surviving chronicles of early Korean culture. The *Samguk Sagi*, written by Kim Pusik in the twelfth century, is modeled on Chinese dynastic histories.

The *Samguk Yusa* exhibits much less interpretive overlay, confirming the belief that Iryŏn compiled the book at his leisure rather than under official sanction. Together, the *Samguk Yusa* and *Samguk Sagi* provide the oldest surviving examples of Korean narratives. A translation of the former has been offered by Ha Tae-Hung and Grafton K. Mintz under the title, *Samguk Yusa: Legends and History of the Three Kingdoms of Ancient Korea* (Seoul: Yonsei University Press, 1972).

48. Ibid., 250.

49. Araki Kengo, "Confucianism and Buddhism in the Late Ming," in *The Unfolding of Neo-Confucianism*, ed. William Theodore de Bary (New York: Columbia University Press, 1975), 56.

50. Plaks, "Towards a Critical Theory of Chinese Narrative," 348.

51. For a general introduction into Tambiah's methodology, see the introductory chapters of his works such as *Buddhism and the Spirit Cults in Northeast Thailand* (Cambridge: Cambridge University Press, 1970); *World Conqueror and World Renouncer* (Cambridge: Cambridge University Press, 1976); and *The Buddhist Saints of the Forest and the Cult of Amulets* (Cambridge: Cambridge University Press, 1984).

52. Tambiah, *Spirit Cults in Northeast Thailand*, 4.

53. Ibid.

54. Thomas Carlyle, *On Heroes, Hero-Worship and the Heroic in History*, The World's Classics, no. 62 (London: Oxford University Press, 1904), 1–2.

55. Quinn, "Tragic Dilemmas," 151.

Chapter 2. Narratives and the Autobiographical Process

1. See Peter Lee, *Korean Literature: Topics and Themes* (Tucson: University of Arizona Press, 1965).

2. W. E. Skillend, "Nineteenth Century Books with Stories in Korean," in *Korean Classical Literature*, ed. Chung Chong-wha (London: Kegan Paul International, 1989), 105.

3. Lee, *Korean Literature*, 71.

4. See Hwang P'aegang, "Kososŏl ŭi kaenyŏm" [The concept of the classic novel], in *Han'guk kososŏllon* (Seoul: Asea Munhwasa, 1991).

5. Uchida Michio, "Tōdai shōsetsu no okeru yume to gensetsu" [Dreams and illusion in Tang tales], *Shūkan Tōyōgaku* (May 1959): 11–12.

6. Kenneth DeWoskin, "The Six Dynasties *Chih-Kuai* and the Birth of Fiction," in *Chinese Narrative: Critical and Theoretical Essays*, ed. Andrew H. Plaks (Princeton: Princeton University Press, 1977), 22.

7. Victor Mair, "The Narrative Revolution in Chinese Literature: Ontological Presuppositions," *Chinese Literature: Essays, Articles, Reviews* 5 (July 1983): 1–27.

8. Sheldon Hsiao-peng Lu offers a succinct and focused study of the Chinese views of history and fiction in *From Historicity to Fictionality* (Stanford: Stanford University Press, 1994). See in particular chapters 3 and 4 for his discussion of the Chinese ontological presuppositions concerning the meaning of historical narrative.

9. Pei-yi Wu states that the division between *shi* and *wen*, which he describes as a division between the public and objective, and the private and subjective, respectively, "was consistently maintained in China." (*The Confucian's Progress: Autobiographical Writings in Traditional China* [Princeton: Princeton University Press, 1990], 6.)

10. Plaks, "Towards a Critical Theory of Chinese Narrative," 318.

11. DeWoskin, "The Six Dynasties *Chih-Kuai*," 51.

12. Certainly the persistence of the prestige of history was the main reason authors of fiction attempted to cloak their works in its aura. Y. W. Ma gives further explanation of this phenomenon within the Tang tales, stating that they were primarily written by examination candidates who sought attention but shunned open flirtation with literary creativity: "But if they could demonstrate their narratives as historically true and ethically exemplary, these 'factual reports' might be able to work in their favor. In a word, T'ang story writers had their eyes on the realistic rewards to their exploration of fantasy." ("Fact and Fantasy in T'ang Tales," *Chinese Literature: Essays, Articles, Reviews*, 2 [1980]: 180).

13. Anthony C. Yu, "History, Fiction, and the Reading of Chinese Narrative," *Chinese Literature: Essays, Articles, Reviews* 10 (1988): 6.

14. Sŏp'o, which literally means "Western port," was Kim Manjung's literary name. I will use this designation from here on.

15. See the discussion by Karl Weintraub in *The Value of the Individual: Self and Circumstance in Autobiography* (Chicago: University of Chicago Press, 1978), xi–xix.

16. Ibid., xv.

17. Weintraub makes a very similar point about ancient Greece. The basic social and economic unit formed by the family (which resulted in strong kinship ties), and the civic demands necessary for upholding the polis, were factors that retarded the development of autobiography as understood in the modern sense. See ibid., 1–17.

18. Robert Hegel, "An Exploration of the Chinese Literary Self," in *Expressions of Self in Chinese Literature* (New York: Columbia University Press, 1985), 6.

19. Pei-yi Wu, *The Confucian's Progress*, 84.

20. See Patricia Spacks, *Imagining a Self* (Cambridge: Harvard University Press, 1976), 18.

21. Martin Huang asserts that in China, the autobiographical sensibility definitively moved from formal biographical writings to fiction in the eighteenth century. Citing the political repressiveness of the Qing dynasty and the increasing complexity of literati identity, Huang suggests that the mask of a "fictional other" was the only means for individuals to critique conventional Confucian roles and create alternative options. See *Literati and Self-Re/Presentation* (Standford: Stanford University Press, 1995).

22. There is no Western-language translation of this novel. Daniel Bouchez reports that there are two works of this title—a xylograph in Korean, and a manuscript in Chinese, both of which are conserved in Paris. Several Korean editions of the novel have been published in Korea, mostly in the late fifties and sixties, but little information is given on which version they follow.

I will be following the Chinese version that appears in the *Hanguo Hanwen Xiaoshuo Quanji* series, volume 7, pp. 3–62, hereafter cited as *NJG*.

23. For an account of neo-Confucianism and the establishment of the Chosŏn dynasty, see Chai-sik Chung's "Chŏng Tojŏn: 'Architect' of the Yi Dynasty Government and Ideology" in *The Rise of Neo-Confucianism in Korea*, ed. William Theodore de Bary and JaHyun Kim Haboush (New York: Columbia University Press, 1985), 59–88.

214 EMBRACING ILLUSION

24. See JaHyun Kim Haboush, "The Education of the Crown Prince: A Study in Confucian Pedagogy" for a history of the Royal Lecture, which was an official body which sought to educate the king in Confucian concepts of the benevolent ruler. Haboush also deals with the politicization of this body. In *The Rise of Neo-Confucianism in Korea*, cited above, 161–222.

25. The work of John Duncan argues against the commonly accepted thesis that the establishment of the Chosŏn dynasty entailed the revolutionary rise of a whole new class of political elites. What Duncan demonstrates instead is that the majority of the leading clans of the Koryŏ continued their prominent positions in the Chosŏn as well. The establishment of the Chosŏn dynasty simply added to the swelling ranks of the Yangban; specifically eight new clans are accounted for in Duncan's study, four of which were military in origin. See Duncan, "Social Background to the Founding of the Chosŏn Dynasty".

26. For an account of the so-called "literati purges," see Edward Wagner, *The Literati Purges: Political Conflict in Early Yi Korea* (Cambridge: Harvard University Press, 1974).

27. Korea departed from the example of Chinese institutions with this practice. Primogeniture was strictly observed, and the denial of political opportunity to secondary sons was fiercely upheld as necessary to maintain social distinctions and ultimately, social order. For an excellent study of this situation, see Martina Deuchler, " 'Heaven Does Not Discriminate': A Study of Secondary Sons in Chosŏn Korea," *Journal of Korean Studies* 6 (1988–89); 121–64.

28. Fujiya Kawashima has conducted a series of studies on the *hyangan*, or "local gentry association," of Chosŏn Korea. He states that the impetus for the organization was fueled by the " . . . ever growing number of degree-less and unemployed yangban who sought to preserve their status on the local level." See Kawashima, "The Local Gentry Association in Mid-Yi Dynasty Korea: A Preliminary Study of the Ch'angnyŏng Hyangan, 1600–1838," *Journal of Korean Studies* 2 (1980); 123.

29. Tradition has it that *KUM* was written during Sŏp'o's third exile in 1687 to Sŏnch'ŏn. This claim has been confirmed by So Chaeyŏng, based on the discovery of the text known as *Sŏp'o Yŏnbo* (Annals of Sŏp'o) at Tenri University in Japan. See "Kososŏl palttalsa" [Development of the classical novel], in *Han'guk Kososŏllon* (Seoul: Asea Munhwasa, 1991), 37.

Daniel Bouchez states that *NJG* was written between 1689 and 1692, the years of Sŏp'o's last exile. (*Tradition, traduction et interpretation d'un roman coréen: Le Namjŏng ki* [Paris: Collège de France, 1984], 9.)

30. This is my translation of Bouchez's French rendering of the original. "Le roman coréen Nam-jŏng ki, et l'affaire de la reine min," in Journal Asiatique 264(1976), 407.

31. The gap between history and fiction was perhaps most understandably bridged by historical fiction and romances such as Romance of the Three Kingdoms and The Water Margin. The value of these novels were vindicated precisely by their closeness to history. See Li Zhi (1527–1602) and Yuan Hongdao's (1568–1610) assessments of Shuihuzhuan and Jinpingmei, respectively, in Chou Chih-p'ing's Yuan Hung-tao and the Kung-an School (Cambridge: Cambridge University Press, 1988), 25–26 and 54–60.

32. A translation of this novel, by Kim Chong-un, appears in Virtuous Women: Three Classic Korean Novels (Seoul: Royal Asiatic Society, 1974) with a brief introduction.

33. Chou Chih-p'ing, The Kung-an School, 57.

34. Bouchez, "Le roman coréen Nam-jŏng ki," 431.

35. Bouchez, "Buddhism and Confucianism," 446.

36. The Lisao is contained in an anthology of poems, many of which are attributed to Qu Yuan, known as Chu Ci, or The Songs of the South. A translation of this anthology, along with an informative introduction, is offered by David Hawkes, The Songs of the South (Harmondsworth: Penguin, 1985).

37. Ibid., 69.

38. Bouchez, "Le roman coréen Nam-jŏng ki," 434.

39. NJG, 32.

40. NJG, 34.

41. Hawkes, Songs of the South, 72.

42. Bouchez, "Le roman coréen Nam-jŏng ki," 433.

43. Anthology of Korean Literature: From Early Times to the Nineteenth Century, compiled and edited by Peter H. Lee (Honolulu: University of Hawaii Press, 1981), 110.

44. See Daniel Bouchez, "Les propos de Kim Ch'un-T'aek sur le Nam-jŏng ki," Melanges de coreanologie offerts à M. Charles Haguenauer (Paris: Collège de France, 1979), 1–43.

45. Bouchez conducts a detailed examination of the extant manuscripts of NGJ in order to determine their genealogical descent vis à vis each other and

to settle upon the closest facsimile of Sŏp'o's original text. In *Tradition, traduction et interpretation d'un roman coréen: Le Namjŏng ki.*

46. Ibid., 234.

47. Ibid., 233.

48. Ibid., 225.

49. Ibid., 226.

50. An examination of the trends in late Ming literary theory and practice which support Pei-yi Wu's thesis about the convergence between fiction and autobiography falls outside of the purview of this study. Emerging scholarship on the Gongan literary school of the late Ming, however, offers much supportive insight on this period's push toward individual expressions of self and emotion through literature. Chih-p'ing Chou's title, *Yuan Hung-tao and the Kung-an School,* offers a helpful introduction along with an extensive bibliography of recent studies.

51. This translation is taken from David Hawkes' introduction in *Songs of the South,* 55–56.

52. This is taken from David Hawkes' introduction to an earlier edition of *Ch'u Tz'u: The Songs of the South* (Oxford: Clarendon Press, 1959), 17.

53. See for example, Patrick Hanan, "Fiction of Moral Duty: The Vernacular Story in the 1640s," in *Expressions of Self in Chinese Literature* (New York: Columbia University Press, 1985); and Robert Hegel, *The Novel in Seventeenth Century China* (New York: Columbia University Press, 1981).

54. Arthur Waley, trans. *Chinese Poems* (London: George Allen and Unwin, Ltd., 1946), 151–52.

55. Daniel Bouchez, "Kim Manjung et le *Sanguo Zhi,*" in *Cahiers d'Études Coréennes: Twenty Papers on Korean Studies Offered to Professor W. E. Skillend* (Paris: Collège de France, 1989), 17.

56. Ibid., 27.

57. Ibid., 26.

58. Joseph S. M. Lau, "Duty, Reputation, and Selfhood in Traditional Chinese Narratives," in *Expressions of Self in Chinese Literature,* ed. Robert E. Hegel and Richard C. Hessney (New York: Columbia University Press, 1985), 367.

59. Paul Ricoeur, *Time and Narrative: Volume One* (Chicago: University of Chicago Press, 1984), 74.

60. Ibid.

Chapter 3. The Symmetry of Illusion and Reality

1. In most instances I will use the 1974 translation of *KUM* by Richard Rutt in *Virtuous Women*, which he entitles *A Nine Cloud Dream* and which will be cited hereafter as *NCD*. For corresponding passages from the original text, I will refer to the text published in *Hanguo Hanwen Xiaoshuo Quanji* [*A compilation of Korean novels written in Chinese*], ed. Lin Ming-teh, vol. 3 (Taibei: Jongguo Wenhua Xueyen), 327–449. This text will hereafter be cited as *KUM*.

   NCD, 24; *KUM*, 333.

2. The song that Shaoyou plays is entitled "The Phoenix Seeks its Mate" (*feng qiu huang*). The renowned poet Sima Xiangru (179–117 B.C.E.) supposedly played this song in order to seduce and marry Zhuo Wenjun (150–115 B.C.E.), a young widow and poet in her own right. The recollection of this story is also repeatedly made in the Yuan drama *The Western Chamber* (*Xixiangji*), which was extremely popular in seventeenth-century Korea. It is not unlikely that Sŏp'o followed the example of the drama in his use of this poetic allusion.

3. *NCD*, 40; *KUM*, 345.

4. *NCD*, 57; *KUM*, 358.

5. *NCD*, 109; *KUM*, 395.

6. *Jiuyunmeng*, ed. Wei Xusheng (Shanshi: Beiyue Wenyi Chubanshe, 1984), 10.

7. Kim Kidong, *Yijo sidae sosŏllon* [Study of the novels of the Yi dynasty] (Chŏngyŏn-sa, 1964), 285.

8. Nussbaum, "Transcending Humanity," *Love's Knowledge*, 390.

9. Chung Chong-wa, "Korean Classical Fiction," 8.

10. *The Tale of Hong Kiltong* is translated in abridged form by Marshall Pihl in Peter Lee's *Anthology of Korean Literature*, 119–47.

11. Many of these tales were unauthored, oral narratives (derived from *pansori* performances), which were much more widely dispersed than a classical novel such as *KUM* as popular entertainment. Some of the more highly regarded tales included *Tale of Sim Ch'ŏng*, *Tale of Hŭngbu*, and perhaps Korea's best-loved story, the *Tale of Ch'unhyang*.

12. Chung Chong-wa, "Korean Classical Fiction," 5.

13. The "talented scholar–beautiful maiden" narratives developed into a popular fictive genre in the seventeenth and eighteenth centuries in China. Robert Hegel characterize them as "genius and beauty romances":

Their characters are wooden, on the whole, with stereotyped features, aspirations, and talents. All the men, and usually the women
too, are brilliant writers; all are extraordinarily attractive. [*The
Novel in Seventeenth Century China*, 173]

The inner dream tale of *KUM* fits into this strain of fictive narratives,
reflecting the popularity of the *chuanqi* in Korea.

14. *The Strange Tales of Liaozhai*, a collection of short stories written by Pu
Songling (1640–1715) in the early Qing dynasty, is one of the better known
examples of stories that continue the *chuanqi* tradition well beyond the Tang
dynasty.

15. See Chung, "Korean Classical Fiction," 7. A translation of one of the *Kŭmo
Sinhwa* tales, "Student Yi Peers Over the Wall" is translated in Peter Lee's
Korean Literature, 79–91.

16. See Robert Hegel's discussion of the criterion of realism as it relates to the
seventeenth century Chinese novel in *The Novel in Seventeenth Century China*,
230–33.

17. Plaks, "Full-length *Hsiao-shuo* and the Western Novel: A Generic Reappraisal," in *China and the West: Comparative Literature Studies*, ed. William
Tay, et al. (Hong Kong: Chinese University Press), 169-70.

18. Plaks points out, for example, that the continuum of epic, romance, and
novel does not adequately describe the Chinese case, which never had an epic
tradition, and whose literary beginnings is more properly traced to historiog-
raphy. Ibid., 164–65.

19. Ibid., 171–73, 175.

20. Lu, *From Historicity to Fictionality*, 9.

21. Ibid., 77–82.

22. Hegel, *The Novel in Seventeenth Century China*, 232.

23. Plaks, "Full-length *Hsiao-shuo*," 172.

24. *KUM*, 446. This is my own translation. Richard Rutt's version of this passage is rather truncated.

25. Hwang offers one of the more sophisticated analyses of the literary structure and religious meaning of *KUM* within Korean scholarship. He overwhelmingly affirms the religious import of the novel, claiming that it is a
"representative instance . . . of a novel which confirms the proposition that

literature is one of the methods of salvation available to humanity." *Chosŏn wangjo sosŏl yŏn'gu,* 228.

26. Plaks, *Archetype and Allegory,* 223.

27. Michel Strickmann, "Dreamwork of Psycho-Sinologists: Doctors, Taoists, Monks," in *Psycho-Sinology: The Universe of Dreams in Chinese Culture,* ed. Carolyn T. Brown (Lanham: University Press of America, 1988), 26.

28. Alex Wayman discusses the dream in India and Tibet in terms of its classification, prophetic uses, and ontology. Wayman's discussion is helpful and forms an interesting comparative context for looking at the professional dream literature of China. (Alex Wayman, "Significance of Dreams in India and Tibet," *History of Religion* 7, no. 1 [August 1967]: 1–12.)

29. Dell Hales, "Dreams and the Daemonic in Traditional Chinese Short Stories," in *Critical Essays on Chinese Literature* (Hong Kong: Chinese University of Hong Kong, 1976), 80.

30. See Choe Samyong's discussion of the use of dreams in Korean narratives in "Sojaeron" [Source materials], in *Han'guk kososŏllon* [Korean classic novel] (Seoul: Asea Munhwasa, 1991), 195–201.

31. See Kim Kwangsun's classifications in "Yuhyŏngnon," [Typologies] in *Han'guk kososŏllon* [Korean classic novel] (Seoul: Asea Munhwasa, 1991), 280–83.

32. David R. Knechtges, "Dream Adventure Stories in Europe and T'ang China," *Tamkang Review* 4, no. 2 (October 1973): 101–19. Knechtges provides summaries of all the European, Islamic, and Chinese tales that he places under his category of the dream adventure tale.

33. From William H. Nienhauser's translation in *Traditional Chinese Stories,* ed. Y. W. Ma and Joseph S. M. Lau (New York: Columbia University Press, 1978), 435–38.

34. The *Taiping Guangji,* which contains "The Pillow of Jiaohu," "The World Inside a Pillow," "The Magistrate of the Southern Branch," and "The Cherry Maid," was introduced to Korea during the Koryŏ dynasty under the reign of King Kojong (1214–1259).

35. A translation of this story is provided by E. D. Edwards in *Chinese Prose Literature* (London: Stephen Austin and Sons, 1938), 206–12.

36. Chang Han-liang conducts a structural analysis (in the manner of Claude Levi-Strauss' approach to mythic story cycles) on "The Pillow of Jiaohu," "The

World Inside a Pillow," "Magistrate of the Southern Branch," and "The Cherry Maid." Using the Six Dynasties "Pillow of Jiaohu" as the original source, the three derivative Tang tales are broken down into stuctural components and analyzed in relation to each other. Chang concludes that the tale cycles conform to Tzvetan Todorov's definition of "gnoseological narrative," which deals primarily with the hero's rite of passage from ignorance to knowledge.

See Chang Han-liang, "The *Yan Lin* Story Series: A Structural Analysis," in *China and the West: Comparative Literature Studies* (Hong Kong: Chinese University Press, 1980): 195–216.

37. "The Dream of Lu Tung Pin," in *The Eight Immortals of Taoism: Legends and Fables of Popular Taoism*, trans. and ed. by Kwok Man Ho and Joanne O'Brien (New York: Meridian, 1990), 72.

38. I am using the Shuen-fu Lin and Larry J. Schulz translation, *The Tower of Myriad Mirrors* (Berkeley: Asian Humanities Press, 1978).

39. See Larry Schulz's "Introduction" in *The Tower of Myriad Mirrors*, 6.

40. Ibid., 183.

41. Ibid., 192.

42. Ibid., 186.

43. Robert Hegel reports that Dong Yue was an "amateur psychologist in the area of dreams." His fascination with dreams is attested by the fact that Dong Yue went to the point of organizing a dream society, as well as writing four prose pieces on the nature of dreams. For a discussion of Dong Yue and *The Tower*, see Hegel, *The Novel in Seventeenth Century China*, 142–66.

44. Ibid., 166.

45. Pak Sŏng'ŭi, *Han'guk kodae sosŏllon kwa sa* [Theses and history of the Korean classic novel] (Seoul: Chimmundang, 1992), 273–81.

46. Sŏl Sŏnggyŏng, *Han'guk kojŏn sosŏl ŭi ponjil*, 98.

47. Chŏng Kyubok traces this theory to the Song scholar Hong Mai (1123–1202) and his book *Rongzhai Suibi* (*Random Notes from the Tolerant Study*). In *Kuunmong yŏn'gu* [Research on *Kuunmong*] (Seoul: Korea University Press, 1974), 334.

48. A. C. Graham, trans. *The Book of Lieh-tzu*, (London: Butler & Tanner, 1960), 63.

49. The *Sūtrālamkāra* has been translated into French by Edouard Huber in *Sūtrālamkāra: Traduit en Francais sur la Version Chinoise de Kumārajīva* (Paris: La Société Asiatique, 1908). The story of Śaranapiku appears on pages 342–55.

50. Edouard Chavannes offers a summary in *Cinq Cents Contes et Apologues: Extraits du Tripitaka Chinois* (Paris: Société Asiatique, 1911), 23.

51. Pei Puxian advances this theory in *Zhongyin Wenxue Guanxi Yanjiu* [Research into the relationship between Chinese and Indian literature] (Taiwan: Xing Funu Xiezuo Xiehui, 1959), 25.

Chŏng Kyubok also strongly adheres to this thesis in *Kuunmong Yŏngu*, 340.

52. Wendy O'Flaherty, *Dreams, Illusion, and Other Realities* (Chicago: University of Chicago Press, 1984), 82.

53. Although it is not my goal to offer textual proof of the continuity between Indian and Chinese dream tales, it is comforting to note the significant Chinese literary scholars who insist on the direct influence of Indian traditions on Chinese literature. Besides Pei Puxian and Chŏng Kyubok, E. D. Edwards, Jaroslav Průšek, Victor Mair, and Anthony C. Yu all have made much of the Indian impact, even though they do not always focus on the same literature or periods.

54. Roberto Ong, *The Interpretation of Dreams in Ancient China* (Bochum: Herausgeber Chinathemen, 1985), 102.

55. Yu, "The Quest of Brother Amor," 81–82.

56. C. T. Hsia, "Time and the Human Condition in the Plays of T'ang Hsien-tsu" in *Self and Society in Ming Thought*, ed. William Theodore de Bary (New York: Columbia University Press, 1970), 272.

57. *NCD*, 175; *KUM*, 448.

58. For a translation of this story, see Burton Watson, trans. *The Complete Works of Chuang Tzu* (New York: Columbia University Press, 1968), 49.

59. Graham, *The Book of Lieh-tzu*, 65.

60. An example of such exhortation is delivered through another well-known episode—that of Zhuangzi's conversation with a skull. When the skull extols the world of the dead, Zhuangzi counters, "Suppose I could get the Clerk of Destinies to make your frame anew, to clothe your bones once more with flesh and skin, send you back to father and mother, wife and child, friends and

home, I do not think you would refuse." The skull shoots back, "How can you imagine that I would cast away joy greater than that of a king upon this throne, only to go back to the toils of the living world?" (*Anthology of Chinese Literature: From Early Times to the Fourteenth Century*, ed. Cyril Birch [New York: Grove Press, 1965], 83).

61. *KUM*, 448. This passage is not fully rendered in the Rutt translation.

62. *NCD*, 61; *KUM*, 360.

63. *NCD*, 65; *KUM*, 363.

64. *KUM*, 448. Richard Rutt's slightly truncated translatation can be found in *NCD*, 176.

65. O'Flaherty offers the tale in full in *Dreams, Illusions*, 134.

66. Ibid., 199.

67. A. C. Graham has repeatedly made the argument that Taoism does not fit into the Western category of philosophy. He bases this position on at least two points. First, Taoism is not rational discourse, but on the contrary an anti-rationalist reaction. Secondly, he states that the Taoist concept of the Way is not equivalent to the Western metaphysical concept of Being. Taoists do not strive for a final reality as much as they seek the way of proper action. Graham attributes China's divergent path away from neo-Platonic speculations to its language, which has no equivalent for the concept of Being.

See " 'Being' in Western Philosophy Compared with *Shih/Fei* and *Yu/Wu* in Chinese Philosophy" in *Studies in Chinese Philosophy and Philosophical Literature* (Singapore: Institute of East Asian Philosophies, 1986), 322–59.

68. O'Flaherty, *Dreams, Illusions*, 114.

69. This tale is from the *Yogavāsistha* and is given in full by O'Flaherty in *Dreams, Illusions*, 132.

70. Graham, *The Book of Lieh-tzu*, 68–69.

71. Translation by Winnie Leung in *Contemporary Literature in Translation* 18 (Spring 1974): 21–22.

72. An expanded version of this story is offered in the Tang tale of "Scholar Chang." It is translated by Donald Gjertson in *Traditional Chinese Stories*, 439–40.

73. *KUM*, 394; *NCD*, 107.

74. Translated in *Sourcebook of Korean Civilization*, 661.

75. Jaroslav Průšek says about karma,

"In the creation and spread of this theme, the religious narrator had exercised a very profound influence on the Chinese novel and, in many respects, an unfortunate one. Chinese literature, . . . [has] through this facile moral explanation been stripped of all the tragedy and pathos of undeserved misfortunes, and in this manner a good number of novels, stories, as well as dramas, became no more than unreal moral schemes." ["The Narrators of Buddhist Scriptures and Religious Tales in the Sung Period," *Archiv Orientální* 10 (1938): 386]

76. Anthony Yu, "History, Fiction, and the Reading of Chinese Narrative," 16.

77. Kenneth DeWoskin, *Doctors, Diviners, and Magicians of Ancient China: Biographies of Fang-shih* (New York: Columbia University Press, 1983), 30.

78. Anthony Yu remarks that *Journey to the West* is the only work of Ming fiction whose perspective is not "firmly trained on the human world" ("History, Fiction, and the Reading of Chinese Narrative," 14).

Chŏng Kyubok attaches considerable significance to what he calls the "fantasy structure" of *KUM*, claiming that it derives directly from the author's intimate familiarity with *Journey to the West*. Chŏng offers point-by-point correlations between fantastic elements of both novels, such as cloud somersaulting; and episodic themes, such as the *topoi* of the Dragon King (and other fantastic beasts) transformed into a white-robed scholar in order to listen to Buddhist sūtras (*Kuunmong Yŏngu*, 277–97). It is unclear to me to what extent such themes derive exclusively from *Journey to the West*, or from a broader fund of literary motifs. In any case, there is no reason to doubt Chŏng's overall assertion of Sŏp'o's knowledge of the Chinese Ming novel.

79. DeWoskin, *Doctors, Diviners*, 31.

80. Taken from the translation by Anthony C. Yu (Chicago: Chicago University Press, 1977), vol. 1, 241.

81. Sheldon Lu states,

The fantastic opens up new horizons of existence and creates visions of possible worlds beyond the conventionally known. All this contributes to a perceptual and conceptual disorientation and ultimately to the decentering of the homogeneous, autonomous Confucian subject. [*From Historicity to Fictionality*, 117]

Lu refers mainly to the *chuanqi* and the result of its discourse on the fantastic. My argument seeks to wed this process to a specifically Buddhist view of reality.

82. Victor Mair, *T'ang Transformation Texts* (Cambridge: Harvard University Press, 1989), 49.

83. Pei-yi Wu, *The Confucian's Progress*, 6, footnote 4.

Chapter 4. A Metaphysics in Search of Expression

1. Plaks, "Towards a Critical Theory of Chinese Narrative," 349.

2. Ibid., 348.

3. O'Flaherty, *Dreams, Illusions*, 203.

4. Ibid.

5. See Thomas Kasulis, "Philosophy as Metapraxis," in *Discourse and Practice*, ed. Frank Reynolds and David Tracy (Albany: State University of New York Press, 1992), 169–95.

In this article, Kasulis offers the case study of the Japanese Buddhist monk Kūkai (774–835), who worked to integrate the metapractical and ontological aspects of Buddhism. Kasulis suggests the need for Western philosophy to attempt a similar balance of metaphysical and metapractical theories.

6. *Buddhism in Translations*, trans. Henry Clarke Warren (New York: Atheneum Press, 1979), 121.

7. See D. T. Suzuki, *An Introduction to Zen Buddhism* (New York: Grover Press, 1964) and *Essays in Zen Buddhism*, second series. (London: Rider, 1970).

More recently, the cry of anti-intellectualism has been sounded by Hsueh-li Cheng, in "Psychology, Ontology and Zen Soteriology," *Religious Studies* 22 (1986): 459–72.

8. Robert Buswell and Robert Gimello have proposed that historically, a breakdown in religious praxis has often *preceded* and *led* to metaphysical constructions—most often in the form of systematic orderings of the Buddhist path (*mārga*). Such conceptual systems were created, they suggest, in order to justify the validity of Buddhist experience in the very face of its apparent meaninglessness. See the introductory essay in *Paths to Liberation* (Honolulu: University of Hawaii Press, 1992), 19–20.

My point does not dispute this chronology. A breakdown in the rationale and efficacy of religious praxis may lead to intellectual readjustments, but this order of events still maintains the priority of metaphysics in the sense that in any confessional tradition, actions are justified in relation to beliefs about reality rather than the other way around.

9. The characteristics of impermanence (*anitya*), egolessness (*anātman*), and suffering (*duhkha*) form the three marks (*lakshana*) of conditioned existence in Buddhist theory. See Edward Conze's discussion in *Buddhist Thought in India* (Ann Arbor: University of Michigan Press, 1967), 34–46.

10. The Buddhist concern with the nature of speech and knowledge is evident from the very beginning of the tradition when Buddhists engaged in debate with orthodox Hindu philosophers. For example, the contention of the *Purva Mimamsa* that there is an ontological connection between words and their meaning was supposedly countered by the Buddha with the argument that the meaning of words are conventional and that one must utilize speech without being led astray by it. See K. N. Jayatilleke, *Early Buddhist Theory of Knowledge* (Delhi: Motilal Banarsidass, 1980), 314–17.

11. According to David Kalupahana, this subtle but important distinction between the Theravāda and Mahāyāna view of words points to a significant divergence in philosophical positions between the two. Whereas the early tradition denied any realm of metaphysical absolutes, the later tradition refers explicitly to a transcendent and absolute reality. The Chinese construction of Buddhism quite definitely takes on the latter mode, as we shall see. Kalupahana generally believes that the notion of an Absolute reverses and contradicts early Buddhist doctrine. This issue will not be evaluated here. See *Buddhist Philosophy: A Historical Analysis* (Honolulu: University of Hawaii Press, 1976).

12. See Robert A. F. Thurman, *The Holy Teaching of Vimalakīrti* (University Park: Pennsylvania State University Press, 1976), 73–78.

13. For an account of the debate between the Prāsangikas and Svātantrikas, see Nathan Katz, "An Appraisal of the Svātantrika-Prāsangika Debates," *Philosophy East and West* 26, no. 3 (July 1976): 253–67.

14. Robert E. Buswell, Jr., "Ch'an Hermeneutics: A Korean View," in *Buddhist Hermeneutics*, ed. Donald Lopez. Kuroda Institute Studies in East Asian Buddhism, no. 6 (Honolulu: University of Hawaii Press, 1988), 246.

15. Chung-ying Cheng, "On Zen Language and Zen Paradoxes," *Journal of Chinese Philosophy* 1 (1973); 91.

16. Ibid., 93.

17. A period which Peter Gregory and most historians of Chinese Buddhism date to the Sui (581–617) and Tang (618–907) dynasties. This era grew out of an earlier period of relatively unsophisticated translating and interpretive

practices and became much more accurate in representing Indian ideas and creative in synthesizing its own.

18. Robert Gimello, "Apophatic and Kataphatic Discourse in Mahāyāna: A Chinese View," *Philosophy East and West* 26, no. 2 (1976): 119.

An indispensable account of the Huayan school and its position on religious discourse is given in Peter Gregory's *Tsung-mi and the Sinification of Buddhism*.

19. Katz, "Svātantrika-Prāsangika Debates," 255.

20. This is from David Kalupahana's translation in *Nāgārjuna: The Philsophy of the Middle Way* (Albany: State University of New York Press, 1986), 333.

21. Conze, *Buddhist Thought in India*, 250.

22. Garma C. C. Chang states, "The importance of Śunyatā in every field of Mahāyāna Buddhism cannot be overstressed, and in the Doctrine of Totality of the Hwa Yen school, it is especially significant" *(The Buddhist Teaching of Totality: The Philosophy of Hwa Yen Buddhism* [University Park: Pennsylvania State University Press, 1974], 60).

23. See Gregory, *Tsung-mi and the Sinification of Buddhism*, 93–135, for an account of *panjiao* generally and its evolution in the Huayan school.

24. This threefold *panjiao* scheme of Zongmi is outlined by Gregory in *Tsung-mi and the Sinification of Buddhism*, 206–14. Zongmi offered two *panjiao* schemes, one in his *Inquiry into the Origins of Man* and one in his preface to the *Collected Writings on the Source of Chan*. Gregory shows how despite the differing strategies of classification used in these two sources, the effect and content are basically the same.

25. Ibid., 214.

26. Zongmi's *Inquiry into the Origins of Man* (*Yuanren Lun*) has been translated by Yoshito S. Hakeda in *The Buddhist Tradition in India, China, and Japan*, ed. William Theodore de Bary (New York: Vintage, 1969), 179–96. See in particular 182–85 for Zongmi's criticism of native Chinese doctrines.

Peter Gregory provides an excellent discussion of Zongmi's critique of and impact on the broader Chinese intellectual tradition in *Tsung-mi and the Sinification of Buddhism*, 255–313.

27. Han Yu's criticisms of Buddhism are most notable in two works, the *Yuandao*, which Wing-tsit Chan renders as *An Inquiry on the Way* in *A Source Book of Chinese Philosophy* (Princeton: Princeton University Press, 1963), 454–56; and *Memorial on the Buddha's Bone*, which is translated in

Edwin O. Reischauer's *Ennin's Travels in T'ang China* (New York: Ronald Press Company, 1955), 221–24.

28. Sung-peng Hsu summarizes the difference between Chinese and Buddhist views of the universe as follows: "Chinese philosophies develop metaphysics in order to justify the values of life in this world, but Buddhist philosophies develop metaphysics in order to show the illusoriness of the universe so that it can be transcended." In *A Buddhist Leader*, 112.

29. Gregory, *Tsung-mi*, 7.

Gimello's "Apophatic and Kataphatic Discourse" is primarily a study of this aspect of Dushun's thought, which is contained in the *Huayan Fajie Guanmen* (*Discernments of the Dharma Element of the Avataṃsaka*, T 1878, 45.652b12–654a28). Gimello concludes that this text

> ... had the intention of validating and enhancing the phenomenal world by showing that phenomena are not merely the mute things and events in which we are enmeshed by reason of our ignorance and craving. Rather they are all eloquently significant, charged with meaning by the liberating principle that all things are indeterminable. A particular phenomenon, after all, is above all else an instance of that truth. ["Apophatic and Kataphatic Discourse," 129]

30. From the Hakeda translation, 191. See footnote 26.

31. For an account of this shift in language and ideology, see Buswell, *Formation of Ch'an Ideology*, 75; and "Ch'an Hermeneutics," 244–45.

32. My description of the *Trimśikā* is based on Thomas Wood's translation and discussion of *Trimśikā* verses 21–25 in *Mind Only: A Philosophical and Doctrinal Analysis of the Vijñānavāda* (Honolulu: University of Hawaii Press, 1991), 49–60.

33. *The Lankāvatāra Sūtra*, trans. D. T. Suzuki (London: George Routledge and Sons, 1932), 190.

34. See Buswell's discussion of the doctrine of *amalavijñāna* ("immaculate consciousness") and how its development created a bridgehead between opposing theories of mind within Mahāyāna schools, and which favored the doctrine of original purity. In *Formation of Ch'an Ideology*, 92–104.

Diana Y. Paul offers a comprehensive discussion of the development of and conflicts in Chinese Yogācāra theories of levels of consciousness, particularly in regard to the question of purity and impurity. See chapter two, "The

Dissemination of Paramārtha's Ideas," in *The Philosophy of Mind in Sixth-Century China* (Stanford: Stanford University Press, 1984), 38–72.

35. Peter Gregory's portrayal of Guifeng Zongmi consistently stresses the latter's attempts to push Buddhism to greater metaphysical explicitness in order to explain "how the world of delusion and defilement, the world in terms of which beings experience themselves, evolves out of a unitary onto-logical principle that is both intrinsically enlightened and pure" ("What Happened to the 'Perfect Teaching'?: Another Look at Hua-yen Buddhist Hermeneutics," *Buddhist Hermeneutics*, ed. Donald S. Lopez, Jr. [Honolulu: University of Hawaii Press, 1988], 219).

36. See Yoshito S. Hakeda's introduction in *The Awakening of Faith*, trans. Yoshito S. Hakeda (New York: Columbia University Press, 1967), for this argument.

37. Ibid., 31.

38. Buswell, *Formation of Ch'an Ideology*, 83.

39. Wŏnhyo's commentary on the *Awakening of Faith* has been studied in depth by Sung-bae Park in "Wŏnhyo's Commentaries on the *Awakening of Faith in Mahāyāna*" (Ph.D. diss., University of California at Berkeley, 1979).
    See also Sung-bae Park, *Buddhist Faith and Sudden Enlightenment* (Albany: State University of New York Press, 1983).

40. I take this observation directly from Buswell, *Formation of Ch'an Ideology*, 116.

41. See Hu Shih, "Ch'an (Zen) Buddhism in China and Its History and Method," *Philosophy East and West* 3, no. 1 (April 1953): 3–24; and "Development of Zen Buddhism in China," *Chinese Social and Political Science Review* 15 (1931–32): 475–505.
    For Suzuki, see bibliography.

42. The pervasiveness of the praxis of deconstruction within the Buddhist tradition is evident in all its phases. Witness Winston King's discussion of the concept of *nirvāna/nibbāna* in the Theravāda tradition and its primarily negative characterization as "extinction," which is likened to a flame which "goes out." King states, ". . . the Buddhist negativity concerning the final goal (Nibbāna) was intended as a methodological and psychological device rather than an ontological statement; later on in the growth of the tradition and its conflict with other traditions, such statements were ontologized into 'descriptions' of the Supreme Reality" (*Theravāda Meditation: The Buddhist Transformation of Yoga* [University Park: Pennsylvania State University Press, 1980], 23).

43. David W. Chappell, "Hermeneutical Phases in Chinese Buddhism," in *Buddhist Hermeneutics*, ed. Donald Lopez (Honolulu: University of Hawaii Press, 1988), 193.

For a description of how the Chan textual tradition of the *yu-lu* itself follows the conventions of Buddhist scriptures, see Judith A. Berling, "Bringing the Buddha Down to Earth: Notes on the Emergence of *Yu-lu* as a Buddhist Genre," *History of Religions* 27, no. 1 (August 1987): 56–88.

44. I make this assessment from David Chappell's description of what he calls the "canonical" phases of Buddhism in China. See Chappell, "Hermeneutical Phases," 177.

45. From Chinul's *Encouragement to Practice*, trans. Robert Buswell in *The Korean Approach to Zen* (Honolulu: University of Hawaii Press, 1983), 103.

46. Quoted by Hee-jin Kim, "'The Reason of Words and Letters': Dōgen and Koan Language," in *Dōgen Studies*, ed. William R. LaFleur (Honolulu: University of Hawaii Press, 1985), 54.

47. Chinul did much to bring together the Sŏn and Hwaŏm schools, claiming that the philosophy of the latter formed an understanding of the practice of the former. See Buswell's translation of *The Complete and Sudden Attainment of Buddhahood* in *The Korean Approach to Zen*, 198–237.

48. According to Bernard Faure, the opposition between sudden enlightenment and gradual cultivation was a later sectarian development within Chan which betrayed an earlier and harmonious understanding of these two paths as a twofold truth. The overall Chinese tendency to integrate apparently contradictory concepts and practices is demonstrated by Faure as he uses the rubric of the "two truths" to discuss a range of semantically overlapping dualisms that emerged in the Chan tradition. In addition to sudden/gradual, there is essence/function, meditative/scholastic, and *upāya/prajñā*. Chinul's own syncretic tendencies evokes the spirit of the two truths model. See Faure, *The Rhetoric of Immediacy* (Princeton: Princeton University Press, 1991), 53–78.

49. *The Zen Teachings of Master Lin-chi*, trans. Burton Watson (Shambala: Boston, 1993), 31.

50. Ibid., 75.

51. The concept of the two truths was more likely to be invoked by Chinul through the concept of the noumenal and phenomenal mind derived from *The Awakening of Faith*. The noumenal mind represented the mind of original purity which could not be accessed intellectually. The phenomenal mind generated the conditioned and relative world which appears real to the

unenlightened. Rather than forming two opposing and mutually exclusive principles, the noumenal and phenomenal minds are originally one and relate dynamically to each other. For a lucid discussion of Chinul's theory on the dual nature of the mind, see Buswell's introductory essay in *Korean Approach to Zen*, 56–61.

52. *Encouragement to Practice*, trans. in Buswell, *Korean Approach to Zen*, 105.

53. The question of Hyujŏng's *dharma* lineage and its relationship with Chinul's own line is discussed by Hee-Sung Keel in *Chinul: The Founder of the Korean Sŏn Tradition* (Seoul: Po Chin Chai Ltd., 1984), 167–78. Keel is ultimately satisfied to point to the doctrinal similarities between the two figures rather than settling the question definitively.

54. Keel reports that the *Diamond Sūtra* was one of the most frequently published and circulated Buddhist texts in the Chosŏn dynasty, in great part due to its compactness. See ibid., 177, n. 37.

See Chigwan's article, "Yŏnt'aek mit Inok ŭi sagi wa kŭ ŭi kyohakkwan" in *Han'guk pulgyo sasangsa* for a discussion of this era's Buddhist literature. In addition to the study of canonical texts and commentaries, late Chosŏn dynasty Buddhists were active in producing their own treatises. These texts (*sagi*, "private records") encompassed personal anecdotes about departed masters, as well as interpretations of and commentary on difficult canonical passages. Chigwan examines two of the most influential *sagi* writers, Yŏnt'aek Yuil (1720–1799), who was an acknowledged master of the Hwaŏm Sūtra; and Inok Ŭijŏm (1746–1796), who was recognized for his proficiency in the Four Teachings.

55. In his monumental study of Chosŏn dynasty Buddhism, Takahashi Tōru cites *KUM* as an example of "free thinking" which utilized literary means to assert the superiority of Buddhism over and against the reigning ideology of neo-Confucianism. This observation is made within his larger assertion about the persistence of Buddhist thought not only amongst women and the common people, but within court circles as well. See *Richō Bukkyō*, (Tokyo: 1929) 794–95.

56. Quoted in Yu Pyŏnghwan, "Kuunmong ŭi pulgyo," 474.

57. The "two access" theory is discussed in chapter five of the *Vajrasamādhi Sūtra*, "Approaching the Edge of Reality," which is translated by Buswell in his *Formation of Ch'an Ideology*, 215–16. Buswell's own discussion of this teaching appears on pp. 126–37.

58. Buswell, *Formation of Ch'an Ideology*, 134.

59. *Rhetoric of Immediacy*, 75.

60. Paramārtha's reputation as one of the most preeminent translators of Buddhist texts in China was established on the basis of his near-exclusive translations of Yogācāra texts. In addition to the *Vimśatikā*, his translations include Vasubandhu's *Abhidharmakośa, Madhyāntavibhāga, Trimśikā*, and the *Mahāyāna-samgraha-bhāsya*. He also translated Asanga's *Mahāyānasamgraha* and *Yogācārabhūmi*.

61. I am using Paul Griffiths unpublished translation of the *Vimśatikākārikā & Vrtti* (*Twenty Verses and Elucidation*). University of Chicago Divinity School, October 1991.

62. Burton Watson, trans. *The Complete Works of Chuang Tzu* (Columbia University Press, 1968), 47–48.

63. Mair uses the phrase "localized intensification" to describe the Indian theory of drama: ". . . the whole world is thought to be a transformational appearance. The drama is a localized intensification of the transformational process. This conception of theatrical art is unlike that of *mimesis*, in which the drama is held to be an imitation of reality" ("Narrative Revolution in Chinese Literature," 16–17).

64. See William LaFleur's first chapter, particularly page 8, in *The Karma of Words* (Berkeley: University of California Press, 1983) for a discussion of the Japanese appropriation of Bo Zhuyi.

65. From Mervyn Sprung's translation of the *Prasannapadā: Lucid Exposition of the Middle Way: The Essential Chapters from the Prasannapadā of Candrakīrti* (London: Routledge & Kegan Paul, 1979), 184.

66. LaFleur, *Karma of Words*, 23.

67. Ibid., 87.

Chapter 5. Philosophy in Narrative Action

1. Michael Riffaterre, *Fictional Truth* (Baltimore: Johns Hopkins University Press, 1990), xiii.

2. Sŏl Sŏnggyŏng, "*Kuunmong ŭi kujojŏk yŏn'gu*" [On the structure of *Kuunmong*], part 1 *Inmun Kwahak* 27/28 (1972): 231–76; part 2 *Ŏnŏ munhwa* 1 (1974): 72–103; part 3 *Kugŏ kungmunhak* 58/60 (1972): 291–319.

3. Ibid., part 1, 238–42.

4. I am following the A. F. Price and Wang Mou-lam translation for its readability and faithfulness to Kumārajīva's Chinese translation. *The Diamond Sūtra and Sūtra of Hui Neng* (Boulder: Shambala Press, 1969), 29. The Chinese text is from the *Taishō Tripitaka* 235.8.748–752c. The citations are followed by page and column numbers. See bibliography under *Jingang boruo boluomi jing* for full reference.

Edward Conze's translation of the *Diamond Sūtra*, which follows the Sanskrit text, renders this passage somewhat differently. Rather than asserting "material characteristics are not, in fact, material characteristics," Conze translates it, "What has been taught by the Tathāgata as the possession of marks, that is truly a no-possession of no-marks." The phrase "material characteristics" is a faithful translation of the Chinese phrase *shenxiang* (身相), whereas "possession of marks" translates the Sanskrit *sampad*, which Conze explains as referring to "the attainments or accomplishments of the individual in the course of his religious career." (See Conze, *Buddhist Wisdom Books* [London: George Allen & Unwin Ltd, 1958], 28.)

The slight variations in translation are to be expected. What is more significant is the consistency of the pattern of the sūtra's discourse. In that case, Conze's Sanskrit translation also follows the *"X* is not *X"* structure.

5. From *The Diamond Cutter of Doubts: A Commentary on The Diamond Sūtra by Ch'an Master Han Shan,* tran. Lu K'uan Yü, in *Ch'an and Zen Teaching,* vol. 1 (York Beach: Samuel Weiser, 1993), 203. Hereafter cited as *DCD.*

6. Price, *Diamond Sūtra,* 60.

7. Hanshan is careful to point out that in making its negations, the *Diamond Sūtra* does not assert annihilation, or nihilism. After the *"X* is not *X"* formula is applied to the forms "particles of dust" and "the universe," Hanshan comments:

> . . . although all dharmas are perceived as non-existent, there is no fall into the false conception of annihilation . . . Mountains, rivers and the great earth, all disclose the body of the King of the Law (Dharmarāja). If one wishes to perceive the Dharma-kāya, one should be provided with the right Diamond-eye. This was why He said: 'The universe is not real but is merely called a universe.' [*DCD,* 178]

8. Price, *Diamond Sutra,* 30–31.

9. Hanshan claims, "One who listens to it (this Dharma) free from alarm, fear, and dread, will be very rare, because what the Buddha expounded is

beyond words and speech. Therefore, He said: 'The first pāramitā is not but *is merely called* the first pāramitā' [emphases mine]" (*DCD*, 181–82).

10. Price, *Diamond Sūtra*, 37.

11. Conze, *Buddhist Wisdom Books*, 47.

12. Sŏl Sŏnggyŏng, "*Kuunmong* ŭi kujojŏk yŏn'gu," 236.

13. Conze's translation often includes the word "therefore" where the Chinese version does not explicitly give it. A side-by-side reading of Conze and Price brings out the strikingly different semantic impact imparted by the translation that something is "therefore called *X*" as opposed to "merely called *X*."

14. Price, *Diamond Sūtra*, 33.

15. Conze, *Buddhist Wisdom Books*, 39.

16. Gregory Schopen's translation of the Gilgit (sixth-century Sanskrit) text of the *Diamond Sūtra* slightly alters the "*X* is not *X*; it is called *X*" formula to read instead: "*X* is not *X*; in that sense '*X*' is used." For example: "That which is the possession of characteristic marks is said to be not the possession of characteristic marks by the Tathāgata. In that sense 'possession of characteristic marks' is used." (p. 127)

The use of quotation marks around the category in question, along with the explanatory phrase that it is "in that sense" that "*X*" is used, suggests a cautionary attitude which recognizes the category's ultimate unreality. Schopen's rendition of the formula, however, suggests even more strongly the sūtra's desire to demonstrate the proper use and understanding of language.

See *Studies in the Literature of The Great Vehicle*, ed. Luis O. Gomez and Jonathan A. Silk (Ann Arbor: University of Michigan, 1989), 123–31.

17. *DCD*, 181.

18. Price, *Diamond Sūtra*, 58.

19. Ibid., 63.

20. *DCD*, 185.

21. Chŏng Kyubok, "Kuunmong ŭi sasangjŏk yŏn'gu," in *Kŏjŏn sosŏl yŏn'gu* (Seoul: Chŏmŭmsa, 1982), 297–331.

22. Ibid., 317.

23. Rutt, *Virtuous Women*, 175.

24. See Kim Iryŏl, "Kuunmong shin'go," in *Han'guk kososŏl yŏn'gu* (Seoul: Iu Ch'ulp'ansa, 1988), 373–88.

25. Kim Iryŏl is rather critical of the realism of the dream sequence. He points out that Sŏp'o devotes most of the novel's pages to the dream sequence; however, the depiction of Shaoyou's realization of the brevity of his life, in Kim's opinion, is trite and facile (see ibid., 374). Kim's critique is based largely on literary grounds. In his view, Shaoyou's abrupt conclusion that life is ephemeral and therefore illusory after a long life of rich rewards and fulfillment is lacking in verisimilitude and pathos. My assertion of "realism" here, however, is meant to refer primarily to the dream sequence's historical setting in contrast to the immortal peak that Xingzhen occupies.

26. Sheldon Lu reports that in Tang dream tales, dream time takes longer to narrate than historical time. Conventional realism is subverted by making dream time more prominent, but what exists within the dream frame is also ambiguous: Are they the narrator's assertions or the subjective creations of the dreamer? "Objectivity is entangled in the vision of the protagonist, existence is enmeshed in perception, and ontology is qualified by epistemology" (Lu, *From Historicity to Fictionality*, 126).

27. Riffaterre, *Fictional Truth*, xiv.

28. I take this definition of a subtext from Michael Riffaterre's glossary entry in ibid., 131. He defines a subtext as a "unit of significance" for the text in which it appears: "The subtext reflects the entire fiction when its structure is identical to the matrix of the novel . . ."

29. Of all the prodigious works on Buddhist logic, Xuanzang translated the *Nyāyamukha* by Dignāga and the *Nyāyapraveśa* by Sankarasvāmin into Chinese. F. Th. Stcherbatsky comments on these choices: *Buddhist Logic*, vol. 1 (New York: Dover, 1962), 54

> "What may have been the reasons which induced Hsuen Tsang, who is believed to have studied the logical system of Dignāga in India . . . to choose for translation only two nearly identical, short manuals, it is difficult for us at present to decide. The most plausible explanation would be that he himself was much more interested in the religious side of Buddhism and felt only a moderate interest in logical and epistemological inquiries."

30. I am using Frederick Streng's translation in *Emptiness: A Study in Religious Meaning* (Nashville: Albingdon Press, 1967), 222.

31. Bimal Krishna Matilal, "Buddhist Logic and Epistemology," in *Buddhist Logic and Epistemology*, ed. Bimal Krishna Matilal and Robert Evans (Dordrecht: Reidel, 1986), 26.

32. Ibid., 28.

33. Streng, *Emptiness*, 227.

34. Ibid.

35. Lisa Raphels, *Knowing Words: Wisdom and Cunning in the Classical Traditions of China and Greece* (Ithaca: Cornell University Press, 1992), 3.

36. This kind of claim has been most frequently made for Japanese Buddhism. In *Flowing Traces: Buddhism in the Literary and Visual Arts of Japan*, the editors assert: "Buddhism's beginnings in Japan had the arts at their center. Ever since that time, . . . it has proven difficult—some might say impossible—for the Japanese to conceive of Buddhism except in conjunction with concrete aesthetic embodiments" (p. 3). Eds. James H. Sanford, William R. LaFleur, and Masatoshi Nagatomi (Princeton: Princeton University Press, 1992)

The editors make clear that this thesis is not a tribute to Japanese uniqueness. The Japanese focus on aesthetic expression took its cue from Korean Buddhist artisans of the fifth century. Both groups in turn were also undoubtedly influenced by Chinese cultural traditions which blurred the lines between the artistic and the spiritual. For an account of late imperial Chinese aesthetic theory in relation to religious enlightenment, see Richard John Lynn, "Orthodoxy and Enlightenment: Wang Shih-chen's Theory of Poetry and Its Antecedents," in *Unfolding of Neo-Confucianism*, ed. William Theodore de Bary (New York: Columbia University Press, 1975).

37. Gadjin Nagao, "The Silence of the Buddha," in *Mādhymika and Yogācāra*, trans. Leslie Kawamura (Albany: State University of New York Press, 1991), 45.

38. Ibid.

39. Malcolm David Eckel, *Jñānagarbha's Commentary on the Distinction Between the Two Truths* (Albany: State University of New York Press, 1987), 43–49.

40. Ibid., 47.

41. Yu, "The Quest of Brother Amor," 85.

42. Yu, "History, Fiction, and the Reading of Chinese Narrative," 16–17.

43. Ibid.

44. Anthony C. Yu, "The Stone of Fiction and the Fiction of Stone: Reflexivity and Religious Symbolism in *Hung-lou meng*," *Studies in Language and Literature* 4 (October 1990): 29.

45. Ibid., 28.

46. Rutt, *Virtuous Women*, 176.

Chapter 6. Remythologizing the Comparative Enterprise

1. Martha Nussbaum, *The Fragility of Goodness*, 14.

2. Philip Quinn, "On Demythologizing Evil." Paper presented at the American Academy of Religion, New Orleans, November 1990.
    The actual article which this presentation is concerned with appears under the same title in *Discourse and Practice*, ed. Frank Reynolds and David Tracy (Albany: State University of New York Press, 1992), 111–40.

3. See chapter 4, footnote 5 of this work.

4. Quinn, "On Demythologizing Evil."

5. Huston Smith, "Postmodernism's Impact on the Study of Religion," *Journal of the American Academy of Religion* 58, no. 4 (Winter 1990), 657.

6. The "real above" is Plato's own term which he uses in book nine of the *Republic*. See Nussbaum, *Fragility of Goodness*, 136–64, for a discussion of Plato's concept of perfect reason.

7. Clifford Geertz uses this metaphor, which is taken from Robert Solow, in "Thick Description: Toward an Interpretive Theory of Culture," in *The Interpretation of Cultures* (New York: Basic Books, 1973), 30.

8. See Jonathan Z. Smith's introduction in *Imagining Religion: From Babylon to Jonestown* (Chicago: University of Chicago Press, 1982).

9. See Jonathan Z. Smith's essay "Sacred Persistence: Toward a Redescription of Canon," in ibid., 36–53.

10. Jonathan Z. Smith, *To Take Place* (Chicago: University of Chicago Press, 1987), 104.

11. Ibid., 108.

12. Wendy Doniger O'Flaherty, *Other Peoples' Myths* (New York: Macmillan, 1988), 139.

13. Mair, "Narrative Revolution in Chinese Literature," 9.

14. Ibid., 8.

15. Ibid., 7.

16. Victor Mair, *Painting and Performance* (Honolulu: University of Hawaii Press, 1988).

17. E. T. Kirby, *Ur-Drama: The Origins of Theatre* (New York: New York University Press, 1975.

18. Mair, *Painting and Performance,* 70.

19. Graham, *The Book of Lieh-tzu,* 63.

20. Stephen Toulmin, "Beyond Anti-Anti-Relativism." Unpublished paper delivered to the Religions in Culture and History conference, University of Chicago Divinity School, October 1986.

21. Graham, *The Book of Lieh-tzu,* 65. See Isabelle Robinet, "Metamorphosis and Deliverance from the Corpse in Taoism," *History of Religion* 19, no. 1 (August 1979): 37–70, for a fuller discussion of Taoist powers.

22. Charles Taylor, "Comparison, History, Truth," in *Myth and Philosophy,* ed. Frank Reynolds and David Tracy (Albany: State University of New York Press, 1990), 42.

23. To be sure, it is not the case that all schools of Buddhist philosophy rejected the separation of the world into the relatively and absolutely real. In fact, the Sthaviravadins posited the relative unreality of the mundane world—calling it illusion—compared to the absolute reality of *nirvāna.* The distinction between relative and absolute realities is therefore a familiar one in Buddhist ontology. The ontology present in *KUM,* however, is the brand which argues for the immanence rather than transcendence of absolute reality. In Edward Conze words, "The most startling innovation of the Mahāyāna is . . . the identification of the Unconditioned with the conditioned" (*Buddhist Thought in India,* 226).

24. Nussbaum, *Love's Knowledge,* 183.

25. O'Flaherty, *Other Peoples' Myths,* 141.

Selected Bibliography

Western Sources

Bachelor, Stephen, ed. *The Way of Korean Zen,* by Kusan Sunim. New York: Weatherhill, 1985.

Bantly, Francisca Cho. "Buddhist Allegory in the *Journey to the West.*" *Journal of Asian Studies* 48, no. 3 (August 1989): 512–24.

———. "Buddhist Philosophy in the Art of Fiction." In *Discourse and Practice,* edited by Frank Reynolds and David Tracy. Albany: State University of New York Press, 1992.

———. "Myth and Cosmology in *The Book of Poetry.*" In *Myths and Fictions,* edited by Shlomo Biderman and Ben-ami Scharfstein. Leiden: E. J. Brill, 1993.

Berling, Judith. *The Syncretic Religion of Lin Chao-en.* New York: Columbia University Press, 1980.

———. "Bringing the Buddha Down to Earth: Notes on the Emergence of *Yu-lu* as a Buddhist Genre." *History of Religion* 27, no. 1 (August 1987): 56–88.

Birch, Cyril, ed. *Anthology of Chinese Literature: From Early Times to the Fourteenth Century.* New York: Grove Press, 1965.

Bouchez, Daniel. "Le roman coréen Namjŏng ki et L'affaire de la Reine Min." *Journal Asiatique* 264 (1976): 405–51.

———. "Les Propos de Kim Ch'un-T'aek sur le *Nam-Jŏng ki.*" In *Melanges de Coreanologie Offerts à M. Charles Haguenauer,* vol. 1: *Mémoires du Centre d'Études Coréennes.* Paris: Collège de France, 1979.

239

———. *Tradition, Traduction et Interpretation d'un roman coréen: Le Namjŏng ki.* Paris: Collège de France, 1984.

———. "Buddhism and Neo-Confucianism in Kim Manjung's *Random Essays (Sŏp'o manp'il).*" In *The Rise of Neo-Confucianism in Korea,* edited by William Theodore de Bary and JaHyun Kim Haboush. New York: Columbia University Press, 1985.

———. "Kim Manjung et le *Sanguo zhi.*" In *Twenty Papers on Korean Studies Offered to Prof. W. E. Skillend,* vol. 5: *Cahiers d'Études Coréennes.* Paris: Collège de France, 1989.

Buswell, Robert E. *The Korean Approach to Zen: The Collected Works of Chinul.* Honolulu: University of Hawaii Press, 1983.

———. "Ch'an Hermeneutics: A Korean View." In *Buddhist Hermeneutics,* edited by Donald S. Lopez, Jr. Kuroda Institute Studies in East Asian Buddhism, no. 6. Honolulu: University of Hawaii Press, 1988.

———. *The Formation of Ch'an Ideology in China and Korea.* Princeton: Princeton University Press, 1989.

Buswell, Robert E. and Robert M. Gimello, eds. *Paths to Liberation: The Mārga and Its Transformations in Buddhist Thought.* Kuroda Institute Studies in East Asian Buddhism 7. Honolulu: University of Hawaii Press, 1992.

Chan, Wing-tsit. "The Evolution of Neo-Confucian Concept of *Li* as Principle." *Tsing Hua Journal of Chinese Studies* 4 (1964): 123–48.

Chang, Garma C. C. *The Buddhist Teaching of Totality: The Philosophy of Hwa Yen Buddhism.* University Park: Pennsylvania State University Press, 1974.

Chappell, David W. "Hermeneutical Phases in Chinese Buddhism." In *Buddhist Hermeneutics,* edited by Donald S. Lopez, Jr. Kuroda Institute Studies in East Asian Buddhism, no. 6. Honolulu: University of Hawaii Press, 1988.

Chavannes, Edouard. *Cinq Cents Contes et Apologues: Extraits du Tripitaka Chinois.* Paris: Société Asiatique, 1911.

Cheng, Chung-ying. "On Zen Language and Zen Paradoxes." *Journal of Chinese Philosophy* 1 (1973): 77–102.

Cheng, Hseuh-li. "Psychology, Ontology and Zen Soteriology." *Religious Studies* 22 (1986): 459–72.

Chou, Chih-p'ing. *Yuan Hung-Tao and the Kung-An School.* Cambridge: Cambridge University Press, 1988.

Chung, Chai-sik. "Chŏng Tojŏn: 'Architect' of the Yi Dynasty Government and Ideology." In *The Rise of Neo-Confucianism in Korea*, edited by William Theodore de Bary and JaHyun Kim Haboush. New York: Columbia University Press, 1985.

Chung Chong-wha. "The Korean Classical Fiction and the Romance." In *Korean Classical Literature: An Anthology*, edited by Chung Chong-wha. London: Kegan Paul International, 1989.

Conze, Edward. *Buddhist Thought in India.* Ann Arbor: University of Michigan Press, 1967.

———. *Buddhist Meditation.* New York: Harper & Row, 1969.

Deuchler, Martina. "Neo-Confucianism: The Impulse for Social Action in Early Yi Korea." *Journal of Korean Studies* 2 (1980): 71–111.

———. " 'Heaven Does Not Discriminate': A Study of Secondary Sons in Chosŏn Korea." *Journal of Korean Studies* 6 (1988–89): 121–64.

———. *The Confucian Transformation of Korea: A Study of Society and Ideology.* Cambridge: Harvard University Press, 1992.

DeWoskin, Kenneth J. "The Six Dynasties *Chih-Kuai* and the Birth of Fiction." In *Chinese Narratives: Critical and Theoretical Essays*, edited by Andrew H. Plaks. Princeton: Princeton University Press, 1977.

———. *Doctors, Diviners, and Magicians of Ancient China: Biographies of Fang-shih.* New York: Columbia University Press, 1983.

Duncan, John. "The Social Background to the Founding of the Chosŏn Dynasty: Change or Continuity?" *Journal of Korean Studies* 6 (1988–89): 39–79.

Eckel, Malcolm David. *Jñānagarbha's Commentary on the Distinction Between the Two Truths.* Albany: State University of New York Press, 1987.

Edwards, E. D. *Chinese Prose Literature.* London: Stephen Austin and Sons, 1938.

Faure, Bernard. *The Rhetoric of Immediacy: A Cultural Critique of Chan/ Zen Buddhism.* Princeton: Princeton University Press, 1991.

Gale, James, trans. *The Cloud Dream of the Nine.* London: Small, Maynard & Company, 1922.

Gimello, Robert. "Apophatic and Kataphatic Discourse in Mahāyāna: A Chinese View." *Philosophy East and West* 26, no. 2 (1976): 117–36.

Graham, A. C. "'Being' in Western Philosophy Compared with *Shih/ Fei* and *Yu/Wu* in Chinese Philosophy." In *Studies in Chinese Philosophy and Philosophical Literature.* Singapore: Institute of East Asian Philosophies, 1986.

———, trans. *The Book of Lieh-tzu.* London: Butler & Tanner, 1960.

Grayson, James Huntley. *Korea: A Religious History.* New York: Oxford University Press, 1989.

Gregory, Peter. "What Happened to the 'Perfect Teaching'?: Another Look at Hua-yen Buddhist Hermeneutics." In *Buddhist Hermeneutics,* edited by Donald S. Lopez, Jr. Kuroda Institute Studies in East Asian Buddhism, no. 6. Honolulu: University of Hawaii Press, 1988.

———. *Tsung-mi and the Sinification of Buddhism.* Princeton: Princeton University Press, 1991.

Griffiths, Paul, trans. *Viṃśatikākārikā and Vrtti* [Twenty verses and elucidation], by Vasubandhu. Unpublished translation by Paul Griffiths. University of Chicago Divinity School, October 1991.

Ha Tae-Hung and Grafton K. Mintz, trans. *Samguk Yusa: Legends and History of the Three Kingdoms of Ancient Korea,* by Iryŏn. Seoul: Yonsei University Press, 1972.

Haboush, JaHyun Kim. "The Education of the Crown Prince: A Study in Confucian Pedagogy." In *The Rise of Neo-Confucianism in Korea,* edited by William Theodore de Bary and JaHyun Kim Haboush. New York: Columbia University Press, 1985.

———. *A Heritage of Kings: One Man's Monarchy in the Confucian World.* New York: Columbia University Press, 1988.

Hakeda, Yoshida S., trans. *The Awakening of Faith.* New York: Columbia University Press, 1967.

————, trans. *Inquiry into the Origins of Man* by Guifeng Zongmi. In *The Buddhist Tradition in India, China, and Japan,* edited by William. Theodore de Bary. New York: Vintage, 1969.

Hales, Dell. "Dreams and the Daemonic in Traditional Chinese Short Stories." In *Critical Essays on Chinese Literature,* edited by William H. Nienhauser, Jr. Hong Kong: Chinese University of Hong Kong, 1976.

Han Yu. *Memorial on the Buddha's Bone.* Translated by Edwin O. Reischauer. In *Ennin's Travels in T'ang China.* New York: Ronald Press Company, 1955.

————. *An Inquiry on the Way.* Translated by Wing tsit-Chan. In *A Source Book of Chinese Philosophy.* Princeton: Princeton University Press, 1963.

Hanan, Patrick. "The Fiction of Moral Duty: The Vernacular Story in the 1640s." In *Expressions of Self in Chinese Literature,* edited by Robert E. Hegel and Richard C. Hessney. New York: Columbia University Press, 1985.

Hawkes, David. Introduction to *Ch'u Tz'u: The Songs of the South* by Qu Yuan. Oxford: Clarendon Press, 1959.

————, trans. *The Songs of the South.* Harmondsworth: Penguin Books, 1985.

Hegel, Robert. *The Novel in Seventeenth Century China.* New York: Columbia University Press, 1981.

————. "An Exploration of the Chinese Literary Self." In *Expressions of Self in Chinese Literature,* edited by Robert E. Hegel and Richard C. Hessney. New York: Columbia University Press, 1985.

Heine, Steven. "The Zen Koan as Religious Symbol." *Journal of the American Academy of Religion* 58, no. 3 (1990): 357–87.

Ho, Kwok Man and Joanne O'Brien, ed. *The Eight Immortals of Taoism: Legends and Fables of Popular Taoism.* New York: Meridian, 1990.

Hsia, C. T. "Time and the Human Condition in the Plays of T'ang Hsien-tsu." In *Self and Society in Ming Thought*, edited by William Theodore de Bary. New York: Columbia University Press, 1970.

Hsu, Sung-peng. *A Buddhist Leader in Ming China*. University Park: Pennsylvania State University Press, 1979.

Hu Shih. "Development of Zen Buddhism in China." *Chinese Social and Political Science Review* 15 (1931–32): 475–505.

———. "Ch'an (Zen) Buddhism in China and Its History and Method." *Philosophy East and West* 3, no. 1 (April 1953): 3–24.

Huang, Martin W. *Literary and Self-Re/Presentation: Autobiographical Sensibility in the Eighteenth-Century Chinese Novel*. Stanford: Stanford University Press, 1995.

Huber, Edouard, trans. *Sūtralamkāra*. Paris: Société Asiatique, 1908.

Jayatilleke, K. N. *Early Buddhist Theory of Knowledge*. Delhi: Motilal Banarsidass, 1980.

Kalupahana, David J. *Nāgārjuna: The Philosophy of the Middle Way*. Albany: State University of New York Press, 1986.

Kasulis, Thomas. "Philosophy as Metapraxis." In *Discourse and Practice*, edited by Frank Reynolds and David Tracy. Albany: State University of New York Press, 1992.

Katz, Nathan. "An Appraisal of the Svātantrika-Prāsangika Debates." *Philosophy East and West* 26, no. 3 (July 1976): 253–67.

Kawashima, Fujiya. "The Local Gentry Association in Mid-Yi Dynasty Korea: A Preliminary Study of the Ch'angnyŏng Hyangan." *Journal of Korean Studies* 2 (1980): 113–38.

———. "A Study of the *Hyangan*: Kin Groups and Aristocratic Localism in the Seventeenth- and Eighteenth-Century Korean Countryside." *Journal of Korean Studies* 5 (1984): 3–38.

Keel, Hee-Sung. *Chinul: The Founder of the Korean Sŏn Tradition*. Berkeley Buddhist Studies Series 6. Seoul: Po Chin Chai Ltd., 1984.

Kengo, Araki. "Confucianism and Buddhism in the Late Ming." In *The Unfolding of Neo-Confucianism*, edited by William Theodore de Bary. New York: Columbia University Press, 1975.

Kim, Hee-jin. " 'The Reason of Words and Letters': Dōgen and Koan Language." In *Dōgen Studies*, Edited by William R. LaFleur. Honolulu: University of Hawaii Press, 1985.

Kim Chong-an, trans. *The True History of Queen Inhyŏn*. In *Virtuous Women: Three Classic Korean Novels*, edited by Richard Rutt and Kim Chong-an. Seoul: Royal Asiatic Society, 1974.

King, Winston. *Theravāda Meditation: The Buddhist Transformation of Yoga*. University Park: Pennsylvania State University Press, 1980.

Kirby, E. T. *Ur-Drama: The Origins of Theatre*. New York: New York University Press, 1975.

Kitagawa, Joseph M. *On Understanding Japanese Religion*. Princeton: Princeton University Press, 1987.

Knechtges, David R. "Dream Adventure Stories in Europe and T'ang China." *Tamkang Review*, 4 no. 2 (October 1973): 101–19.

LaFleur, William. *The Karma of Words*. Berkeley: University of California Press, 1983.

Lee, Ki-baik. *New History of Korea*. Translated by Edward W. Wagner with Edward J. Shultz. Cambridge: Harvard University Press, 1984.

Lee, Peter H. *Korean Literature: Topics and Themes*. Tucson: University of Arizona Press, 1965.

Lee, Peter H., ed. *Anthology of Korean Literature: From Early Times to the Nineteenth Century*. Honolulu: University of Hawaii Press, 1981.

―――, ed. *Sourcebook of Korean Civilization*. Volume 1. New York: Columbia University Press, 1993.

Leung, Winnie, trans. "Record of the Three Dreams." By Bai Xingjian. In *Contemporary Literature in Translation* 18 (Spring 1974): 21–22.

Lin, Shuen-fu and Larry J. Schulz, trans. *The Tower of Myriad Mirrors*. Berkeley: Asian Humanities Press, 1978.

Lu, Sheldon Hsiao-peng. *From Historicity to Fictionality: The Chinese Poetics of Narrative*. Stanford: Stanford University Press, 1994.

246 EMBRACING ILLUSION

Lynn, Richard John. "Orthodoxy and Enlightenment: Wang Shih-chen's Theory of Poetry." In *The Unfolding of Neo-Confucianism*, edited by William Theodore de Bary. New York: Columbia University Press, 1975.

Ma, Y. W. "Fact and Fantasy in T'ang Tales." *Chinese Literature: Essays, Articles, Reviews* 2 (1980): 167–81.

Ma, Y. W. and Joseph S. M. Lau, eds. *Traditional Chinese Stories*. New York: Columbia University Press, 1978.

Mair, Victor. "The Narrative Revolution in Chinese Literature: Ontological Presuppositions." *Chinese Literature: Essays, Articles, Reviews* 5 (July 1983): 1–27.

———. *Painting and Performance*. Honolulu: University of Hawaii Press, 1988.

———. *T'ang Transformation Texts*. Cambridge: Harvard University Press, 1989.

Matilal, Bimal Krishna. "Buddhist Logic and Epistemology." In *Buddhist Logic and Epistemology*, edited by Bimal Krishna Matilal and Robert Evans. Dordrecht: Reidel, 1986.

Murti, T. R. V. *The Central Philosophy of Buddhism*. London: Unwin Paperbacks, 1980.

Nagao, Gadjin. *Mādhyamika and Yogācāra*. Translated by Leslie Kawamura. Albany: State University of New York Press, 1991.

Nussbaum, Martha C. *The Fragility of Goodness: Luck and Ethics in Greek Tragedy and Philosphy*. Cambridge: Cambridge University Press, 1986.

———. *Love's Knowledge: Essays on Philosophy and Literature*. New York: Oxford University Press, 1990.

O'Flaherty, Wendy Doniger. *Dreams, Illusions, and Other Realities*. Chicago: University of Chicago Press, 1984.

———. *Other Peoples' Myths*. New York: Macmillan, 1988.

Ong, Roberto. *The Interpretation of Dreams in Ancient China*. Bochum: Herausgeber Chinathemen, 1985.

Park, Sung-bae. "Wŏnhyo's Commentaries on the *Awakening of Faith in Mahāyāna*." Ph.D. diss., University of California at Berkeley, 1979.

———. *Buddhist Faith and Sudden Enlightenment*. Albany: State University of New York Press, 1983.

Paul, Diana. *The Philosophy of Mind in Sixth-Century China*. Stanford: Stanford University Press, 1984.

Plaks, Andrew H. *Archetype and Allegory in the Dream of the Red Chamber*. Princeton: Princeton University Press, 1976.

———. "Towards a Critical Theory of Chinese Narrative." In *Chinese Narrative: Critical and Theoretical Essays*, edited by Andrew H. Plaks. Princeton: Princeton University Press, 1977.

———. "Full-length *Hsiao-shuo* and the Western Novel: A Generic Reappraisal." In *China and the West: Comparative Literature Studies*, edited by William Tay, et al. Hong Kong: Chinese University Press, 1980.

———. *Four Masterworks of the Ming Novel: Ssu ta ch'i-shu*. Princeton: Princeton University Press, 1987.

Price, A. F. and Wang Mou-tam, trans. *The Diamond Sūtra and the Sūtra of Hui Neng*. The Clear Light Series. Boulder: Shambala Press, 1969.

Prüšek, Jaroslav. "The Narrators of Buddhist Scriptures and Religious Tales in the Sung Period." *Archiv Orientální* 10 (1938): 375–89.

Quinn, Philip. "Tragic Dilemmas, Suffering Love, and Christian Life." *Journal of Religious Ethics* 17, no. 1 (Spring 1989): 151–184.

———. "On Demythologizing Evil." Paper presented at the American Academy of Religion. New Orleans, November 1990.

———. "On Demythologizing Evil." In *Discourse and Practice*, edited by Frank Reynolds and David Tracy. Albany: State University of New York Press, 1992.

Raphels, Lisa. *Knowing Words: Wisdom and Cunning in the Classical Traditions of China and Greece*. Ithaca: Cornell University Press, 1992.

Riffaterre, Michael. *Fictional Truth*. Baltimore: Johns Hopkins University Press, 1990.

Robinet, Isabelle. "Metamorphosis and Deliverance from the Corpse in Taoism." *History of Religion* 19, no. 1 (August 1979): 37–70.

Robinson, Richard. *Early Mādhyamika in India and China*. Madison: University of Wisconsin, 1969.

Ruegg, D. Seyfort. "Does the Mādhyamika Have a Thesis and Philosophical Position?" In *Buddhist Logic and Epistemology*, edited by Bimal Krishna Matilal and Robert Evans. Dordrecht: Reidel, 1986.

Rutt, Richard. Introduction to *A Nine Cloud Dream* by Kim Manjung. In *Virtuous Women: Three Classic Korean Novels*. Seoul: Royal Asiatic Society, 1974.

———, trans. *A Nine Cloud Dream*. In *Virtuous Women: Three Classic Korean Novels*, edited by Richard Rutt and Kim Chong-un. Seoul: Royal Asiatic Society, 1974.

Sanford, James H., William R. LaFleur, and Masatoshi Nagatomi, eds. *Flowing Traces: Buddhism in the Literary and Visual Arts of Japan*. Princeton: Princeton University Press, 1992.

Skillend, W. E. "Nineteenth Century Books with Stories in Korean." In *Korean Classical Literature: An Anthology*, edited by Chung Chong-wha. London: Kegan Paul International, 1989.

Smith, Huston. "Postmodernism's Impact on the Study of Religion." *Journal of the American Academy of Religion* 58, no. 4 (Winter 1990): 653–70.

Smith, Jonathan Z. *Imagining Religion: From Babylon to Jonestown*. Chicago: University of Chicago Press, 1982.

———. *To Take Place*. Chicago: University of Chicago Press, 1987.

Spacks, Patricia Meyer. *Imagining a Self: Autobiography and Novel in Eighteenth-Century England*. Cambridge: Harvard University Press, 1976.

Sprung, Mervyn. *Lucid Exposition of the Middle Way: The Essential Chapters from the Prasannapadā of Candrakīrti*. London: Routledge & Kegan Paul, 1979.

Streng, Frederick. *Emptiness: A Study in Religious Meaning.* Nashville: Abingdon Press, 1967.

Strickmann, Michel. "Dreamwork of Psycho-Sinologists: Doctors, Taoists, Monks." In *Psycho-Sinology: The Universe of Dreams in Chinese Culture,* edited by Carolyn T. Brown. Lanham: University Press of America, 1988.

Suzuki, D. T. *An Introduction to Zen Buddhism.* New York: Grover Press, 1964.

———. *Essays in Zen Buddhism,* second series. London: Rider, 1970.

———, trans. *The Lankāvatāra Sūtra.* London: George Routledge and Sons, 1932.

Taylor, Charles. "Comparison, History, Truth." In *Myth and Philosophy,* edited by Frank Reynolds and David Tracy. Albany: State University of New York Press, 1990.

Teiser, Stephen. *The Ghost Festival in Medieval China.* Princeton: Princeton University Press, 1988.

Thurman, Robert A. F. *The Holy Teaching of Vimalakīrti.* University Park: Pennsylvania State University Press, 1976.

Toulmin, Stephen. "Beyond Anti-Anti-Relativism." Unpublished paper delivered to the Religions in Culture and History conference. University of Chicago Divinity School, October 1986.

Wayman, Alex. "Significance of Dreams in India and Tibet." *History of Religion* 7, no. 1 (August 1967): 1–12.

Waley, Arthur, trans. *Chinese Poems.* London: George Allen and Unwin, Ltd., 1946.

Warren, Henry Clarke, trans. *Buddhism in Translations.* New York: Atheneum Press, 1979.

Watson, Burton, trans. *The Zen Teachings of Master Lin-chi.* Boston: Shambala, 1993.

———, trans. *The Complete Works of Chuang Tzu.* New York: Columbia University Press, 1968.

Weintraub, Karl Joachim. *The Value of the Individual: Self and Circumstance in Autobiography.* Chicago: University of Chicago Press, 1978.

Wood, Thomas. *Mind Only: A Philosophical and Doctrinal Analysis of the Vijñānavāda.* Honolulu: University of Hawaii Press, 1991.

Wu, Pei-yi. *The Confucian's Progress: Autobiographical Writings in Traditional China.* Princeton: Princeton University Press, 1990.

Yearley, Lee. *Mencius and Aquinas: Theories of Virtue and Conceptions of Courage.* Albany: State University of New York Press, 1990.

Yu, Anthony C. "History, Fiction, and the Reading of Chinese Narrative." *Chinese Literature: Essays, Articles, Reviews* 10 (1988): 1–19.

———. "The Quest of Brother Amor: Buddhist Intimations in the *Story of the Stone.*" *Harvard Journal of Asiatic Studies* 49, no. 1 (June 1989): 55–92.

———. "The Stone of Fiction and the Fiction of Stone: Reflexivity and Religious Symbolism in *Hung-lou meng.*" *Studies in Language and Literature* 4 (October 1990): 1–30.

———, trans. *Journey to the West.* Volumes 1–4. Chicago: University of Chicago Press, 1977–1983.

Yu, Chun-fang. *The Renewal of Buddhism in China: Chu-hung and the Late Ming Synthesis.* New York: Columbia University Press, 1981.

Yü, Lu K'uan, trans. *The Diamond Cutter of Doubts: A Commentary on The DIamond Sūtra by Ch'an Master Han Shan.* In *Ch'an and Zen Teaching.* Vol. 1. York Beach: Samuel Weiser, 1993.

Non-Western Sources

Chigwan. "Yŏnt'aek mit Inok ŭi sagi wa kŭ ŭi kyohakkwan" [The personal records of Yŏnt'aek and Inok and their scholastic views]. In *Han'guk pulgyo sasangsa.* Iri (Chŏlla bukto): Wŏn Pulgyo Sasang Yŏn'guwŏn, 1975.

Cho Yunje. *Han'guk munhaksa* [History of Korean literature]. Seoul: Tongguk Munhwasa, 1963.

Choe Samyong. "Sojaeron" [Source materials]. In *Han'guk kososŏllon*. Seoul: Asea Munhwasa, 1991.

Chŏng Kyubok. *Kuunmong yŏn'gu* [Research on *Kuunmong*]. Seoul: Korea University Press, 1974.

————. *Kuunmong wŏnjŏn ŭi yŏn'gu* [Textual studies on *Kuunmong*]. Seoul: Ilchisa, 1977.

————. "Kuunmong ŭi sasangjŏk yŏn'gu" [Research on *Kuunmong* thought]. In *Kojŏn sosŏl yŏn'gu*. Seoul: Chŏmŭmsa, 1982.

————. *Kim Manjung yŏn'gu*. [Research on Kim Manjung]. Seoul: Saemunsa, 1983.

Han Kidu. "Paekp'a wa Ch'oŭi sidae Sŏn ŭi nonjaengjŏm" [Controversial points in Sŏn at the time of Paekp'a and Ch'oŭi]. In *Han'guk pulgyo sasangsa*. Iri (Chŏlla bukto): Wŏn Pulgyo Sasang Yŏn'guwŏn, 1975.

Hong Kisam. "Han'guk pulgyo munhaknon" [Korean Buddhist literature]. In *Ch'oesin kungmunhak charyo nonmunjip (sokp'yŏn)*: vol. 2 *Hyŏndae munhak (sanmun p'yŏn)*. Seoul: Taejegak, 1990.

Hwang P'aegang. *Chosŏn wangjo sosŏl yŏn'gu* [A study of the romances of the Chosŏn Dynasty]. Seoul: Hanguk Yŏn'gu-in, 1986.

————. "Kososŏl ŭi kaenyŏm" [The concept of the classic novel]. In *Han'guk kososŏllon*. Seoul: Asea Munhwasa, 1991.

Jingang boruo boluomi jing [The Diamond sūtra]. In Taishō shinshū daizōkyō 235.8.748c–752c. Edited by Takakusu Junjirō and Watanabe Kaikyoku. Tokyo: Daizōkyōkai, 1924–1935.

Kim Chinse. "Kososŏl ŭi chakja wa tokja" [The writer and reader of the classic novel]. In *Han'guk kososŏlon*. Seoul: Asea Munhwasa, 1991.

Kim Iryŏl. "Kuunmong sin'go" [New Reflections on *Kuunmong*]. In *Han'guk kososŏl yŏn'gu*. Chŏng Kyubok et al. Seoul: Iu Ch'ulp'ansa, 1988.

Kim Kidong. *Yijo sidae sosŏllon*. [Study of the novels of the Yi dynasty]. Chŏngyŏn-sa, 1964.

Kim Kwangsun. "Yuhyŏngnon" [Typologies]. In *Han'guk kososŏllon*. Seoul: Asea Munhwasa, 1991.

Kim Manjung. *Kuunmong* [Dream of the nine clouds]. In *Hanguo Hanwen Xiaoshou Quanji* [A compilation of Korean novels written in Chinese]. Edited by Lin Ming-teh. Volume 3. Taibei: Jongguo Wenhua Daxue Chubanbu, 1980.

———. *Sassi Namjŏnggi* [The southern expedition of Madame Sa]. In *Hanguo Hanwen Xiaoshuo Quanji* [A compilation of Korean novels written in Chinese]. Edited by Lin Ming-teh. Volume 7. Taibei: Jongguo Wenhua Daxue Chubanbu, 1980.

———. *Jiuyunmeng* [Dream of the nine clouds]. With a foreword by Wei Xusheng. Shanshi: Beiyue Wenyi Chubanshe, 1984.

Kim Yŏngt'ae. *Han'guk pulgyosa kaesŏl* [Outline of Korean Buddhist history]. Seoul: Purok Han'guk Chongp'asa, 1986.

Pak Sŏng'ŭi. *Han'guk kodae sosŏllon kwa sa* [Theses and history of the Korean classic novel]. Seoul: Chimmundang, 1992.

Pei Puxian. *Jongyin Wenxue Guanxi Yanjiu* [Research into the relationship between Chinese and Indian literature]. Taiwan: Xing Funu Xiezuo Xiehui, 1959.

So Chaeyŏng. "Kososŏl palttalsa" [Development of the classic novel]. In *Han'guk kososŏllon*. Seoul: Asea Munhwasa, 1991.

Sŏl Sŏnggyŏng. "*Kuunmong* ŭi kujojŏk yŏn'gu" [On the structure of *Kuunmong*]. Part 1 *Inmun kwahak* 27/28 (1972): 231–76. Part 2 *Ŏnŏ munhwa* 1 (1974): 72–103. Part 3 *Kugŏ kungmunhak* 58/60 (1972): 238–42.

———. *Han'guk kojŏn sosŏl ŭi ponjil* [The essence of the Korean classic novel]. Seoul: Kukhak Charyowŏn, 1991.

Takahashi Tŏru. *Richō Bukkyō* [Yi dynasty Buddhism]. Tokyo: 1929.

Uchida Michio. "Tōdai shōsetsu ni okeru yume to gensetsu" [Dreams and illusion in Tang tales]. *Shūkan Tōyōgaku* (May 1959): 2–12.

Yi Kiyŏng. *Han'guk ŭi pulgyo*. [Korean Buddhism]. Seoul: Sejong Taewang Kinyŏm Saŏphoe, 1974.

Yu Pyŏnghwan. "Kuunmong ŭi pulgyo sasangjŏk yon'gu rŭl wihan chiban." [Foundations for research on the Buddhist thought of *Kuunmong*]. In *Ch'oesin kungmunhak charyo nonmunjip (sokp'yŏn):* vol. 5 *Kojŏn munhak (sanmunp'yŏn)*. Seoul: Taejegak, 1990.

Index

ālayavijñāna concept, 130
allegory
  in Chinese fiction, 115
  self-reflexive, 146–47
  *The Southern Expedition of
    Madame Sa* as, 51–53, 58–59, 66
  Western, 12, 14, 115
anātman doctrine. *See* selflessness
  (*anātman*)
Araki Kengo, 28
art
  meaning of, 144–45
  as medium to examine
    philosophical questions, 151–52
assertion
  in circle of emptiness, 165
  of impermanence, 121–22
  moving from assertion to negation
    to, 165
  negation as form of, 154–55
  nonassertion, 167, 168, 171
awakening metaphor, 152
The Awakening of Faith (Aśvaghoṣa ?)
  impact of, 131
  influence of, 16
  as one of Four Teachings, 138
  understanding of the mind, 130–31

Bai Xingjian, 104–5, 108
Bodhidharma (ca. 530?), 126

Bouchez, Daniel, 4, 45, 51, 53–55,
  58–59, 63, 65
Bo Zhuyi (772–846), 62, 145
the Buddha
  ordering of revelations, 140
  resort to trickery, 147
  stance against metaphysical
    discourse, 120–21
Buddhism
  central lesson of, 203
  Chinese appropriation of, 128–29
  as conceptual agent in *KUM*, 106,
    117
  conflict with Confucianism in
    KUM, 26
  emotions as failings in, 9
  hierarchies of doctrines in, 16, 26
  highest goals of, 25
  of Kim Manjung, 19–27
  non-propositional discourse in, 169
  ontology of illusion in, 63
  perspectives in *KUM*, 13
  relation to literature, 22–23
  speech and discourse in realization
    of enlightenment, 120
  teaching of emptiness, 9
  truth claim of, 152
  world as illusory creation, 110–11
Buddhism
  Yogācāra school, 103, 126

253

Buddhism, Chan
  development of, 16
  dreams in literature of, 142
  emergence of school of, 132
  metaphysics of, 186–87
  realignment of metaphysics and
    metapractice in, xi
  Song dynasty, 123
Buddhism, Chan/Sŏn, 16
Buddhism, Chinese
  emptiness (kong) in, 126
  language of emptiness (kong), 126
  unity of relative and absolute
    truth, 125–26
  Yogācāra factor in, 126–27
Buddhism, Chosŏn
  Hyujŏng's contribution to, 137–38
  neo-Confucian environment of, 15
Buddhism, East Asian, 15
  influence of Lotus Sūtra on, 146
  tathāgatagarbha concept in, 129
Buddhism, Indian, 16
  dream adventure tales, 95–96
  emptiness doctrine of
    Mādhyamika school, 126
  influence in China, Korea, and
    Japan, 126
  Mādhyamika school of, 126–27
Buddhism, Korean
  in context of Chosŏn dynasty,
    16–18
  division between scriptural studies
    and meditation, 135
  fiction to revalorize, xi
  influence of Awakening of Faith in,
    131–32
  relation to literature, 23
Buddhism, Mahāyāna
  in KUM, 9
  objection to language, 122
  Perfection of Wisdom text, 15, 69
Buddhism, Sŏn
  accesses of principle and practice,
    140

Buddhism, Yogācāra school, 103
Buddhist literature, Chan, 142
Buswell, Robert, 11, 131, 132–33, 140

Candrakīrti, 146
Cao Xueqin, 80
Cheng, Chung-ying, 124
Chinul (1158–1210), 133, 135–39
Chŏng Ch'ŏl (1536–1593), 57–58
Chŏng Kyubok, 97, 160–61
Chosŏn dynasty
  Korean Buddhism in context of,
    16–18
Chosŏn dynasty
  neo-Confucianism during, 47–51
  relationship with Ming China, 46
chuanqi genre, 35, 41, 79, 87
Chung Chong-wha, 77, 78–79
Confucian academies (sŏwŏns), 48–49
Confucianism
  conflict with Buddhism in KUM,
    26
  highest goals of, 25
  Zongmi's criticism of, 128
  See also neo-Confucianism,
    Chosŏn Korea
Conze, Edward, 126, 157, 158
cosmogony, Buddhist, 128
creation
  in Buddhist ontology, 201
  nature of, 197–98
cultures
  metaphysics and metapractices of,
    xi
  role in philosophical discourse, 5

Dahui Zonggau (1089–1163), 123
deceptions in KUM, 100–103
demythologization, xi
devices, literary
  karma as, 108–9
  Sŏp'o's self-conscious use of, 82
  Sŏp'o's use of karma, 82–83
devices, rhetorical, 82
DeWoskin, Kenneth, 39, 108

Diamond Sūtra
emptiness (śunyatā) philosophy of, 94
follow-up to negation strategy, 156–59
in *KUM*, 15, 153–54, 164–65, 174–75
language used as negation in form of assertion, 154–55
negative use of language and follow-up, 156–61
as one of Four Teachings, 138
discourse
in Buddhist philosophy, 120–22
overcoming limitations in *KUM*, 122
See also kataphatic discourse; ontology, Buddhist; philosophical discourse
Dōgen (1200–1253), 133–34
Dong Yue (1620–1686), 91–92
drama
plays of Tang, 89–90, 98
Song dynasty, 44
dream, life as
in dream adventure tales, 87–90
in *Vimśatikā (Twenty Verses)*, 142–43; 142–44
dream adventure tale
Chinese influence, 88–91
The Dream of the Nine Clouds as, 87–88, 93
origins of, 94–97
philosophical origins, 98–107
Samguk Yusa as Korean, 88
Soushenji as Chinese, 88
dream metaphor in *KUM*, 114–15
dream motifs
of Asian literature, 85
in *KUM*, 99–100, 165
as symbol of Buddhist onology of emptiness, 84
The Dream of the Nine Clouds (KUM)
Buddhist philosophical debate, 153–54

in Chinese language, 12
conflict between Buddhism and Confucianism in, 26
consideration of reality in, 81
convergence of metaphysics and metapractice in, xi, 171, 181–85
criticism of, 76, 82, 163
Diamond Sūtra as subtext in, 15, 74, 94, 164–65, 174–75
distinction between illusion and reality, 151
distinction between metaphysics and metapractice in, 28–33
as dream tale, 87
elements of *chuanqi* narrative, 79–80
emptiness doctrine in, 24–25
as example of Chinese literature, 1–12
interpretation of, 4–5, 12, 14–15, 41
lesson of life as a dream, 5
military and dream travel elements in, 93–94
narrative influences, 106
nonassertion in, 168, 171
nonreferentiality of, 118
ontology of illusion in, 26–27
organizational principle in frame tale of, 140–41
philosophical system illuminated by, 15
philosophical views of, 117
receding frames of reality in, 116, 118–19, 139
structural layout, 10
theme of, 3–4
use of Buddhist symbols, 181
The Dream of the Red Chamber [*HLM*] (Cao Xueqin), 13, 80
dream as literary trope, 84
illusion to discourse on illusion, 172

dreams
  as examples of representation,
    142–43
  as instrument of communication,
    85
  interpretations in China, 85
  interpretations in Korea, 85–87
  Korean interpretations of, 85–87
  literary function in China, 85
  meaning in dream adventure tales,
    97–107
  symbolical significance, 152–53
dream sequence
  in KUM, 83
dream tale (mong charyu), Korea,
  87–88
dream travel record (mong yurok),
  Korea, 87
dualism
  double negation to go beyond, 159
  transcendance in Diamond Sūtra,
    160, 162–63
  transcendence in KUM, 164
Dushun (557–640), 129

Eckel, Malcolm D., 170
emptiness
  circle in movement from assertion
    to negation to assertion, 165
  doctrine of Indian Buddhism, 126
emptiness (śunyatā), 5
  basis of, 13
  Buddhist teaching of, 9
  in The Dream of the Nine Clouds,
    24–25, 84
  Kim Manjung's doctrine of, 20
  in Kim Manjung's understanding
    of Buddhism, 20
  Mādhyamika theory of, 5, 126, 146,
    167
  metaphysics of, 182
  Sŏp'o's use of doctrine of, 139

fantasy
  fiction of Sŏp'o to make truth
    claims, 151–52

in KUM, 108
  Sŏp'o's use of, 113
  where karma functions most fully,
    109–10
Faure, Bernard, 142
Fa Zang (643–712), 4
fiction
  Chinese, 80, 116
  criteria and aims of, 6
  as form of philosophical discourse,
    5, 188
  as form of philosophizing, 5
  as form of remythologization, x–xi
  ontological theory of, 63
  origins and rise of Chinese, 38–39
  philosophical significance, 37–45
  philosophy through vehicle of, 6–9
  to provide moral commentary on
    contemporary events, 65–66
  to revalorize Korean Buddhism, xi
  significance of Sŏp'o's writing of,
    44–45
  as Sŏp'o's choice of discourse,
    168–69
  used to invent one's life, 66
fiction, Chinese
  The Dream of the Red Chamber,
    13, 80
fiction, Korean
  novels and memoirs, 36
  The Formation of Ch'an Ideology in
    China and Korea (Buswell), 132
Four Collected Works (sajip), 138
Four Teachings, 138

Geertz, Clifford, 193
Gimello, Robert, 124–25
Graham, A. C., 198
Great Learning (Da Xue), 59
Gregory, Peter, 127–28

Haep'yong clan, 50
Hales, Dell, 85
han'gŭl script, 23, 37
Hanshan Deqing (1546–1623), 155,
  159, 160

Han Yu (768–824), 128
Hawks, David, 60–61
Heart Sūtra
  emptiness in, 15, 129
  paradoxical logic of, 159, 168
Hegel, Robert, 43, 81
Hīnayāna teachings, 127
HLM. See The Dream of the Red
  Chamber [HLM] (Cao Xueqin)
Hŏ Kyun (1569–1618), 35–37, 77
Hong Kiltong, 77
Hong Kiltong (The Life of Hong
  Kiltong), 35–36
Hong Kisam, 22, 23
Hsia, C. T., 98
King Huai (r. 328–299 BCE), 55
Huayan school, 5, 16, 140, 165
Hui Neng, 16
Hu Shih, 132
Hwang P'aegang, 84
Hwaŏm school, 5
King Hyojong (1649–1659), 65
Hyujŏng (1520–1604), 24, 106–7, 137–38

illusion
  Buddhist ontology of, 25–26
  in creation of reality, 62–63
  in examples of Buddhist text, 106–7
  Indian and Chinese senses of, 102–5
  in KUM, 100–3, 117–18, 162–63, 165
  ontology of, 63, 118–19, 152–53
  symmetry of illusion and reality in
    KUM, 112–13
  use of term in Diamond Sūtra, 159
imagination
  process in The Southern
    Expedition of Madame Sa, 66–67
  relation to ontology of creation, 198
  role in comparative religions, ix–x
  role in The Dream of the Nine
    Clouds, 2–3
impermanence, 121–22
Inquiry into the Origins of Man
  (Zongmi), 128, 129
Iryŏn, 27

Journey to the West, The, 14, 36
  functioning of karma in presence
    of fantasy, 109–10
  Xiyoubu as supplement to, 91–93

karma
  in Korean dream tale, 87
  as literary device, 82
  religious meaning in narrative,
    107–13
  structural and religious meaning
    of, 83–84
Kasulis, Thomas, 185
kataphatic discourse, 125, 127, 141
Katz, Nathan, 125
Kim Changsaeng (1548–1631), 50
Kim Ch'unt'aek (1670–1717), 12,
  50–51, 58
Kim clan, Korea, 46–47
Kim Iryŏl, 163
Kim Kidong, 76, 82, 107
Kim Manjung, 3–4, 12, 15
  Chinese influence on writing of, 36
  doctrine of emptiness, 20
  understanding of Buddhism, 20
  use and practice of writing fiction,
    33
  See also Sŏp'o
Kim Sisŭp (1435–1493), 35
Knechtges, David, 87–88, 96
Koryŏ dynasty (918–1392), Korea, 17,
  35–36, 47
KUM. See The Dream of the Nine
  Clouds (KUM)
Kŭmo Sinwha (New Stories from
  Golden Turtle Mountain), 35, 79
Kuunmong (Kim), 30, 36, 37, 93
  See also The Dream of the Nine
  Clouds (KUM)

LaFleur, William, 145, 146–47, 152,
  168
language
  Buddhist objection to, 122
  Lotus Sūtra's lack of discursive,
    166

language *(continued)*
  Mādhyamika school uses of,
    122–24
  negation as form of assertion,
    154–59
  parallel use in *KUM*, 161–62
  reestablishment of, 167
  as symbol in *KUM*, 141
  used to proclaim liberation of
    language, 169–70
  use in *Diamond Sūtra*, 156–60
Lankāvatāra Sūtra, 126, 130
Lee, Peter, 37, 57
Liezi, 94–95, 99
Linji Yixuan (d. 866/67), 135, 136–37
Lisao (Qu Yuan), 55–56, 60
literati, countryside (*sarim*), 48
literature
  as form of ontology, xi–xii
  relation to Buddhism, 22–23
Liuguan, 69–70
Lotus Sūtra, 20, 146
  collapsing of meaning and
    representation, 147
  lack of discursive language in,
    166
  metaphysical lesson of, 152
  use of *upāya*, 148

Mādhyamika school
  emptiness (*śunyatā*) doctrine of, 5,
    126, 146
Mādhyamika school, Indian
  use of language, 122–23
Mahāsatipatthānasutta, 9
Mair, Victor, 39–40, 42, 62, 64, 110–11,
  116, 144, 197–99
Matilal, Bimal, 167
Mazu Daoyi (709–788), 135
metaphor
  of awakening, 152
  of clouds in *KUM*, 101
  of life as a dream, 68
metaphysics
  convergence in *KUM* with
    metapractice, 63, 171

of a culture, xi
demands of *hongaku*, 147
distinct from metapractice, 28–29
in East Asian Buddhist tradition,
  121
of *KUM*, 112–13
priority in philosophical system,
  187, 189
metapractice
  articulation as, 63
  convergence in *KUM* with
    metaphysics, 171
  of a culture, xi
  distinct from metaphysics, 28–29
  in East Asian Buddhist tradition,
    120–21
  forms of expression as, 28
  in *KUM*, 63, 113, 117
  as solution to limitations of
    discourse, 122
mimesis, 144
the mind
  dream as projection of, 142–43
  nature in Indian Buddhism, 129–30
  original nature of, 130–31
  theory of, 127
Mind-only philosophy, 144–45
Ming dynasty, China, 38, 45–46, 65
Mirror for Meditation Students, 106–7
Mudanting (*The Peony Pavilion*). *See
  The Peony Pavilion* (Tang)
Mūlamadhyamakākaikās
  (Nāgārjuna), 125

Nagao, Gadjin, 170
Nāgārjuna, 125, 126, 146, 166–68
Nam Yŏngno (1810–1858), 93
narrative
  birth and prognostication dreams
    in Korean, 85–86
  chuanqi, 79
  conveyance of meaning in East
    Asian novels, 11–15
  to create reality, 33
  of dream adventure tales, 88–91
  as form of expression, 117

as form of philosophy, x
influences on *KUM*, 106
in *KUM*, 10, 67
in *KUM* of reality and illusion,
    100–102, 105–6, 112–13
as metapractice in *KUM*, 29, 63
ontological capacity of, 33
realism in Confucian, 81
receding frame of reality in Indian,
    116
to represent ontological structures,
    115–16
in *The Southern Expedition of
    Madame Sa*, 59–61, 66–67
used to signify one's life, 66
negation
    in circle of emptiness, 165
    double, 165
    as form of assertion, 154–59
    in Mādhyamika school, 166
neo-Confucianism, Chosŏn Korea, 3,
    46–47
nonassertion, 167
novels
    conveyance of meaning in East
        Asian, 11–15
    self-consciousness in Chinese, 82
    significance of pre-nineteenth-
        century Korean, 36–37
Nussbaum, Martha, 6–8, 22, 76, 178,
    179, 180–81, 203

O'Flaherty, Wendy D., 97, 102–3, 115,
    116, 117, 197, 203
Ong, Roberto, 97
ontology
    East Asian Buddhism, 138
    of illusion, 63, 152–53
    of illusion in *KUM*, 105, 118–19,
        201
    literature as form of, xi–xii
    in mandates of karma, 111
    narrative to represent structures of,
        115–16
ontology, Buddhist
    of emptiness (śunyatā), 13

of illusion, 25–26
ontological discourse, 201

Pak Sŏng'ŭi, 93
panjiao system of classification, 16,
    17, 26, 124, 127, 140, 165
paradox
    danger of, 170–71
    in Mādhyamika literature, 168
The Peony Pavilion (Tang), 89
phemonena (*shi*)
    as bearers of reality, 146
    equality of, 145–46
    language about ground of,
        148–49
    numinous nature of, 129
philosophical discourse
    development of Buddhist, 119–28
    focused on metaphysics and
        metapractice, 178
    in *KUM*, 30
    of *KUM*, 112, 119
    meaning in context of study, 5–6
philosophy
    appropriation by Chinese of
        Indian, 127
    common meaning, 5
    meaning in context of study, 6, 28
    priority of metaphysics in, 187, 189
    use of term, 28
Plaks, Andrew, 12–14, 25, 29, 40, 41,
    59, 80–81, 82, 84, 115, 141
Platform Sūtra, 16, 20
practical learning (*Sirhak*), 49
practice access, 140
*Prajñāpāramitā (Perfection of
    Wisdom)* school, 15, 69, 122
Price, A. F., 157
principle access, 140
principle concept (*li*), 25, 129

Qing dynasty, China, 46
Quinn, Philip, x–xi, 7, 10, 33, 183–84
Qu Yuan, 54–57, 60

Random Essays (Sŏp'o manp'il), 4,
    15, 19–21

Raphels, Lisa, 169
realism
    Confucian narratives, 81
    in *KUM*, 107
    Western sense of, 80
reality
    Buddhism's theory of, 125–26
    as a dream, 144
    in *KUM* narrative, 100–1
    narrative's shared view of, 8–9
    receding frames of, 116, 118–19, 139
    as representation in *Vimśatikā*, 142–43
    use of term in *Diamond Sūtra*, 159
"Record of the Three Dreams, The," (*Sanmengji*), 104–5
religious meaning
    in *KUM*, 15
    in karma, 83–84, 107–13
    in narratives, 92
renewed affirmation (LaFleur), 152, 168
representation
    reality in Chinese Buddhism as, 142–43
    receding frames of reality as, 118
Rhetoric of Immediacy (Faure), 142
Ricoeur, Paul, 67
Riffaterre, Michael, 152, 164
The Rites of Passage (van Gennep), 194
The Romance of the Three Kingdoms, 36, 51
    fictional account, 64
    Sŏp'o's comparison with official account, 63–65
    transformation of ideals into action, 178–79

Samguk Yusa, 27
samsāra concept, 25
Samyuktaratnapitakasūtra, 95

Sanguozhi
    official account of *Three Kingdoms* novel, 63
sarim (countryside literati), 48
Sassi Namjŏnggi
    allegorical stratagem, 58
    cultural and historical references, 62
    cultural symbols in, 61
    political affairs in, 51–53
Sejong (1418–1450), 16
self-conception, sinological tradition, 62
self-consciousness
    in Chinese novel, 82
    in *Nine Clouds* and *Southern Expedition*, 81–82
selflessness (*anātman*)
    of Buddhism, 120
    in Hīnayāna teachings, 127
    in Indian views of the mind, 129–30
self-referentiality
    in *KUM*, 117–19
self-representation
    in narrative of *KUM*, 45
    theater as vehicle for, 44
Shaoyou
    dream-state protagonist in *KUM*, 163
Silence (Endo), 10
Silla dynasty (668–918), Korea, 17
Sima Qian (146–86 BCE), 38, 60
Sirhak scholarship. *See* practical learning (*Sirhak*)
Skillend, W. E., 36
skillful means principle (*upāya*), 147–48
Smith, Huston, 191, 193–95
Smith, J. Z., 194
Sŏl Sŏnggyŏng, 93–94, 153–54, 157–58
Song dynasty (960–1279), China, 44
King Sŏnjo (1567–1608), 50, 57
Sŏn school, Korea
    establishment of, 135
    role of Chinul in, 135

Sŏp'o
autobiographical tone in fiction of,
59–60, 61
career, 46, 50
death of, 50
life of, 42
lineage of, 49–50
use of fiction by, 60
use of narrative, 62–63
See also Kim Manjung
Sŏp'o manp'il (Random Essays), 4,
15, 19–21, 138–39
soteriology
Buddhist, 145
in KUM, 14
Southern Expedition of Madame
Sa, The
allegory in narrative of, 66
Southern Expedition of Madame Sa,
The, [NJG] (Kim Manjung), 12
autobiographical sense of, 45,
52–53, 66–67, 180
Buddhist lesson in, 181
dilution of original message, 58
interpretation of, 51–53
sŏwŏns. See Confucian academies
(sŏwŏns)
Strickmann, Michel, 85
King Sukchong (1674–1720), 51
śunyatā. See emptiness (śunyatā)
Śurangama Sūtra, 20, 138
Sūtralamkāra, 95
Sūtra of Perfect Enlightenment, 138
Suzuki, D. T., 121, 124, 132
symbols
cultural, 61
dream motifs as, 84
dreams as, 152–53
in Japanese form of Buddhism, 145
in KUM, 181
language as, 141

Tale of Ch'unhyang, 86
Tambiah, Stanley, 31–32
Tang dynasty (618–907), China, 17, 90

Tang Xianzu (1550–1616), 89–90, 98
Taoist thought, 98–99
tathāgatagarbha concept, 20, 129–31
Taylor, Charles, 201–2
Teiser, Stephen, 17, 28, 31
theater
focus of Sŏn theater in Korea, 139
self-presentation orientation, 44
See also drama
Three Kingdoms, The. See The
Romance of the Three Kingdoms
Tiantai school, 5, 16, 140
topoi, 23
Toulmin, Stephen, 200
Tower of Myriad Mirrors, The, 91–93
Toyotomi, Hideyoshi, 137
Tracy, David, ix
True History of Queen Inhyon, The, 52
truth
affirmation and negation of
Mādhyamika, 166
in Lotus Sūtra, 147–48
nature of, 197
unity of relative and absolute,
125–26
truth claims, 151–52

Uchida Michio, 38–39
Ŭisang (625–702), 55
upāya. See skillful means principle
(upāya)

Vajrasamadhi Sūtra, 132–33, 140
van Gennep, Arnold, 194
Vasubandu, 142–44
Vigrahavyāvartanī (Nāgārjuna),
166–68
Vimalakīrtinirdeśa Sūtra, 20, 122
Vimśatikā (Vasubandu), 142–43, 152

Wei Xusheng, 76
Wŏnhyo (617–686), 54, 131
words
See language
Wu Pei-yi, 44, 60, 111

Xingzhen
  waking state protagonist in *KUM*,
    163–64, 174
Xingzhen as Shaoyou, 69–70
Xuanzang (596–664), 166

Yangban class, Korea
  commitment to neo-Confucianism,
    46–50
  political rebellion, 49
  ranking system, 47
Yearley, Lee, 1–2
Yogācāra school, 126–27
  in China, 130
  of ontic equivalence, 144

Yogavāsistha, 102–3
Yu, Anthony C., 14, 41, 97, 107,
    172–73
yuan, 82–83
Yulgok (1536–1584), 50
Yu Pyŏnghwan, 21

Zhenzhongji, 88–89
zhiguai tradition, 108
Zhi Yi (538–597), 4
Zhuangzi, 143–44, 197–98
Zhugeliang, 65
Zhuxi, 20, 25
Zongmi Guifeng (780–841), 127,
    128–29, 136, 138–39